BEHAVIORAL INSIGHTS FOR SUPERVISION

BEHAVIORAL INSIGHTS FOR SUPERVISION

SECOND EDITION

RALPH W. REBER

General Supervisor, Personnel Development
Champion International Corporation
Pasadena, Texas

GLORIA VAN GILDER

Director, Human Resources Development
Memorial Hospital System
Houston, Texas

PRENTICE-HALL, INC, Englewood Cliffs, New Jersey 07632

Library of Congress Cataloging in Publication Data

Reber, Ralph W.
　　Behavioral insights for supervision.

　　Includes bibliographies.
　　1. Psychology, Industrial.　2. Supervision of
employees.　I. Van Gilder, Gloria E.
II.　Title.
HF5548.8.R38 1982　　　658.3'02　　　81–15687
ISBN 0-13-073114-5　　　　　　　AACR2

1–03

Editorial production/interior design: Margaret McAbee
Cover design: Tony Ferrara Studio
Manufacturing buyer: Ed O'Dougherty

Printed in the United States of America

10　9　8　7　6　5　4

Prentice-Hall International, Inc.,　*London*
Prentice-Hall of Australia Pty. Limited,　*Sydney*
Prentice-Hall of Canada, Ltd.,　*Toronto*
Prentice-Hall of India Private Limited,　*New Delhi*
Prentice-Hall of Japan, Inc.,　*Tokyo*
Prentice-Hall of Southeast Asia Pte. Ltd.,　*Singapore*
Whitehall Books Limited,　*Wellington, New Zealand*

CONTENTS

Cases and Role-Playing Exercises

141

PREFACE

In 1975, when the first edition of this book was published, widespread employee dissatisfaction with work, higher turnover and absenteeism rates, lower productivity and quality, more complaints and grievances, increased union activity, and more demands from minorities were some of the problems facing supervisors and their organizations.

As this second edition is completed in 1981, these "people problems" are still with us—if anything, their intensity has increased and shows few signs of lessening. Despite an energy crisis, skyrocketing inflation, increasing governmental interventions, and a host of other roadblocks currently facing organizations, the most demanding challenges for the majority of supervisors in the eighties will still involve employees. Dealing with "people problems" will consume more and more time.

Yet, many supervisors will readily admit that they are poorly equipped to deal with these human problems at work. They simply don't have the level of expertise and skill concerning people that they may have in regard to equipment, techniques, and procedures. Frequently, supervisors are highly skilled people whose backgrounds and training are primarily technically oriented. It is much easier for them to work with inanimate things—facts, figures, machines, techniques, materials, etc. (after all, these things are *predictable*)—than it is with people. Compounding the situation, today's supervisor functions in an increasingly changing work environment. The attitudes and values of the work force continue to be in a state of transformation. Simple reward and punishment systems of motivation, for example—although still used with great frequency—are no longer getting the job done. People are demanding more and more from the work they do, while seemingly willing to give less and less in return. Employee loyalty to the organization often seems only a memory. And, supervisors can frequently be heard moaning, "People just don't want to work anymore like they used to."

To be sure, this little book can't be expected to change all of that—but, if you're realistic about your expectations, it can surely help you.

As you've probably already guessed, this book is written for anyone who is interested in expanding his or her knowledge and skills for more effectively supervising people. Whether you are a potential or newly-appointed supervisor, or a seasoned veteran, this book can provide you with background information essential for understanding—and influencing— the behavior of people at work.

A word of warning, however: The book does *not* attempt to cover *all* of the important information and topics that a supervisor needs to know about the job. It isn't meant to be a complete book on supervision. Rather, it concentrates only on the core interpersonal aspects of supervision—namely, motivation and communication. There are other excellent books that cover such "must know" functions as planning, scheduling, performance appraisal, decision making, safety, time management, on-the-job training, counseling, compensation, budgeting, disciplining, administration of labor agreements, etc.

In writing the book, one objective remained uppermost: No matter how complex the concept may be, try to explain it in such a way that understanding and useful application are possible. Hopefully, the result of this goal is a not-too-lengthy book written in easy-to-read language. Examples of practical application of the concepts presented are sprinkled throughout.

A second objective is the involvement of you, the reader, in the learning process. This is partially accomplished by the inclusion of a section of case studies in the back of the book that describe real problems faced by real supervisors. These cases, along with thought-provoking discussion questions at the ends of chapters, provide the involvement opportunities essential for actively understanding and "trying out" the concepts and ideas discussed in the chapters.

Inasmuch as there are few "rules" that explain the actions of people, the book presents basic information that you must interpret and apply within the framework of your attitudes and abilities and the particular characteristics of your organization and employees. Because every person and situation is different, there can be no common cure-alls. Short "how-to" lists and "off-the-shelf" formulas are thus avoided.

It is hoped that you will be stimulated enough to pursue more information—or even conflicting viewpoints—on certain topics. To aid in this respect, an up-to-date listing of carefully selected "Suggested Additional Readings" follow each chapter. An attempt has been made to include only those articles and books that are readable and can be found in most libraries.

Over the past ten years, these materials have been successfully used with trainees representing varying levels of supervision and a wide assortment of business and industrial organizations—both in college classroom situations and in organizations' in-house supervisory training and development programs. Much of what has been added, deleted, or changed in this second edition is based upon the practical advice and experiences shared by hundreds of practicing supervisors who were exposed to the first edition. Their feedback is sincerely appreciated and has doubtless made this a better book.

Gratitude must also be expressed to John Duhring and Margaret McAbee of Prentice-Hall for their support and exceptional patience while the manuscript was being revised.

It is hoped the experience gained in reading, reflecting upon, discussing, analyzing, and attempting to apply these materials will bring about a real understanding of yourself, your employees, and the tremendous influence that you as a supervisor have in developing a productive work climate in your organization. Good luck!

RALPH W. REBER
GLORIA VAN GILDER

BEHAVIORAL INSIGHTS FOR SUPERVISION

1

UTILIZING HUMAN RESOURCES – TODAY'S SUPERVISORY CHALLENGE

If all you know about supervisory development is what you knew five years ago, your knowledge is out of date. Today's and tomorrow's supervisor must master new knowledge and skills to carry out supervisory work.[1]

George R. Terry

The man who thinks he knows everything about a subject renounces all hope of learning anything more about it.

William J. Stevens

"If my supervisors knew half as much about the people they supervise as they do about machinery, processes, and products, we could double our rate of production." The speaker was the superintendent of a large metal fabricating plant. His statement points out an interesting fact: We have progressed more in adapting ourselves to our machines than to each other.

We have amply demonstrated in this country an ability to cope with scientific and technological problems of immense difficulty. Vast amounts of knowledge have been acquired in such areas as space technology, nuclear energy, and medicine. Our mastery of machinery has been proven repeatedly; yet we have not made comparable progress in learning about human behavior.

What happens when there is a malfunction in the office copier, a computer, a drill press, or a lathe? As a rule, supervisors get together with their employees or the appropriate maintenance personnel, study the problem, have it corrected, and get things under

[1] Reproduced by special permission from the January, 1977 TRAINING AND DEVELOPMENT JOURNAL. Copyright 1977 by the American Society for Training and Development, Inc.

way again. But should anything go wrong with an employee—or worse, with a group of employees—many supervisors don't know where to begin to find out the cause of the problem. They are poorly equipped to deal with the human problems existing in their organizations.

Yet despite the dynamic changes going on in the business and industrial scene, the basic responsibility of today's supervisor remains the same. **The supervisor's fundamental responsibility in any organization is to get work done through people**. In order to reach required objectives effectively, supervisors coordinate the activities of others rather than performing operations themselves. **They are dependent on people for the particular results needed**.

The efficiency of an organization depends more on people than on any other resource. In the final analysis, machines and all other resources of an organization produce nothing without the human element to activate and control them.

Why, then, is there often an apparent difficulty in understanding and dealing with the human elements of supervision? In addition to being the most *important* resource, people are by far the most *complex* resource utilized by an organization. The supervisor is faced with different problems in dealing with people than in dealing with other resources. Unlike machinery and materials, the human resource is not standardized and does not respond to the use of impersonal formulas and techniques. Human beings vary in intelligence, attitudes, emotions, needs, and skills—all of which determine, to a greater extent than we sometimes realize, the quality of their performance on the job. Possibly because the subject seems so complex, many supervisors simply choose to ignore the problem, preferring instead to concentrate on inanimate objects—machines, facts, or figures—while letting people take care of themselves. (Unfortunately, they seldom do!)

The problem often seems to be particularly acute among individuals with scientific or technical backgrounds and training who are moved from technical jobs to supervisory or managerial positions requiring that they work with groups of people. Their experience has usually placed a premium on precision, predictability, and control. Conditioned by the predictability of the laws of the physical sciences, the technically oriented person may expect the people in his work group to act in a similar rational, predictable fashion. This expectation can often lead to an explosive situation; people do not act like machines, and they seldom appreciate being treated as such.

THE BEHAVIORAL APPROACH TO SUPERVISION

In getting things done through people, the supervisor must understand and influence the behavior of these people, both as individuals and as members of groups. **Just as we must study a machine before we can know how to operate and maintain it, we have to study the employee before we can hope to get him or her to cooperate, work willingly, and maintain a high performance level**. To do this effectively requires at least an elementary knowledge of human behavior.

As our society and employees acquire higher levels of education, more affluence, and different attitudes and values about work, the need for understanding human behavior and approaches for solving human problems within organizations has become greater than ever before. Fortunately, increasing efforts and successes have been made in unlocking the mysteries of people at work in organizations. A growing body of knowledge—resting on the principle that **where people work together as groups in order to accomplish objectives, people should understand people**—is available to assist the supervisor in developing good relations with employees and in getting the most from them. This body of knowledge has drawn heavily on the disciplines of *psychology, sociology,* and *anthropology,* collectively known as the *behavioral sciences.* Although the relationships among people at work cannot be the exclusive sphere of any one of these sciences, psychology—the study of human behavior—has probably played the biggest role in influencing management thought.

Both the quantity and quality of research findings in the field have been steadily improving through the years. The newest concepts represent a considerable spin-off from the appealingly simple notions on which the pioneers of the behavioral management school originally concentrated. A common thread running throughout a large majority of behavioral science research findings seems to be: "You are not utilizing human resources at their full capacity. You are appealing to lower-level needs to motivate employees, rather than higher social and psychological needs. You have designed jobs to take advantage of only the minimum performance human beings are capable of."

This research has necessarily upset and torn down many traditional and cherished notions about the direction and motivation of people and has developed new approaches that offer considerable promise for the fulfillment of both individual and organizational goals. As is the case with many new ideas and changing methods, these findings have frequently been resisted or ignored by those who could profit the most from them—namely, supervisors and managers. After all, American enterprise has enjoyed tremendous success through the years using the older methods of management, and "you can't quarrel with success!"

Recently, however, there has been a renewed interest in human behavior and motivation, sparked by the fact that the traditional concepts about the supervision of people are simply not working in all situations as they once did. Thus supervisory and management personnel are increasingly interested in the discoveries of behavioral science that can be applied to the task of improving productivity and profits in their organizations.[2]

Unfortunately, we are dealing with an *inexact science*—if indeed, as many argue, it can even be referred to as a science. The known elements of human behavior in organizations are only a small portion of what is yet to be learned. No one has been able to define and apply very basic principles of human behavior comparable to the precise relationships of the physicial sciences. Certainly we know a great deal about human behavior, but the application of our knowledge is less direct and far more difficult to understand.

The probability appears to be high that much more knowledge will become available and supervisors of the future will possess more factual information for coping with human problems. Yet we can't wait for the perfecting of behavioral management science before attempting to apply it. It may well be another hundred years (if ever) before we have reliable knowledge of precisely what causes people's behavior. In the meantime, supervisors must supervise. Just as physicians must treat cancer patients to the best of their present abilities without waiting for complete scientific understanding, so should supervisors take advantage of what is currently known about human behavior. Although our knowledge admittedly may be inexact and incomplete, enough is known to make examination of the subject quite fruitful. As someone once said, "Just because a problem is large is no excuse for not applying intelligence to it!"

THE SUPERVISOR'S CHANGING ENVIRONMENT

Supervising people has never been easy, but it is harder and more complex today than ever before. Changes of all kinds are creating new problems that challenge the human skills of even the best and most experienced supervisors. Together, these changes help explain why today's supervisor is finding supervision in its traditional form so difficult to carry out.

The Changing Values of Today's Work Force

Many segments of our society are experiencing a transition from traditional values and attitudes. Nowhere is this more noticeable than in the youth of the work force—those under 35, the group once known as the "post-war baby boom" that has now reached young adulthood. In the eyes of the "old timers," there is definitely a "new breed" in the work force.

A long-term research study by the firm of Yankelovich, Skelly and White has recently shown that changes over the last fifteen years have greatly affected the way American workers—especially younger ones—view the role of work in their lives and the values they bring with them to work. During the late 1940s and the 1950s, the values people lived and worked by were such traditions as *commitment to the job, conformity to social standards, a fair day's work for a fair day's pay, dedication to family,* and *faith in the rewards of the future.* Belief in the "work ethic" held that if you worked hard, saved, and behaved yourself, eventually you would get your just reward; you would achieve "The American Dream." Money, material goods, and job security were all highly valued. But in the early years of "the turbulent 1960s," this foundation of traditional values began to be questioned, and the after-effects are easily seen in the "new breed"— whether they be white-collar or blue-collar.

The general trend against "the establishment" that began in the 1960s is marked today by continued opposition to the authority of traditional institutions and values. Young people are much less inclined to defer automatically to their elders simply because their elders are more experienced. Being more independent, the young are not so often awed by their employers. With the lessening acceptance of the status quo, many of this generation seem to be in an almost constant state of dissatisfaction with what *is* relative to what *could be*. They are better educated and have higher expectations. Many are unhappy with meaningless work; they are revolting against the dum-dum jobs of the world.[3]

Historically, the unwritten contract of American work has been: "A fair day's work for a fair day's pay." Not very long ago, management could assume that if it kept its end of that contract—namely, providing the jobs, the money, the expected fringe benefits, and reasonable working conditions—employees would respond by fulfilling their part of the bargain. Today, however, the Yankelovich studies point to a "holding back phenomenon" —an increasing tendency for employees to demand and expect more without necessarily giving anything more in return.[4]

Combined, these shifts in values change most of our customary ideas about how to motivate—and communicate with—this portion of the work force. If supervisors are to lead this new breed of employees effectively, they must recognize the presence of such changes and adjust to them on a rational basis, regardless of whether they personally view the changes in values and attitudes as good or bad.

Increased Independence and Mobility of the Work Force

Simple reward-and-punishment systems that were hallmarks of earlier concepts of motivation were based largely on the fact that employees could not switch jobs easily. Because workers feared losing their jobs, the threat of dismissal could always be used to move them to action; even after the depression years of the 1930s were over, this fear persisted.

Not so today. The "fear" factor has lost considerable clout in motivating today's workers. Being fired is no longer seen as the ultimate disaster. Having never experienced a real depression, younger workers especially are more likely to view losing a job as a temporary inconvenience than as a tragedy.[5] Job security is now almost taken for granted by many. It is often viewed as a *right,* to be demanded and guaranteed. Even if the worst does happen, one can always fall back on unemployment compensation, welfare, and similar benefits.

Because alternative employment opportunities are more readily available, today's workers are also relatively more mobile and independent than the typical workers of only a generation ago. People are changing jobs more frequently. In fact, personnel experts forecast that, on the average, today's workers will change jobs and occupations as many as seven times during their careers. The "new breed" no longer chooses their first employer as the place to make a lifetime career, but as a stepping stone to something better. Those who attempt to make a career in one job in one organization are clearly in the minority. "The Company" is not the all-powerful influence on an employee's life that it used to be.

Desire for Meaningful Work

The youth of the work force are also entering their first jobs with a much higher level of educational attainment than any previous generation. In 1940, for example, Americans received an average of eight years of schooling; in 1975, the total had increased to thirteen years. The percentage of high-school graduates among employees is today the highest in history, and the number of college graduates has increased 500 percent during the past thirty years.[6]

Not only do people stay in school longer than before, they are also the targets of a different kind of education than their elders received. It is an education characterized by encouraging people to think for themselves, to question, to discover themselves, and to seek their own identity. The extreme of this is the "open classroom" concept, where children are taught to set their own goals and plan their own schedules. In any case, education is pushed as "the way" to have the good things in life. What school-age children are not told that, if they stay in school, they'll get a good, high-paying job and won't have to do a "nothing job" or manual labor like perhaps their parents did?

Thus many of today's workers have been conditioned to setting their expectations in life higher than previous generations. And they also have high expectations concerning things other than high earnings. Typically, the more education workers have, the less satisfied they are with routine, unchallenging work. Organizations that once employed elementary school dropouts now often hire those with two or more years of college— workers whose entire education has encouraged them to think for themselves. Their boredom tolerance is usually quite low. They want and *expect* meaningful, challenging work. Seldom looking for the routine, "secure" jobs that prior generations were often attracted to, they generally expect to be more involved in responsible work as soon as possible. They actively seek more participation in decisions affecting them—to help control their work, not be controlled by it. As will be discussed further in Chapter 3, they expect their supervisors to recognize and utilize whatever skills, talents, and knowledge they have to offer. Fulfilling these expectations is usually a large order for many supervisors—to say the least.[7]

The problem, of course, is that jobs have failed to change in step with these increased educational attainments and higher expectations. It is quite possible that younger people have been encouraged to have *unrealistic* expectations about the real-world life of work. Employers have probably contributed to the situation by continuing to raise educational requirements for jobs without changing the nature and design of the jobs. Fred Herzberg, an authority on motivation in the work place, summed up this dilemma when he pointed out that "we're educating more and more to do less and less."

Faced with the tedium of over-specialized, routine jobs, many employees become frustrated and creatively spend their excess mental energies causing problems for their supervisors. Or, in lieu of meaningful job satisfaction, they just leave. Young workers especially seem quite willing to "job hop" until they find a place that offers more satisfying work.

While it is not easy to generalize about all workers' viewpoints, such studies as the Department of Health, Education, and Welfare's 1973 report on *Work In America* express the needs that workers at all levels seem to have:

> What the workers want most, as more than 100 studies in the past 20 years show, is to become masters of their immediate environments and to feel that their work and they themselves are important—the twin ingredients of self-esteem. Workers recognize that some of the dirty jobs can be transformed only into the merely tolerable, but the most oppressive features of work are felt to be avoidable: constant supervision and coercion, lack of variety, monotony, meaningless tasks, and isolation. An increasing number of workers want more autonomy in tackling their tasks, greater opportunity for increasing their skills, rewards that are directly connected to the intrinsic aspects of work, and greater participation in the design of work and formulation of the tasks.

Adjusting to a Changing Environment

Additional changes, such as the justified demands of racial minorities, women, and the handicapped for equal employment opportunities; increased government action in all sectors of business; the revitalized power of labor unions; and the technological advances that must be kept up with, add still more complexity to the role of the supervisor, leaving little time for complacency.

The dramatic increase in the number of women pouring into the nation's work force deserves special mention. In fact, some labor experts believe this is one of the most significant changes in American worklife since World War II. Women now represent more than 45 per cent of all jobholders—double the number in the early 1920s—and the percentage continues to grow.[8] The women's movement has focused considerable attention on eliminating traditional inequities, such as occupational sex-typing, dissatisfying jobs, and earnings differences between men and women doing the same kind of work.

Given this dynamic state of affairs, today's and tomorrow's supervisors need to know much more about how to get things done through people than ever before. They have to be better prepared.

Adjusting to this changing environment is not always easy because for many supervisors it involves an entirely new philosophy of managing people. For instance, it is increasingly evident that supervisors can no longer simply "make" their employees perform in a desired manner. In the past, authoritarian means—threats of job loss, demotion, wage reduction, verbal abuse, and so on—may have been quite effective in forcing people to work harder. However, most current research—as well as practical experience—indicates that strict reliance on autocratic supervision and various forms of negative motivation have little relevance in today's work environment. Supervisors must currently rely heavily on the *voluntary cooperation* of employees to help accomplish the organization's goals Power alone can no longer generate the initiative and resourcefulness needed for such cooperation.[9]

THE UNIQUE ROLE OF
THE FIRST-LINE
SUPERVISOR

Supervisory functions, of course, occur at all management levels in an organization. Therefore, much, if not all, of what we will discuss in the following chapters is also applicable to individuals in higher management positions. However, this book is primarily focused on the increasingly important role of the first-line supervisor in an organization.

As the first level of management above the rank-and-file operative worker, the first-line supervisor occupies a unique and strategic position in the hierarchy of management. The importance of this position to the success of the organization's management and to the satisfaction of employees is frequently understated. First-line supervisors are responsible for directing the largest portion of an organization's work force. As management's representative at the point of immediate contact with workers and as the workers' liaison with management, the supervisor is a vital link in the organization's downward and upward flow of communication. All the policies and plans of top management flow through the supervisor to be implemented by those who work under his or her direction.

Because each supervisor has a direct effect on the satisfaction employees derive from their jobs, he or she becomes a key individual in their lives. Employees look to their supervisor as a source of information, guidance, counsel, decisions, recognition, and so on. To rank-and-file workers, their supervisor is "management."

Often, in a unionized organization, the supervisor may feel like a sitting duck for a union that whittles away at his or her power in the work group. The union may be more influential in hiring, making promotions, increasing salaries, and firing than is the supervisor in fact.

Often referred to as the "man-in-the-middle," the supervisor is constantly confronted by pressures from two groups—employees and higher management. To be accepted and respected by both groups, the supervisor must be a *member* of both groups, dividing attention and loyalty between them. Each group has its own set of expectations concerning the supervisor's role; frequently these expectations are in conflict. Management usually expects the supervisor to put priority on higher production, lower costs, and exacting schedules. Employees, on the other hand, expect the supervisor to be understanding of their work problems, fair, helpful, and friendly, and to represent them in their dealings with higher management. Each group expects the supervisor to be loyal to it—to "be on its side." Needless to say, living up to both sets of expectations is seldom an easy task, but it is one to which the supervisor must become accustomed. When the goals and expectations of employees and management are in direct conflict, it is usually up to the supervisor to work out a fair compromise.

How Are New Supervisors Selected?

In most organizations, employees are selected for new supervisory positions based on their demonstrated technical skills and experience in line-level jobs. In other words, they are picked because they were the best (or sometimes the most senior) "producers"— the best machine operator, the best electrician, the best nurse, and so on. Management takes these hard-working, skilled employees, tells them how grateful it is for their past contributions, symbolically gives them white hardhats, and promotes them to supervision. In a matter of minutes, they are expected to become supervisory miracle workers. These proven operators, craftsmen, or whatever, are no longer expected to produce with their hands, but rather miraculously to be able to lead and motivate *others* to produce as well or better than they did in their old jobs.

Now it isn't necessarily bad that management selects supervisors from employees who have good technical knowledge to do the jobs that they will be supervising. But neither is it necessarily good.

More often than not, the newly appointed supervisors are poorly prepared for these new responsibilities. They soon find themselves in a job that requires a brand new set of skills—such as *planning, motivating, communicating, counseling, disciplining, organizing, appraising,* and *training,* to mention only a few. Yet management expects them to begin performing like "pros" almost overnight. The fact that many supervisors don't perform effectively at first really shouldn't be that much of a surprise.

Again, this doesn't mean that technical skills should be downgraded or that they are unimportant to a supervisory job. Nor, as stated before, does it mean that there is anything wrong with picking supervisors who have good technical skills. It *does* imply, however, that technical experience and expertise do not guarantee supervisory success, and that further training and development are normally needed for learning how best to get work accomplished through the efforts of other people.

Preparation and Training for Supervision

Unfortunately, supervisors and management personnel are a group that has probably had less formal training in how to do their jobs effectively than any other group of employed people!

If you disagree with that statement, stop and think about it. Most other employees receive some formal training and preparation in how to do their jobs before they are expected to function effectively. Would you, for instance, put a person who has no formal training in an electrician's job? Would you make somebody who has no formal training an accountant or a nurse or an engineer? How about a chemist, a secretary, or a racing car driver? Yet organizations place people in supervisory positions all the time without providing or requiring special training and preparation!

Oh, perhaps if the supervisor's boss is so inclined, there may be some personal coaching and counseling on a sporadic basis. Far more often, though, the new supervisor learns by "trial-and-error" or "sink-or-swim."

Although it is true that more and more organizations are recognizing the need to provide some kind of formal training for new supervisors–either in-house or by attending various public seminars–such organizations are still in the minority. It is as if the supervisor is expected to be a "born leader."

Supervisory Skills Can Be Learned

And that brings up an interesting question: Is there such a thing as a "born leader"? You've doubtless heard that term used to describe someone who seems to possess good leadership skills; "Old Joe is just a 'born leader.'"

It is often suggested that good supervisors–like good athletes–are born, not made. This simply isn't true, even though organizations typically promote supervisors from the ranks as if they do have a "natural" talent for managing the work of others. People *do not* instinctively know how to plan, motivate, communicate, counsel, organize, and all the other normal activities required of a supervisor. Somewhere, somehow, people must have the opportunity *to learn* these skills–and *to practice* them. Certainly, these skills can be learned in many ways other than formal classroom training or by reading a book. As mentioned before, supervisory skills can be learned through on-the-job coaching by a good boss or, more typically, through trial-and-error. But, trial-and-error can often be expensive for the organization–and is usually very frustrating to the new supervisor.

True, people are born with different potentials, degrees of intelligence, physical attributes, and other characteristics. A good athlete is made when a person's natural endowments are developed by learning, effort, practice, and experience. The same thing is true for developing supervisors. Natural characteristics can be developed only through learning, practice, and experience. The skills involved in supervising are as learnable as the skills involved in playing football or tennis.

Making the Transition to Supervision–"Doing" versus "Supervising"

The transition from worker to effective supervisor, already made difficult by inadequate training and preparation, can be further complicated if a new supervisor has difficulty "letting go" of the "doing" activities he or she has been used to performing.

As already discussed, a supervisor's job is supposed to be one of getting work done through the efforts of other people, rather than doing the work personally. But it doesn't always work out that way. A lot of new supervisors (as well as older, more experienced ones) succumb to what can be called the "dirty hands syndrome." This describes supervisors who regularly get involved in nonsupervisory tasks. They can be found trying to do much of the work themselves, work that could and should be done by their employees. They get more involved in performing routine production and clerical tasks than they do in performing the functions of supervision. Very often, it seems easier–and more fun–to go back and "get your hands dirty."[10]

A new supervisor may also discover that it often takes longer to give directions and to supervise someone else doing the work than it does to do it oneself. There may be a real temptation to save time and effort by stepping in and doing the job rather than going through the process of training someone else to do it, and then spending time checking up to see if the job has been done right. It is tempting to think, "I can do it better myself." Yet, this is the essence of the difference between "doing" and "supervising."

Of course, there are times when supervisors should demonstrate a willingness to work along with their employees and "help out in a pinch." But this can lead to the point where supervisors end up neglecting many of the very responsibilities they have in fact been promoted to do–planning, motivating, organizing, training, and so forth. In order to meet these responsibilities, supervisors have to *delegate* as much routine work to others as is possible–not do such work themselves.

Undoubtedly, supervision requires a whole new perspective. Acquiring that perspective isn't easy. New supervisors may have been at "the top of the ladder" as experienced, proven, and knowledgeable workers. But now they're at the *bottom* of another ladder as the newest and least-experienced supervisors. Instead of being the superstars, they are now the ones who don't know the ropes and have a lot to learn. Their status and self-confidence have taken a turnaround. They can easily become insecure and frustrated.

This insecurity and frustration can lead to "dirty-hands" supervision. Supervisors may fear that they aren't capable of performing their new tasks up to management's expectations. Or they may lack confidence in their employees' abilities, fearing errors and mistakes. Or they may actually fear that their jobs may be done *better* by someone else.

All of these fears and frustrations are probably normal. But, again, the point is that "doing" activities are normally performed at the expense of one's supervisory duties.

FUNDAMENTAL SKILLS OF MANAGEMENT

Supervision, as a subject for study, should not concern itself exclusively with human behavior, as this topic constitutes only a part (although an integral part) of the total field, just as algebra is merely a part of the total field of mathematics. In other words, skill in dealing with human behavior is not the only responsibility a supervisor has, nor is it the only knowledge needed.

It is generally agreed that successful managers *at any level* in an organization must exhibit three distinct yet related skills in carrying out their jobs effectively: (1) *technical skill,* (2) *human skill,* and (3) *conceptual skill.* The relative importance of these three

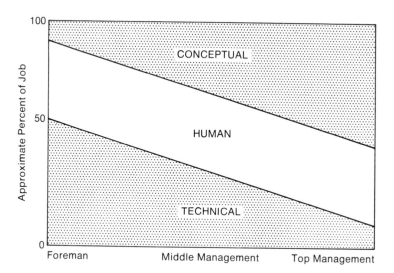

FIGURE 1–1. Relative Importance of Skills at Different Management Levels

skills varies with the level of management; a rough approximation of this relationship is shown in Figure 1-1.

Technical skill refers to a person's proficiency in, and understanding of, the specific techniques, processes, methods, and procedures required in carrying out a particular job. The skills of accountants, computer programmers, engineers, typists, nurses, scientists, and mechanics are examples.

Human skill is the ability to interact effectively with people. It includes the ability to motivate and influence others toward achieving stated goals, to win cooperation and develop an effective work team, to communicate intelligibly, and to gain acceptance of change.

Conceptual skill enables a manager to visualize the organization as an integrated whole, recognizing how a change in any one part affects all the other parts. It's the ability to see "the big picture." For example, a top-level manager of a manufacturing firm must sense the total interrelationships of such diverse functions as engineering, production, sales, advertising, finance, and personnel. Of course, this process also extends to viewing the organization within the external environments that it is influenced by and, in turn, influences—the *social, economic,* and *governmental environments.* [11]

In summary, technical skill is basically concerned with *things,* while human skill deals with *people,* and conceptual skill deals with *ideas.*

Technical skill is obviously the most important skill at the operative level. However, as shown in Figure 1-1, as people are promoted above the operative level and given leadership responsibilities, the need for this skill becomes proportionately less. Why? Because they can normally depend on their employees' technical skills. (Remember that supervisors get work done through others). At higher levels of management, technical skill is often almost nonexistent.

Human skill, in contrast, seems to be a basic requirement for managers at *any* organizational level. However, it would appear to be most important at lower and middle levels where the number of direct contacts with employees is usually greatest.

As managers move up the organizational hierarchy, their need for conceptual skill increases rapidly. They must increasingly deal with long-range planning decisions that are outside the realm of any particular group within the organization; such decisions must take into account the *overall* relationships between various other groups, both within and outside the organization.

Although we certainly cannot discount the importance of either technical knowledge and proficiency or an ability to see the organization as a whole, this book is devoted to the analysis and development of human skills—those involved in getting work done through others. Success in this area appears to be the most difficult challenge today's supervisor faces.

INGREDIENTS FOR THE DEVELOPMENT OF HUMAN SKILLS

Many qualities and attitudes contribute to the improvement of a supervisor's effectiveness in interpersonal relationships with employees. Although it would be difficult to make a complete list of such qualities and attitudes, we can easily single out five that definitely need to be cultivated: *empathy, self-awareness, acceptance of individual differences, perceptual awareness,* and *an employee orientation.* Their importance to you as a supervisor will become increasingly apparent as we examine the various topics of the following chapters.

Empathy

Empathy, perhaps the key requirement for the development of effective human skills, may be defined as **the ability to project oneself imaginatively into the thoughts, feelings, and probable reactions of another person while maintaining an objective viewpoint.** Put a bit more simply, it is the capacity to put yourself in the shoes of the other person and look at things from his or her point of view.

Note that empathy does not imply *agreement* with another's feelings; it does imply *respect* for those feelings. Nor is empathy a case of asking, "What would I do if I were in your position?"; any one of us would bring quite different attitudes and experiences to a particular position. We are truly empathic only when we can sense how the other person feels and reacts to a given situation.

It is also necessary to make a clear distinction between empathy and *sympathy,* for the two are quite different. In sympathy, you come to feel the same way as the one for whom you sympathize; you allow yourself to become emotionally involved. If you empathize, however, you know how the other person feels, but you don't allow these feelings to determine your own. Empathy requires an *objective attitude* toward the behavior of another. The viewpoint needed by the supervisor is similar to that of a physician. Good physicians understand their patients' feelings and needs—that is, they are empathic. But their emotional involvement with patients must be limited if they are to make an objective diagnosis.[12]

Empathy requires the development of an instinctive awareness of what people want and need. Most truly successful sales people exhibit this talent. Empathy enables them to intuitively sense the prospect's *true*—as opposed to *stated*—needs. They can direct their sales presentations to demonstrating how their products can satisfy these needs.

In practice, the ability to empathize well is largely a result of sincere and continued effort by the supervisor. It is seldom easy, especially when you are attempting to understand the attitudes and needs of someone who has a completely different background from your own, as is often the case in relationships with employees. Yet, improvement in this ability should be a continuing goal of every supervisor. If you are to effectively motivate and communicate with your employees, this capacity to project yourself into another person's position is indispensable; it is a foundation for working more effectively with people. Armed with a full understanding of the worker's feelings, your decisions and actions will invariably be more effective.

Self-Awareness

Along with empathy, a prerequisite for increasing your effectiveness in dealing with people (a primary objective of this book) is *a basic awareness of yourself as an individual.* Developing this awareness necessitates a serious examination of your own personality and behavior patterns, often an initially painful process when it results in recognition of the need to change.

Knowledge of the particular impact you have on the behavior of others is of utmost importance in your job as a supervisor. You should know your own inclinations toward, say, taking action hastily, being brusque with employees who don't understand your instructions the first time, and so on. Only through an awareness of your own particular prejudices, values, weaknesses, habits, and the impression you make on others can you begin to make any changes in your attitudes and behavior that would be beneficial to you and your work group.

Acceptance of Individual
Differences

As a supervisor, your job would be much easier if all of your employees had the same abilities, personalities, interests, intelligence, and needs. All you would need would be a magic formula applicable to every individual in your work group. Minimal human skill would be needed, and the long-sought "1-2-3 approach" for dealing with employees would be a practical reality.

The sad truth is, though, that there are no "sure-fire" formulas or "tried-and-true" techniques for dealing with people. Each employee has a unique personality, having been exposed in his or her lifetime to different people, things, situations, and learning experiences that make that individual different from every other person in the world.

Therefore, you must try to understand and work with the distinct personalities and behavior patterns of each of your employees. This reinforces the desirability of knowing employees individually and attempting to understand their unique attitudes, values, aspirations, habits, fears, frustrations, and so on. Only through understanding these factors can you deal with the *variable*—not the fixed—responses of each individual.

Nevertheless, while we all differ from one another, there are many things that we also have in common. As we shall see in Chapter 2, there are general needs to which you can appeal when motivating others and many effective ways of dealing with employees in groups.

Perceptual Awareness

Closely related to our acceptance of individual differences, but worthy of separate mention, is the topic of *perception*. By perception we simply mean the way each individual views the world. It should be obvious to anyone who reflects on the matter that **no two people perceive the same event or situation in exactly the same way.** Each person will perceive the event based on his or her own needs, expectations, interests, background, and previous experiences. In this sense, then, each of us does not react to the world as it is but as we *interpret* it; in other words, it is our "mental image" that counts, not objective reality. That people see and interpret everything through their own "rose-colored glasses" is a well known (and quite true!) cliché.

As a simple example of perceptual differences, let us consider the common house cat, Felix Domesticus. To a bird-lover, the cat is a menace to the world; to the householder, he may be a walking mousetrap. To another cat, he is a fellow creature. To the dog, the cat is something to be chased and eradicated. To a mouse, the cat is a monster to be feared. Each has a different perception of the cat that determines his or her reactions.[13]

In the same way, a job requiring overtime for your department may be perceived quite differently by various people. The salesperson may view it as a way of impressing customers with prompt service; you, the supervisor, may see it as a drain on your overtime budget; your employees may perceive it as extra money on payday or as an imposition that interferes with a bowling game that evening.

As we shall fully discuss in Chapter 7, awareness of perceptual differences is particulary important in all attempts at communication. What one person may consider a simple to-the-point statement or action may be interpreted by another in a completely different light. For example, there is the old story of a supervisor who told one of his production employees, "How about cleaning up this mess around here?" A couple of hours later, the supervisor found the employee just returning to the job he had previously been working on, that of preparing a component that was a rush order for a special customer. His machine and the entire area surrounding it, however, were spotlessly shining. Upon asking the man why the job was not completed on schedule, the employee replied, "I've been cleaning up like you said. See, I've cleaned the entire machine." The supervisor was slightly aghast. The mess he had referred to was only a small oil spill on the floor, an obvious safety hazard. He had, of course, meant for the man to wipe up the spill and return to his work. Who was to blame in this situation—the employee or the supervisor? Each interpreted the statement in his own way and *assumed* that the other person understood it as he did.

Again—at the risk of being repetitious—no two people perceive the same event in exactly the same way; employees react to the supervisor, the organization, and their jobs according to their individual perceptions. Awareness and acceptance of this fundamental fact of life can go a long way toward alleviating potential conflicts and misunderstandings and helping you more easily to influence and understand human behavior.

An Employee Orientation

It was once commonly believed that by giving constant close attention to production activities, results of high quantity and quality would naturally follow. Contrary to this belief, there is consistent evidence that *employee-oriented* supervisors generally achieve somewhat higher production than their solely *productivity-oriented* counterparts.

What are some of the attributes and qualities that are needed by and useful to an employee-oriented supervisor?

1. High expectations that employees have the potential to perform effectively and contribute valuable ideas;
2. A genuine personal interest in employees, viewing each as a unique and worthwhile individual deserving of attention and fair treatment;
3. A willingness to train employees carefully and help them to develop their full capabilities on the job;
4. The viewpoint that responsibility and initiative must be developed within employees rather than commanded by the supervisor.

Note that there is not an inherent dichotomy between an employee orientation and high levels of production. Employee-oriented supervisors are not unconcerned about production; certainly, supervisors must produce or else they cease to be supervisors. In fact, the most successful supervisors seem to be those who combine both orientations, giving more emphasis to an employee orientation.

Why can an employee orientation usually achieve better results? From what we have already discussed in this chapter, the answer should be apparent. Although we must recognize that production of either goods or services and their resultant profits are our primary objectives and necessary for the survival of any type of organization, these objectives are attained principally through human endeavor and cooperation. Employees achieve the productivity. As a supervisor, you can achieve your particular goals only through your employees. If they are not motivated to produce, production won't occur. [14]

Thus, **our goal should be sustained superior productivity from satisfied, motivated employees.** High job satisfaction and better job performance usually go hand in hand, just as low output, frequent mistakes, accidents, grievances, high turnover, and absenteeism are factors often related to low job satisfaction.

MUTUALITY OF INTERESTS

Running throughout our discussions in the following chapters is this general premise: **As we help satisfy an employee's personal goals, he or she will be more ready to cooperate in achieving the organization's goals.** Put another way, our objective is to integrate people into a work environment in such a way that the goals of both the organization and its individual members can be successfully realized. Through close cooperation, the individual and the organization can shape each other in order that both may achieve their objectives. Under such an ideal condition, the individual and the organization may realize a *mutuality of interests.* In other words, the employee prospers as the organization becomes more productive and efficient. In turn, the organization gains higher performance as the individual's respective needs are reasonably satisifed.

Obviously, this is a far from easy goal to attain, and it is doubtful that supervisors acting *alone* can completely achieve such a climate in their particular work groups. There must be an *overall* atmosphere of mutual trust, respect, and confidence among all levels of management and all employees. Nevertheless, such an environment is a very worthwhile goal for any organization to constantly strive for. It is especially worthwhile when one considers that, if employees' goals and objectives are not the same as those of the organization, conflicts, friction, and frustrations are likely to result.

The general philosophy expressed in this book assumes that the individual employee is the most important unit in any organization. Therefore, only to the extent that the particular economic, social, and psychological needs of each are reasonably satisfied is the organization able to make the best use of its human resources.

NO "COOKBOOK APPROACH" TO SUPERVISION

Many supervisors would undoubtedly like a collection of simple, concise, proven rules that they might use in effectively dealing with their employees, thus providing an appropriate solution to any problem. But, contrary to the advice of hundreds of "how-to-do-it" human relations books and the prescriptions of many "quick-and-easy" seminars, such a set of rules unfortunately does not exist, and probably never will. Because every person and every situation is different, there can seldom be any common cure-alls that can be applied to ensure high motivation and morale.

This is mentioned not to discourage anyone but to emphasize again that human beings are a most complex phenomenon and there is simply no one method or collection of methods that will solve all problems in dealing with them. Within wide limits, virtually all sorts of supervisory methods and techniques are successful in certain situations and unsuccessful in others. Therefore, no "cookbook approach" to supervisory problems will be offered in this book. To do so would be naive and frustrating to you as a supervisor when you discover that such universal panaceas aren't always successful.

There are no simple "off-the-shelf" formulas that a supervisor can apply without first carefully diagnosing the particular situation and its problems as they exist at a specific time. An approach that works extremely well in one situation may not work or may be less effective in a different situation, even though the problems may appear to be very similar. What seems to work one day may not work another day. What seems to turn on one employee may leave another employee cold. **A unique supervisor who deals with unique employees in a unique set of circumstances must usually seek unique solutions.**[15]

So, as you examine the material in the following chapters, keep in mind that many of the concepts presented are at best general rules. As with all generalizations, there are always exceptions!

CAN WE REALLY
APPLY BEHAVIORAL
SCIENCE THEORIES?

That's a question often asked by many supervisors after their first exposure to formal supervisory training. Other commonly expressed reactions include: "This stuff is written by people who don't know what it's like in the *real* world." Or, "These ideas are for dreamers." "Not practical." Or, "I've tried it and it doesn't work."

Such comments are often understandable. In their book, *Management of Organizational Behavior: Utilizing Human Resources,* Paul Hersey and Kenneth Blanchard agree that learning to apply the theoretical concepts of some training courses, books, and so forth, is seldom easy:

> Learning to apply the behavioral sciences is much like learning anything; for example, how does one learn to hit a baseball? One learns to hit a baseball by getting up there and attempting to hit—by practice, by doing what you are attempting to learn. There is no way you are going to learn to hit a baseball by merely reading books, even by those people considered to be experts in the field, or watching, in person or on slow motion film, great hitters. All that will do is to give you more conceptual knowledge of hitting a baseball. And yet, the psychologist defines learning as a change in behavior—being able to do something differently than you were able to do before. So in reading and watching others, all that we can get is perhaps a change in our knowledge or a change in attitudes. But if we actually want to

make something a learning situation, we have to "try on" or practice that which is learned to make it a part of our relevant behavior.

Another thing to keep in mind in terms of learning is—how did you feel the first time you ever tried to hit a baseball? If you were like most, you felt anxious, nervous, and uncomfortable. This is the way most of us feel any time that we attempt to do something that is new; something significantly different from the things we are already comfortable doing within our behavioral patterns.

Hersey and Blanchard suggest that learning to use the behavioral sciences isn't any different. Much of what you hear or read in this book or in a training session may have an impact on your knowledge and attitudes, but it only becomes relevant if you are willing to "try on" some new behaviors. If you are willing, you need to recognize that the first time you use a new pattern of behavior you probably will feel ill at ease and uncomfortable. It is this "unfreezing" that we have to go through if we want to learn.

Another caution—the first time you are up at bat attempting to hit a baseball, what is the probability that when the pitcher first delivers the ball, you are going to get a solid hit? The probability is low. It is not any different in learning behavioral science theory. The first time you attempt to behave differently based on theory, we can predict that you will probably be more effective using your old style of behavior rather than the new (although in the long run the new style may have a higher probability of success).

This is why so often supervisors who go through a training experience, in which they learn new knowledge as well as attitudes, find that in "trying on" some new behavior for the first time, it doesn't work. As a result, they may begin to respond negatively to the whole training experience, saying such things as: "This won't work in our organization." "Too idealistic." "This doesn't work in the real world."

All of us have to recognize that just like hitting a baseball, it takes practice. The first few times up, the probability of success is quite low. But the more we practice, the more we attempt to get relevant feedback, the more we can predict that the probability of success will increase.[16]

IN PERSPECTIVE—
THE NATURE AND
NURTURE OF HUMAN
RESOURCES

Without doubt, people are the chief resources of any supervisor, the primary raw material with which he or she works. The efficiency with which any organization can be operated depends to a considerable extent on how effectively its human resources can be utilized and developed. Consequently, it is becoming more and more necessary that every supervisor become thoroughly acquainted with the basic factors and forces influencing and causing human behavior at work. You, as the supervisor, simply cannot influence an employee you do not understand. Unless you have insight and knowledge about *why* your employees behave as they do—very often in ways that actually seem irrational or unreasonable—their behavior will make little sense to you. Furthermore, your not knowing why can be costing your organization time and money.

A successful supervisor might well be viewed as a "human relations engineer," one who has a high degree of skill in diagnosing complex human problems on the job and applying knowledge of human behavior and understanding of one's people to arrive at a solution. Development of this skill requires study in several areas:

Certainly, in your supervisory position, you must understand the fundamental concepts of employee *motivation*. You also need an awareness of the problems involved in the planning and implementation of *change* within your work group or organization. Perhaps no human skill is more important (and less understood) than *communication*, the passing of information and understanding from one person to another; thus, the effective supervisor must recognize the factors that promote and prevent mutual understanding among people in the work situation. Helping you to develop insight and understanding into each of these critical areas is the goal of the following chapters. Read on!

QUESTIONS FOR REVIEW AND DISCUSSION

1. a. "The major problems facing supervision today are 'people problems.'" Do you agree? Explain.
   b. What part of an average day do *you* spend dealing with "people problems"? What seem to be the bases for most of these problems?
2. A high rate of turnover is obviously expensive to an organization. Specifically, estimate what it would cost your organization to replace you.
3. "There isn't all that much to learning how to supervise. It basically involves knowledge that everyone—if he or she is half-way intelligent—already has. It's just a matter of using common sense and 'doing what comes naturally.' Getting along with your employees is nothing more than practicing the Golden Rule." Evaluate these comments.
4. Think of a particular individual you regard as an outstanding supervisor. List the characteristics you feel are responsible for his or her success. Can these characteristics be *developed* by someone who does not possess them? Explain.
5. Picture yourself 10 years from now, or 10 years ago. What do you believe would be (or would have been) your response to an announcement that your department was being abolished? Why might your responses at another time be different from your current response to such an announcement?
6. How does a higher level of education influence the expectations of an individual?
7. a. Name and explain the three skills needed for effective management at any level.
   b. Discuss the relative need for each of these skills at various levels of management.
   c. To what degree is each of the skills necessary to *you* and *your job*?

8. a. What specific methods would you suggest for developing each of the three skills—*technical, human,* and *conceptual*—in supervisors?
   b. Through a series of promotions, a once outstanding department head has now become an incompetent company vice-president. What fundamental skill is this person probably lacking? How might he or she have acquired this skill?
   c. Is the type of human skill required in dealing with managerial personnel the same as is needed by a first-line supervisor?
9. a. Name and discuss briefly the five ingredients for the development of human skills.
   b. How relevant is each of these requirements to your job?
   c. Can you add qualities and attitudes to this list that contribute to a supervisor's effectiveness in human skills?
10. a. How does *empathy* differ from *sympathy*?
    b. What do you foresee as the major problem in practicing empathy effectively?
    c. Cite a recent example in which you feel that you used empathy effectively in dealing with another person.
11. What differences exist among members of this class? Do these differences result in different opinions and viewpoints? Why?
12. a. Why is it that no two people perceive the same situation in the same way?
    b. Based on your own experiences, recall a problem that occurred because of perceptual differences. Could the incident have been avoided? How?
13. "Supervisors should be employee-oriented so that they are able to please their employees better and therefore make employees happier." Do you agree? Explain.
14. "I can't help it if his son is having trouble in school," remarks a supervisor about one of her employees. "He should leave his personal problems at home; he has a job to do here, and I intend to see that he does it." How would you respond to this situation? What skills may be needed to resolve a potential conflict?
15. Explain the concept of "mutuality of interests."

REFERENCES

1. Terry, George R., "The Supervisor of the (Near) Future," *Training and Development Journal,* Jan. 1977, p. 41.
2. Gellerman, Saul W., "Business Discovers Behavioral Science," *Guidelines for Better Management,* Vol. II. Houston: Hydrocarbon Processing/Gulf Publishing Company, 1969, pp. 142–144.
3. Zimney, Stephen A., "The Changing American Worker," *The Champion Magazine* (an employee publication of Champion International Corporation), No. 2, pp. 24–29.
4. Yankelovich, Daniel, "Yankelovich on Today's Workers," *Industry Week,* Aug. 6, 1979, pp. 61–68.
5. *Ibid.,* p. 62.
6. Terry, *op. cit.,* pp. 41–43.

7. *Work in America* (Report of a Special Task Force to the Secretary of Health, Education, and Welfare). Cambridge, Mass.: The MIT Press, 1973, pp. 49, 134–137.
8. Linden, Fabian, "Keys to the '80s–Youth and Affluence," *Across the Board,* Dec. 1979, pp. 35–36.
9. Miljus, Robert C., "Effective Leadership and the Motivation of Human Resources," *Personnel Journal,* Jan. 1970, pp. 36–40.
10. Archer, Earnest R., "Delegation and the 'Dirty Hands' Syndrome," *Supervisory Management,* Nov. 1977, pp. 31–34.
11. Katz, Robert L., "Skills of an Effective Administrator," *Harvard Business Review,* Sept.-Oct. 1974, pp. 90–100.
12. Newman, William H., Charles E. Summer, and E. Kirby Warren, *The Process of Management,* 2nd ed. Englewood Cliffs, N. J.: Prentice-Hall, Inc., 1967, pp. 587–588.
13. Douglas, John, George A. Field, and Lawrence X. Tarpey, *Human Behavior in Marketing.* Columbus, Ohio: Charles E. Merrill Books, Inc., 1967, pp. 24–25.
14. Davis, Keith, *Human Behavior at Work,* 4th ed. New York: McGraw-Hill Book Company, 1972, pp. 112–114.
15. Sartain, Aaron Q., and Alton W. Baker, *The Supervisor and His Job,* 2nd ed. New York: McGraw-Hill Book Company, 1972, pp. 153–155.
16. Hersey, Paul and Kenneth H. Blanchard, *Management of Organizational Behavior: Utilizing Human Resources,* 3rd ed. © 1977, pp. 11–12. Reprinted by permission of Prentice-Hall, Inc.

Suggested Additional Readings

Archer, Earnest R., "Delegation and the 'Dirty Hands' Syndrome," *Supervisory Management,* Nov. 1977, pp. 31–34.

Brown, David S., "Rethinking the Supervisory Role," *Supervisory Management,* Nov. 1977, pp. 2–10.

Carroll, Archie, and Ted Anthony, "An Overview of the Supervisor's Job." *Personnel Journal,* May, 1976, pp. 228–31.

Cooper, M. R., B. S. Morgan, P. M. Foley, and L. B. Kaplan, "Changing Employee Values: Deepening Discontent?" *Harvard Business Review,* Jan-Feb. 1979, pp. 117–125.

Katz, Robert L., "Skills of an Effective Administrator," *Harvard Business Review,* Sept-Oct. 1974, pp. 90–100.

Massey, Morris, *The People Puzzle.* Reston, Va.: Reston Publishing Company, Inc., 1979. 283 pp.

Sasser, W. Earl, Jr., and Frank S. Leonard, "Let First-level Supervisors Do Their Job," *Harvard Business Review,* March-April, 1980, pp. 113–121.

Yankelovich, Daniel. "Yankelovich On Today's Workers," *Industry Week,* Aug. 6, 1979, pp. 61–68.

2

MOTIVATION–THE "WHY"
OF HUMAN BEHAVIOR

*I can charge a man's battery, and then recharge it, and recharge it
again. But it is only when he has his own generator that we can
talk about motivation. He then needs no outside stimulation. He
wants to do it.*[1]

Frederick Herzberg

Year after year, business costs keep mounting. Wages and fringe benefits continue their
upward climb. Vacations grow longer and work days shorter. At the same time, management at all levels finds itself in an unending search for new ways to get the most out of
each payroll dollar and to obtain maximum employee cooperation in achieving the organization's objectives. Means are constantly sought for increasing productivity and reducing
errors, poor work, waste, turnover, absenteeism, and other costly problems. And yet, it is
widely recognized that in the majority of cases employees are still not motivated to perform at a level anywhere near that of which they are capable.

At one time, it was thought that the only way to get extra effort out of employees
was to pay them more or to reward them with additional fringe benefits. If that didn't
work, there was always the threat of dismissal.

Now, organizations are finding that neither more money nor more fringe benefits
automatically leads to more productivity. Neither does the threat of firing; barring any
long-term economic recession, it simply isn't that difficult for almost anyone to find
another job.

Hence, more and more organizations are realizing that the motivation of employees
isn't the simple matter they once viewed it as. In reality, human motivation is a very complicated subject, deserving much more attention and study than has been given it in the
past.

[1] Reprinted by permission of the *Harvard Business Review*. Excerpt from "One More Time:
How Do You Motivate Employees?" by Frederick Herzberg (January-February 1968). Copyright ©
1968 by the President and Fellows of Harvard College; all rights reserved.

Essentially, the study of motivation is concerned with the "why" of human behavior. Why do people behave as they do? Why do some workers devote all their energy to their jobs, while others are satisfied with what appears to be only a half-hearted effort? Why does one worker enjoy performing a job while another loathes it?

The answer to all these questions can be at least partially explained in one word: *motivation.*

As a supervisor, you must understand why people are motivated to behave as they do. Only then can you make the types of decisions that will encourage your employees to direct their efforts toward helping to achieve the organization's goals.

WHAT IS MOTIVATION?

There are a great number of individual theories on the subject of human motivation—often seemingly as many as there have been psychologists! This does not mean that nothing concrete is known about the subject, but rather that there is more than one interpretation of it.

While there is not universal agreement on the makeup of the complex process of motivation, one of the concepts that has traditionally been found useful in understanding it is that of *human needs.*

Psychologists tell us that all human behavior, whether on a conscious or unconscious level, is caused by a person's *need structure.* Thus, a person is motivated to do something because of what he or she needs and wants.

Or, put another way, **all human behavior is motivated or caused, in that it is directed toward the satisfaction of the individual's physiological or psychological needs.**

We can define motivation in its simplest form as **goal-seeking behavior.** Such goal-seeking behavior revolves around the desire for need satisfaction. This process is presented in Figure 2-1. An unsatisfied need causes a state of *tension* which is uncomfortable to the individual.* Action is then taken to reduce, eliminate, or divert the tension state. The need for food, for example, produces a tension state that we call hunger. A goal to be sought (depending on your tastes and degree of affluence) might be a steak dinner. Action would be taken to seek this goal; and if the action were successful, the tension would be removed and the need, at least temporarily, fulfilled.

FIGURE 2-1. Motivation as Goal-seeking Behavior

*The dictionary defines a *need* as a condition requiring supply or relief; it is a lack of something desirable or useful. It is also a feeling of inadequacy; it is the restlessness that results from dissatisfaction with the present state of affairs. It is desiring what you do not have; it is the conviction that you are not enjoying maximum personal satisfaction.

The Hierarchy of Human Needs

If we accept the premise that behavior is goal-directed toward need satisfaction, it seems obvious that you, the supervisor, have but two choices if your motivational efforts are to be successful: (1) you can create felt needs within the employee, or (2) you can offer a means for satisfying needs already within the employee. Either way, it is essential to have a basic understanding of the fundamental needs of people.

For this, we turn to psychologist Abraham Maslow, who has supplied what many consider to be the core theory of human motivation. Maslow suggested that all of us are subject to a *hierarchy of needs*. This simply means that we all share certain fundamental needs that can be ranked in the sequence in which they normally occur. This hierarchy is pictured in Figure 2-2.

According to Maslow, individuals tend to satisfy their needs in the order of priority shown in the hierarchy. Thus, needs in the first two categories are usually met first; these are often called the *primary* needs. Needs in the remaining three categories are *secondary* needs; they are satisfied after the primary needs are met.

Although the need hierarchy does not give us a complete understanding of human behavior or the means to motivate people—nor does any other such theory—it is a helpful starting point in understanding ourselves and those with whom we work.

Physiological needs. First in the Maslow hierarchy of needs are those basic physio-

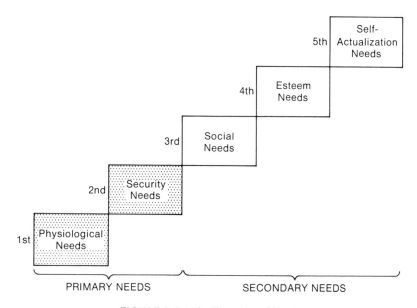

FIGURE 2-2. The Hierarchy of Needs

logical drives that people require for survival and subsistence, including the need for food, drink, rest, air to breathe, shelter, and satisfactory temperatures.

Little conscious thought is typically given to these needs unless something jeopardizes their satisfaction. For example, if you haven't eaten in a week, you will be totally motivated by the need for food. "Man lives for bread alone when there is no bread." Your needs for social status, sex, or recognition are inoperative when your stomach has been empty for a while. But when you eat regularly, hunger ceases to be an important motivator of your behavior.

In the work situation, these physical needs are primarily satisfied by salaries and other economic benefits supplied by management and, to an extent, by the physical conditions of the job—for example, adequate lighting and ventilation, restrooms, drinking fountains, rest periods, and other physical facilities needed to satisfy these primary drives. However, because most organizations do a reasonably good job of taking care of these needs, satisfying them is no longer a prime motivating factor, as it once was.

Security needs. Security needs have both *physical* and *economic* dimensions, with the latter being more significant to management. Although concerned with physical safety, the avoidance of pain, and the seeking of comfort, they can best be seen on the job in attempts to ensure job security and to move toward greater financial support. The desire to fulfill these needs might best be considered as seeking "peace of mind."

Once our physiological needs have been satisfied, we want to feel that they are secure and will continue to be satisfied in the foreseeable future; in other words, having taken care of our physiological needs today, we want a guarantee for tomorrow. Employees specifically seek protection against loss of their jobs and earnings, whether because of illness, accident, old age, arbitrary firing, or other reasons. Security needs are reflected on the job by such things as pension plans, group medical and hospital plans, and all types of job security, especially seniority.

Security is a relative thing. To one person it may mean the ability to maintain a house with fifteen rooms, five servants, and a yacht. To another, it may simply mean some assurance that the rent will be paid next month. But to all, there must be a sense of continuing ability to provide the necessities of life.

Social needs. When our physiological and security needs are reasonably satisfied, social needs become important motivators of our behavior; they are the needs that are satisfied through relationships with other people.

We are social animals. Our social needs include such motives as the need to belong, the need for love and affection, and the need for approval and acceptance by our peers. We want to be participants in activities with others, to be a part of things. We want to identify with a group or groups.

Close friendships, informal work groups, clique formation, and the desire to feel "in" or to be a part of the organization reflect social needs on the job.

In many cases, supervisors become apprehensive about this natural tendency of employees to group together. It's easy to jump to the conclusion that informal work groups are natural threats to the organization and must be immediately broken up. To the contrary, any attempts to prevent informal groups from forming usually result in employee frustration that can lead to uncooperativeness and hostility that never existed before. Indeed, many studies confirm that cohesive, tightly-knit work groups are the most productive.

It is often argued that these needs are (and should be) met mostly outside the job situation. However, if one third to one half of employees' waking hours are spent in the work environment, is it not reasonable to expect that at least *some* of their social needs should be met at work?

Esteem needs. Above the social needs on the hierarchy are the needs for self-esteem: the desire for recognition, appreciation, prestige, status, self-confidence, and the respect of our co-workers. Esteem is often just the good feeling that results when someone makes a positive comment about us or our work or when others demonstrate their respect for us.

Our desire for esteem and recognition dates from an early age. Children soon learn that one of life's best satisfactions is being considered "better than someone else." We want approval of ourselves and of what we do. A fellow, as a gag, once sent one-word telegrams to ten of his friends. The message read simply: "Congratulations." Eight of the ten, thinking that the sender must have learned of one of their recent achievements, promptly sent him notes of thanks!

On the job, sincere praise for a job well done, or a pat on the back in the presence of other workers, are small but important ways of satisfying these needs for the employee. They can also be seen in the employee's desire to have the respect of his or her supervisor, both as a person and as a valued contributor to the organization's goals.

That is not to imply that employees have to receive "verbal bouquets" for every job done correctly. However, when things are done especially well, then the supervisor should offer some type of recognition. Good performance happens more often than we realize! (Have you ever wondered why there aren't more notes of praise than notes of reprimand in employees' personnel files?)

Of course, meaningful praise for a job well done isn't the only way to satisfy the esteem need on the job. Here are some others for your consideration:

1. Involve employees; let them know where they fit in.
2. Keep employees informed about how their jobs contribute to the success of the total operation.
3. Show respect for employees' judgement; allow them to participate in making decisions that affect them.
4. Give employees challenging work; if there isn't a challenge, then there can be no sense of achievement.
5. Set performance goals that are challenging and attainable—and provide feedback to employees on their progress.

We will take a further look at ways to capitalize on the esteem need later in this chapter.

Self-actualization needs.   These needs (also commonly referred to as *self-fulfillment* and *self-realization* needs) reflect our desire to actually achieve that personal development that we are capable of attaining. As Maslow said, "What a man *can* be, he *must* be."[2]

At the workplace, self-actualization becomes a need to work toward or to reach a job level consistent with one's skills, abilities, and aptitudes. Thus, the *work itself* can become a source of gratification, especially if the work includes opportunities for responsibility, a sense of achievement, creativity, challenge, and personal growth. Nonetheless, the jobs of many employees today (if not most) do not provide these kinds of satisfaction, and for some jobs it may be unreasonable to expect that they ever will. The emphasis on job specialization and mass production often offers little chance for rank-and-file employees to feel "self-actualized." In this case, the employees must seek to fulfill their higher-level needs *off the job,* if at all. This perhaps explains why so many people today can be found laboring much harder in their after-hours hobbies and recreational pursuits than they do on their jobs.

Self-actualization is seldom a dominant motivator of behavior because so many people (especially those at the lower levels of the organizational "pecking order") are still attempting to satisfy their social and esteem needs; however, it influences the behavior of nearly everyone. It is usually a constant motivator, as most people will never fully satisfy it.

Much of the discussion in Chapter 3 and in other parts of the book will be aimed at possible ways that these needs (along with the esteem needs) can be better satisfied on the job.

Premises of the Hierarchy

Maslow's theory of human motivation sets forth two fundamental premises that have important implications for supervision:

1. *People's needs are arranged in a hierarchy of importance.* Saying that needs are hierarchical simply means that people are continually "wanting animals"; as they have one need satisfied, they will look up to the next higher order of needs. Conversely, **the higher needs do not become important as motivators until the lower-order needs are relatively well satisfied.**

If needs lower on the hierarchy are not satisfied, people never get around to doing much about the needs higher on the hierarchy. For example, if employees' wage levels are too low to satisfy their basic physiological and security needs, their behavior will be continually dominated by their lower-level needs. It is unlikely that they would respond to incentives designed to satisfy social, esteem, or self-actualization needs. However, once they have achieved a better standard of living, their thoughts will turn to the higher-level needs.

Or, if lower-level needs that have been previously satisfied suddenly face loss of satisfaction, pursuit of higher need fulfillment will cease and attention will again be focused on the lower needs. Anyone who has suddenly become unemployed will vouch for this!

2. *Satisfied needs are no longer motivating.* Perhaps the most important point to remember is that employees are actively motivated by what they are seeking, not by what they already have. As lower-level needs are reasonably satisfied, they become less of a motivational force in a person's behavior.

According to Maslow, a need does not have to be completely satisfied before the next need emerges. If, for example, a worker's physiological and security needs (*primary* needs) are 75 per cent satisfied and the social, esteem, and self-actualization needs (*secondary* needs) are satisfied 30, 20, and 5 per cent, respectively, the worker's behavior will be aimed primarily in the direction of satisfying the higher-level needs. The physiological and security needs would take a subordinate role.

Employees are motivated primarily by the next level of unsatisfied needs in the hierarchy. Thus, in a sense, satisfied needs disappear. Supervisors must look to those needs that are relatively unsatisfied if they wish to influence the behavior of their employees.

The Changing Motivational Emphasis

At one time, management took the view that employees regarded their jobs solely as a means of satisfying their material wants. More recently, with a little help from Maslow and other behavioral scientists, we have come to see that people seek to satisfy other than their purely economic needs.

The role of money. Many supervisors continue to believe that an employee's motivation can be bought. "Money is still the best motivator," they say. Regardless of the problem, they feel that it can be solved either by promising more money or threatening to withhold money.

Certainly, money *is* important. We'd have to be blind or deaf to think otherwise. As previously mentioned, employees' lower-order needs are primarily satisfied through the wages and other economic benefits derived from their jobs. The money that they earn purchases satisfactions for their physiological and security needs. Money can also purchase material goods that people perceive as necessary to satisfy higher-level needs such as belonging, esteem, and status. For example, one might buy an expensive sports car if it was felt necessary to being accepted by a social group. However, it's important to understand that an individual does not satisfy higher-level needs through this type of behavior *on the job*.

To be sure, employees will want and demand more money all the time. But that doesn't necessarily mean that those who get it are going to work any harder. Real motivation simply can't be bought today. Of course, an effective wage and salary program is a "must" for any organization to keep employees from becoming actively dissatisfied with their earnings. But money alone is not going to sufficiently sustain true motivation on the job.

Emphasis on secondary needs. So, although no one discounts the importance of money, it is seldom enough to keep employees motivated today. For a majority of our country's employed workers, there is almost a built-in guarantee that the primary needs (physiological and security) will be reasonably satisfied. As pointed out in Chapter 1, many employees find it less and less necessary to worry about tomorrow. They no longer have an overwhelming feeling that they must work in order to survive and do not take a simple "grin and bear it" attitude toward work. Employees today seek to satisfy more than their economic needs.

Based on the premise that a satisfied need no longer motivates, we can conclude that, as employees' primary needs are satisfied, the incentives needed for motivation must be designed to appeal to the secondary needs (social, esteem, and self-actualization). Yet, this fact is regularly ignored in conventional approaches to motivation.

There must be opportunities at work to satisfy these secondary needs. The failure of many supervisors to realize this is the reason why employees are often dissatisfied even though wages and working conditions are quite good. When their higher-level needs go unsatisfied, employees will often make insistent demands for more money. Such a reaction does not, however, indicate an attempt to further satisfy lower-level needs; rather, money becomes increasingly important for buying the material goods that may provide limited satisfaction of the higher-level needs that are not being satisfied on the job.

Behavior Is Multi-Motivated

Analysis of an individual's behavior would be simple if we could ascribe it to one basic need alone. Needs rarely influence behavior individually, however. Rather, they usually work in combination with each other. Thus, any specific behavior tends to be determined by several of the basic needs simultaneously rather than by only one. For example, the act of eating may be motivated partially by the social needs and the esteem needs (in the case of dining at a gourmet restaurant). As another illustration, sexual behavior in our society is usually multi-motivated. It reflects satisfaction of simple physiological drives as well as aspirations for such needs as belonging, love, esteem, status, and achievement. As we have already seen, earning wages often helps satisfy many of the secondary needs as well as the primary needs.

Thus, we must view Maslow's five-way classification as being somewhat artificial; in reality, the needs are intertwined within the whole person. However, even though the division between the needs is not sharp, it is still usually possible to find one dominant need that is influencing a person's behavior at any one moment. Therefore, their separation for purposes of analysis is still quite useful.

The Influence of
Aspiration Levels

You may argue that some people do not seem to exhibit some of the *secondary* needs at all. As an extreme example, how do you explain the hermit who seeks no social contacts and appears to have little or no need for esteem or self-actualization?

Level of aspiration is probably a major determinant in this case and is directly related to the individual's *expectations of success* in goal achievement. Repeated failures (goal blockages) normally deflate one's self-image of competence and achievement and lead to a downward adjustment of aspirations. By the same token, a sequence of successes tends to reinforce the individual's self-image of competence and ability to achieve, thereby raising his or her level of aspiration.

Thus, the potency of a secondary need depends to a great extent on whether the person expects to be successful in meeting that need. For instance, an employee may have little desire to join the management ranks, saying, "I know I'll never make it"; a fear of failure keeps the individual's level of aspiration low so that he or she will not run the risk of failure.

To understand an employee's need structure, then, we not only have to identify the needs of each and know how well these needs are being met, but we also need to take into account how much more satisfaction of each need a person really expects to attain—his or her level of aspiration.[3]

DETERMINING
EMPLOYEES'
INDIVIDUAL NEEDS

Understanding a theory such as Maslow's need hierarchy by itself does not solve a supervisor's motivation problems. **The supervisor's most difficult task is to judge where employees stand on the need hierarchy and then provide appropriate incentives to satisfy them.** Although it is valuable to know something about human needs in a general sense, it is even more important to know the personal needs of each employee.

In your supervisory job, you obviously must know a great deal about your employees before you can use the "hierarchical ordering" to your advantage. First, you must understand them as individuals. Motivation is personal; it occurs *within the individual.* As such, the incentives that appeal to one employee may be less than successful with another.

Motivation Must Be
Inferred from Behavior

Understanding the motivation of employees is complicated by the fact that it cannot be directly observed, but must be *inferred* from the individual's behavior. We can measure presumed *indicators* of motivation, but not motivation itself.

The measurable indicators of motivation are based on observation of employee action: what a worker does and how he or she behaves. These actions can be expressed in such things as productivity, quality, turnover, grievances, promptness, absenteeism, waste prevention, high interest in the work, and so forth. For example, if we observe Jane Smith producing considerably more than any of her co-workers, we would probably infer that Jane is motivated; however, we did not directly measure her motivation.

This approach, of course, often paves the way for errors of interpretation as we attempt to explain the cause of behavior from the behavior itself.

Differences in
Individual Needs

Further compounding the difficult task of judging where each employee stands on the need hierarchy is the fact that individuals require *varying degrees* of satisfaction of each need. For example, some may feel reasonably secure if they know that they will have their jobs for the next month; others may become quite anxious if they feel that their jobs might be abolished at the end of five years. Likewise, some people require little attention and affection; others seek constant reassurance of their acceptability. Thus, although the need hierarchy in particular cultures and subcultures tends to be similar, **the required degree of need fulfillment varies with individuals** due to differences in interests, attitudes, aptitudes, and past experiences. In addition, the urgency of each need may be vastly greater or smaller within the same individual at different times.

Therefore, you cannot assume that a single approach can be used to motivate all employees toward the accomplishment of the organization's goals. You must come up with an incentive that is meaningful to the individual employee.

How do you find out what the needs of each individual employee are? The answer is not a simple one. Needs are not easily identifiable. They are not lying on the surface in plain view.

It would be relatively easy if you could just ask people what their needs are and rely on their answers. Unfortunately, the answers would seldom be reliable, as people themselves are often not very clear about their own needs and desires. In the case of the secondary needs, their motivations are often unconscious. For example, dissatisfied workers may attribute their dissatisfaction to their wages, only to find later that a salary raise hasn't really satisfied them at all.

There must be considerable *rapport* between you and each of your employees. This takes time, personal involvement, and, above all, *empathy* on your part. Observations of the employee and his or her work record, informal talks, performance ratings, comments from others, and watching the employee's responses to a variety of work assignments and incentives should provide you with a reasonable evaluation of the employee's needs. Knowing these needs, you can then proceed to try satisfying them in the job environment.

The Influence
of Perception

As was discussed earlier, human behavior is goal-seeking or directed rather than being random or illogical. It is important to realize that no form of behavior is irrational or illogical *to the individual*, even though it may seem so to others who do not understand why the person behaves the way he or she does.

People behave in ways that make sense *to them*, based on their perception and understanding of the circumstances in which they find themselves at any point in time. They behave the way they do simply because they believe that they will be better off because of their behavior.

Take the case of a welfare recipient who drives a new Cadillac. You and I may be convinced that this is irrational behavior, declaring that this person doesn't need a Cadillac. We'll never convince the welfare recipient of this, however, because to that person the car is fulfilling definite needs, most likely needs for esteem and status. The person is not motivated by what you or I think ought to be needed and wanted, but by what *he* or *she* needs and wants. In this sense, then, **all behavior is rational.**

The important topic of *perception* is treated in other parts of the book. Suffice it to say at this point that **the process of motivation always operates within the framework of the individual's perception of the situation.** The manner in which the individual perceives or interprets the situation is just as important as what the situation really is in the motivation of his or her behavior. Perhaps this partially explains why the rank-and-file employees typically see their world as far different from that of their superiors.

Do Supervisors Really Know the Needs of Their Employees?

There have been countless studies of what workers want and need. Let us sum up one such typical study:

Three thousand employees were asked two questions:

1. What do you want most from your job?
2. How would you rate these wants in their order of importance?

Later, managers and supervisors were asked to rate the same items in the order they thought employees rated them. Here is the outcome:

Areas of Job Satisfaction Wanted Most by Employees	Employees' Rating by Importance	Management's Rating by Importance
Credit for work they do	1	7
Interest in work	2	3
Fair pay with salary increases	3	1
Understanding and appreciation	4	5
Promotion on merits	5	4
Counsel on personal problems	6	8
Physical working conditions	7	6
Job security	8	2

In comparing the management and employee ratings, it is apparent that management expected employees to be primarily motivated by salary and job security, while the employees stressed satisfaction on the job itself. While management thought employees would show little or no concern for job recognition, employees pointed out that they wanted to be given credit for doing a good job. The results of this study (as well as others) seem to show that some managers and supervisors don't have a true awareness of the wants and needs of their workers; they also illustrate management's traditional emphasis on *primary* needs as motivators.

THE FRUSTRATION
OF GOAL BLOCKAGE

The total satisfaction of human needs, of course, can seldom be met on the job, even when management is willing to try to do so. The realities and constraints of the job will result in certain goals being blocked from satisfaction.

Any time people are unable to satisfy their needs and thereby reduce their tensions, they will experience *frustration.*

Our previous diagram of the motivation process as goal-seeking behavior can be expanded to illustrate the blockage of need satisfaction (see Figure 2-3).

Personal and
Environmental Barriers

The blocks that prevent people's goals from being achieved can be either *personal barriers* (internal to the individual) or *environmental barriers* (external to the individual).[4]

Personal barriers result from people's overestimation or underestimation of their capabilities, either *physical* or *mental*. Examples are the aspiring athlete who does not have the physique to achieve fame as a pro football star and the person who lacks the intelligence necessary to graduate from college, even though these have been life-long goals; in both cases, the individuals *overestimated* their capabilities.

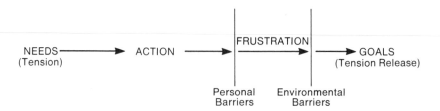

FIGURE 2-3.   Blockage of Need Satisfaction

Or, as an example of a personal barrier resulting from an *underestimation* of capabilities, consider an employee who desires to assume more responsibilty or to learn to operate a new machine. Lacking self-confidence in an ability to attain such goals, the individual may never attempt them or give up before reaching them.

Environmental barriers are those that exist in the situation in which people find themselves. An example of this type of barrier could be the supervisor who stands in the way of a worker's promotion. The job itself or the organization may also be environmental barriers; for instance, a job that affords little or no opportunity for contact with other people represents an environment that precludes workers from adequately fulfilling their social needs at work.

It is important to note that both types of barriers can be either *real* or *imaginary,* depending upon the individual's perception of the situation. As an example, an employee who is afraid to learn to operate a new machine might be imagining that he or she can't do so. However, since the employee *perceives* that he or she can't, the barrier exists. On the other hand, the 135-pound man aspiring to be a football star faces a very real barrier.

Reactions to Frustration

Employees caught in a state of frustration commonly react in ways that will protect their self-concepts and egos from the psychological pain of failure or defeat. These unconscious reactions to frustration are called *defense mechanisms.* Reactions vary from person to person; some people react in a constructive manner while others react in a defensive manner. Regardless, this reactive behavior to frustration can still be considered *goal-seeking behavior* in that it is **directed at the goal of defending the self-concept.** Often, it is behavior not necessarily aimed at accomplishing the organization's goals.

Typical defense mechanisms can be grouped conveniently into three major classifications: (1) *aggressive reactions;* (2) *substitute reactions;* and (3) *avoidance reactions.*

Aggressive reactions.

1. **Aggression:** *Direct* or *indirect* action is taken against the source of frustration. If the barrier happens to be a person, the action taken could be outright physical attack. However, in a work situation, indirect action aimed at the barrier is more likely. For example, verbal aggression, antagonistic behavior, a scowl, subtle sabotage, petty thievery, absenteeism, tardiness, or "malicious obedience."

2. **Displacement:** Here, hostile feelings are *redirected* toward persons or objects *other than* the source of the frustration. In general, the substitute target is one that isn't capable of retaliation. For example, supervisors who have just been reprimanded by their superiors may in turn displace their aggression on subordinate workers who, in turn, may arrive home yelling at their spouses or kicking their dogs.

Lacking any nearby safe objects, the frustrated person may be limited to verbal abuse of such things as the state of the economy, rush hour traffic, minority groups or politicians. Because the world offers a multitude of such "irritations," the displacement of aggression to substitute objects is easy.

Substitute reactions.

1. **Compensation**: This reaction is an attempt to overcome some real or imagined inadequacy. Individuals redirect their behavior away from the unattainable goal toward a *substitute* goal from which they can gain satisfaction.

Thus, a worker who is unable to climb the management hierarchy may try to become a civic-club leader or a union official. Or, as another example, a person who has failed to achieve a desired level of social status in the community may expend a large proportion of income on an expensive car, clothing, and other presumed material indicators of high status.

2. **Rationalization**: Individuals concoct false reasons to justify failure of goal achievement in order to preserve their self-esteem; conclusions that they *want* to believe are arrived at through illogical thinking.

This popular type of reaction often involves blaming something or someone else for one's own failures and inadequacies. For example, an incompetent employee may blame obsolete equipment, poor working conditions, poor supervision, worn-out tools, or those who are "against me," rather than admit personal shortcomings and poor performance.

The person whose ego was severely injured by social contacts in the past may rationalize by saying, "I couldn't care less what other people think of me." This is a way of protecting oneself from being hurt again.

Other examples include the employee who, failing to get a much-desired promotion, says, "I didn't want it anyway because it would require too much extra work," or the salesperson who pads the expense account "because everybody else does it."

3. **Projection**: This reaction is an attempt to protect individuals from conscious awareness of their own undesirable feelings and attitudes by attributing (projecting) them to others; others are blamed for thoughts that are not compatible with one's self-concept.

For example, an employee who is having a bad relationship with his or her supervisor may feel that it is the supervisor who is being nasty and ill-tempered, when in fact this is the behavior of the employee.

Persons who cannot accept the fact that they are racially prejudiced (if this attitude is inconsistent with their self-concept) may ascribe this attitude to others and become "champions" for the cause of racial equality.

4. **Identification**: The achievements of a successful person become the conquests of the frustrated "little man." Individuals get pleasure from the successes of other people when their own successes are blocked. This process frequently leads to internalizing the beliefs and mannerisms of those being identified with. For example, a rank-and-file employee may start talking, dressing, and acting like his or her admired boss. Identification, of course, is what "hero worship" is all about.

Avoidance reactions.

1. **Regression**: When confronted with frustration, some people attempt to return to immature, childlike behavior. This reaction evidently allows them to escape the realities

of adult responsibilities. Desk-pounding, temper tantrums, horseplay, and a desire to return to "the good old days" are examples. Or, a supervisor who has been blocked in some pursuit may become busy with clerical duties more appropriate for employees.

2. **Repression**: People lose conscious awareness (or "forget") incidents or feelings that would cause frustration and anxiety if permitted to remain at the conscious level. Thus, employees may "forget" to tell their boss about personally embarrassing or painful incidents.

3. **Withdrawal**: In this reaction, people retreat from reality by leaving the situation in which frustration is experienced. The withdrawal may be *physical* (actually leaving the scene) or *psychological.*

Increased absenteeism, extended lunch hours or coffee breaks, extra days off, and increased turnover represent examples of ways employees may seek to withdraw physically from jobs that provide little need satisfaction.

Fantasizing and daydreaming provide examples of psychological withdrawal from a frustrating work environment.

4. **Apathy**: Frustrated individuals resign themselves to the fact that a situation exists beyond their control. Typical behavior evidencing this reaction includes doing the bare minimum required to retain the job, doing nothing to correct a malfunction, or simply not caring if something is done right or not.

Implications for
the Supervisor

You can no doubt think of examples of your own reactions to frustration that illustrate the basic defense mechanisms. All of us use these defense mechanisms at one time or another because they perform an important function in protecting our self-concepts and helping us adjust to reality. Thus, as a supervisor, you should find a knowledge of them beneficial in understanding the behavior of your employees as well as yourself.

Unless carried to an extreme degree, such behavior is considered normal. However, when defense mechanisms dominate behavior (as is especially likely with the avoidance reactions) a serious personality problem may exist, requiring professional help.

An understanding of defense mechanisms should give you greater empathy in your everyday interactions with employees. However, it is important to view such reactions on the part of employees as *symptoms* of underlying causes. Take the example of an employee who frequently takes longer than allowed for a lunch break. This might be a withdrawal reaction to an unchallenging, boring job. If at all possible, your action in this case would best be aimed at eliminating the basic *cause* of the frustration (the boring and unchallenging job), not at severely reprimanding the employee for tardiness (the symptom).

The employees' use of defense mechanisms can often serve as valuable clues to the degree to which their needs are being fulfilled. When possible, you can then help to reduce the environmental and personal barriers to their goal achievement.

MOTIVATION
IS INTERNAL

Some supervisors still believe that the only motivation needed to get a job done is a direct order: "Do it—or ELSE!" Such supervisors who think their authority is motivation enough will answer in any discussion about motivation, "I'm too busy to go around coddling my people. I give them an order and the job gets done; but if they goof off, they'll hear from me soon enough." This reaction is common, sometimes understandable; but it reflects a basic misconception about how people are best motivated.

If you are willing to accept our previous concepts of motivation, you can readily see that one cannot truly "motivate" anyone else. "Motivation" does not mean something that supervisors try to "do" to other people.

When you get right down to it, people must motivate themselves. Motivation should be viewed as coming from *within the individual* (internalized) rather than from the employee's supervisor. As motivation expert Frederick Herzberg has said, "I can charge a man's battery, and then recharge it, and recharge it again. But it is only when he has his own generator that we can talk about motivation. He then needs no outside stimulation. He *wants* to do it."[5]

Actually, the only thing a supervisor can do to achieve genuine cooperation from employees is to create an atmosphere in which each individual wants to move in the direction of achieving the organization's goals while at the same time achieving his or her own personal goals; in other words, the supervisor can provide a *motivating environment*. The supervisor cannot force employees to accept the goals of the organization or to seek fulfillment of all their needs on the job. But the supervisor can create an environment—an atmosphere—where employees are encouraged and able to seek such satisfaction for themselves.

Hence, your task as a supervisor is not so much that of "motivating others" as it is of "unleashing" in the right direction the motivation that is already within your people.

OUR ASSUMPTIONS
ABOUT PEOPLE—
"THEORIES X AND Y"

Much discussion has evolved from Maslow's original concept of the need hierarchy, most of it indicating that the motivational methods that may have worked well enough a generation ago are increasingly ineffective today. One of the most important efforts along these lines is the work of the late Douglas McGregor.

McGregor saw the emergence of two basic sets of *assumptions* or *beliefs* about human behavior that characterize management styles. He labeled these sets of assumptions "Theory X" and "Theory Y." These two theories reflect completely different approaches to the motivation of people and have spurred much of the research done since the early 1960s on leadership styles and motivation.

Theory X

Theory X represents the "traditional approach" to the management of people. According to McGregor, it assumes that people are inherently lazy, that they dislike work and avoid it if possible; that they prefer being directed and told what to do, avoid responsibility, and have little ambition.

Managerial style under Theory X assumptions tends to depend on methods of *coercion,* which uses the threat of termination as a means of compelling a person to work, and *compensation,* which uses the reward of money as a means of attracting the person to perform activities needed by the organization. Both methods assume that people have to be subjected to some form of *external control* to ensure productivity; in other words, the supervisor must maintain close surveillance if the organization's objectives are to be obtained.

Whether we like it or not, many organizations today are modeled on Theory X beliefs; many management policies and practices seem to reflect these assumptions. Is it small wonder that conflict and strain often develop between management and workers when managers and supervisors consciously or unconsciously communicate the way they feel about the people who work for them?

Theory Y

On the other hand, Theory Y holds that, given the opportunity and incentive, most people want to work. People will not only accept but, in many cases, seek responsibility. McGregor contended that management, instead of depending solely on direction and control, should concentrate on creating an environment that releases potential, fully utilizes an employee's talents and training, creates opportunity, removes obstacles to individual initiative, and encourages individual growth.

A Theory Y environment attempts to integrate the organization's objectives with the individual's needs. If a worker is committed to the objectives of the organization, he or she will exercise *self-discipline* and *self-control.*

What Did McGregor Really Mean?

On the surface, the distinction between these two theories is deceptively simple, and many people try to oversimplify it. For example, some mistakenly equate Theory X with "hard," "production-oriented," or "authoritarian" leadership, while Theory Y is seen as "soft," "democratic," "permissive," or "employee-oriented." Actually, this is far from what McGregor had in mind. In fact, he said that Theory X assumptions about people could lead to either "hard" or "soft" supervision:

At one extreme, management can be "hard" or "strong." The methods for directing behavior involve coercion and threat (usually disguised), close supervision, tight controls over behavior. At the other extreme, management can be "soft" or "weak." The methods for behavior involve being permissive, satisfying people's demands, achieving harmony. . . .

There are difficulties with the "hard" approach. Force breeds counterforces: restriction of output, antagonism, militant unionism, subtle but effective sabotage of management objectives. This "hard" approach is especially difficult during times of full employment.

There are also difficulties in the "soft" approach. It leads frequently to the abdication of management—to harmony, perhaps, but to indifferent performance.

People take advantage of the soft approach. They continually expect more, but they give less and less.[6]

It is especially important to note that McGregor did *not* deny that employees' behavior in the average organization often reflects the traditional assumptions of Theory X. Realistically, there *are* many employees who appear to be lazy, unambitious, irresponsible, and need to have close direction and control. But McGregor was also sure that people are not like this by nature; instead, they *become* this way because of past experiences and conditioning in Theory X organizations. The traditional approach, according to McGregor, is based on the mistaken notion of what is *cause* and what is *effect*.

In simplest terms, Theory X implies that motivation is *external to the individual,* and Theory Y implies that motivation comes *from within the individual.* Essentially, Theory X represents the traditional "carrot-and-stick" (reward-punishment) model of motivation. As Harry Levinson has said in *The Great Jackass Fallacy,* "If the first image that comes to mind when one thinks 'carrot-and-stick' is a jackass, then obviously the unconscious assumption. . . is that one is dealing with jackasses who must be manipulated and controlled. Thus, unconsciously, the boss is the manipulator and controller, and the subordinate the jackass . . . . The characteristics of a jackass are stubbornness, stupidity, willfulness, and unwillingness to go where someone is driving him. These, by interesting coincidence, are also the characteristics of the unmotivated employee."[7]

The following quote (source unknown) is also useful in illustrating the effectiveness of the "carrot-and-stick" approach: "When you light a fire under a donkey, how far will he go? Just far enough to get away from the fire." This simply points out that there is a distinct difference between *movement* obtained through external reward-and-punishment systems and true *motivation* that is internalized in the individual.

In further differentiating the two sets of beliefs, Theory X is more concerned about *current behavior* of people than with their *capacities* for developing more effective behavior. In contrasts, Theory Y is more concerned with potential for growth and development—that is, *capacity* (what the employee *could* do). An employee may in fact be acting in a lazy, irresponsible fashion and may show a definite dislike for work. The reality of that behavior would necessitate close control and direction by the supervisor. But does that mean that we have to hold Theory X assumptions about this employee? Not at all. *At this particular time,* that employee's behavior requires close direction and control—but this particular time is not his or her entire working lifetime. That employee may *poten-*

tially have the capacity to function effectively and responsibly. Hence, a true Theory Y supervisor will genuinely believe that all employees are *to some degree* capable of more than they have shown. Theory Y in effect says that people are perfectible, though not necessarily perfect.

Another key to understanding the differences between the two theories is *rigidity* versus *flexibility*. Theory X allows for very little flexibility in supervisory style, while Theory Y suggests a wide range of styles, depending on the particular employee and the situation.

Certainly, as we shall see, the kinds of assumptions that we make about people– whether Theory X or Theory Y–have a tremendous impact upon the things we say and do and lead to completely different approaches to motivation.

THE "SELF-FULFILLING PROPHECY" EFFECT THE POWER OF EXPECTATIONS

In his writings, McGregor felt that our assumptions and expectations about people– whether they be "X" or "Y"–can bring about a *self-fulfilling prophecy*. In other words, by our actions, our assumptions and expectations are subtly and often unintentionally communicated in ways that influence other people's behavior. For example, if you assume and expect that people are naturally lazy, dependent, irresponsible, and the like, ("Theory X" assumptions) and you *treat* them as such, they tend to become that way. Or, if you assume that people have the capacity or potential to be responsible, creative, and so on ("Theory Y" assumptions) and treat them as such, they tend to become so.

George Bernard Shaw's play, *Pygmalion* (the basis for the hit musical, "My Fair Lady"), makes essentially the same point: **People may have an extraordinary influence on others–an effect of which they often aren't aware.**

In the play, Professor Henry Higgins, through his abilities and efforts, is able to take an ill-mannered London flower girl–Eliza Doolittle–and, in only a few months, transform her into a soft-spoken "lady" and pass her off as a princess at a celebrity ball. However, Eliza explains to another of the play's characters–Colonel Pickering–that her fantastic development was not entirely the result of Professor Higgins' teaching abilities:

> You see, really and truly, apart from the things anyone can pick up (the dressing and the proper way of speaking, and so on) the difference between a lady and a flower girl is not how she behaves, but how she's treated. I shall always be a flower girl to Professor Higgins, because he always treats me as a flower girl, and always will; but I know I can be a lady to you, because you always treat me as a lady, and always will.

Put simply, the idea of a self-fulfilling prophecy (or "Pygmalion Effect," as it's also often called) states: **People sometimes become what others expect them to become.** In effect, our expectations and assumptions about another person can actually influence the behavior of that person.

Our assumptions and expectations about others are easily "telegraphed" to them both *verbally* by our choice of words and tone of voice, and *nonverbally* by means of facial expressions, gestures, eye contact, and other personal actions. We are *always* communicating and influencing the behavior of others.

The medical profession has long realized that a doctor's expectations can have a sizeable influence on a patient's health and chances of recovery. In other words, the doctor's prognosis—whether optimistic or pessimistic—can act as a self-fulfilling prophecy.[8]

We predict (prophecy) that something is going to happen and then behave in such a way that we make it happen. There are numerous illustrations of the phenomenon: A person who is afraid of dogs is often the first to get bitten. Employees who believe they will make a mistake in front of their boss will often make such a mistake. Supervisors who are always thinking, "These young people today just don't want to work," most assuredly convey—even unintentionally—these thoughts to their employees and are likely to encounter problems. The same is true for employees who think, "This is a miserable company to work for!"

Employees tend to perform so as to meet the supervisor's expectations of them, whether those expectations are positive or not. As an example, if you as a supervisor have an assumption that a particular employee—Sarah—is nonmotivated and basically lazy, you probably wouldn't assign her to do a challenging job. And why should you? You figure, "She'll only foul it up." Right? But when you assign a job to her that is simple and so routine that she couldn't possibly mess up, you may be *contributing* to her continued lack of motivation. Or, as another illustration, the instructions you give this particular employee may be much more detailed, and you may check on her performance more frequently than usual. The implications of your behavior—namely, that you *don't trust* the employee—will usually come through loud and clear enough to affect her behavior. But instead of making her more effective and responsible, the *opposite* is likely to occur. The employee may well "live down" to your expectations.[9]

So perhaps you're thinking: "O.K., I'll start acting as if I really trust and believe in my employees." Well, it doesn't seem to be that simple. Until you *do* sincerely believe, you probably won't be effective. Supervisors can't hide their true feelings about their employees. It's virtually impossible to mask negative attitudes. Indeed, supervisors often communicate most when they think they are communicating least. How supervisors *treat* others will communicate their expectations much more convincingly than what they may say. For example, if you delegate a project to an employee and say, "I really trust you and know you can handle this by yourself," but then you drop by to check the employee's work every ten minutes and constantly question his or her methods, the employee will probably conclude that your words weren't very meaningful.[10]

In summary, positive expectations do not guarantee positive results, but they certainly promise better results than do negative ones.

USING "POSITIVE REINFORCEMENT" AS A MOTIVATIONAL TOOL

Closely tied to our earlier discussion of the *esteem need* is the concept of *positive reinforcement*. In its simplest form, this concept can be stated in one sentence: **When we do something and are rewarded, we will tend to repeat the act.**

In other words, if good things happen to us after we take a certain action or behave in a certain way, there's a better chance that we'll use that behavior again or take that same action. In other words, our behavior has been *positively reinforced*.

So, what value does this concept have to supervision? Just this: If you want high levels of performance from your people, **reinforce them when they perform well.**

What Reinforces?

Some supervisors may jump to the conclusion that money is the strongest available reinforcer. Money can be used as a reinforcer, but it has some definite limitations. First, in order for money to be a successful reinforcer, there must be a clear link between the money and the performance that earned it. In most organizations today, this simply isn't possible. Salary increases are largely determined by seniority systems, union agreements, and cost-of-living considerations. At best, performance is only indirectly a factor. Even bonuses are frequently viewed as being automatic. Second, as pointed out earlier, there is a point at which additional money stops being highly valued by most employees.

Luckily, rewards can take many forms other than money. Such so-called *social reinforcers* as attention, recognition, sincere praise, a well-deserved "attaboy," and expressed approval by the supervisor all have high value as reinforcers. And an added advantage is that these reinforcers are free!

There are also more tangible rewards that are useful as reinforcers, such as gifts, awards, and certificates of achievement. But, for our purposes, we'll concentrate on the social reinforcers.

Using Reinforcement to Improve Performance

Let's see how positive reinforcement might work. Assume that one of your employees, John, has had an absenteeism problem. In fact, John has missed eight days in the last six months.

As John's supervisor, you have counseled him about this problem and, only last month, he was given a written disciplinary warning. One possible way to improve John's attendance would be for you to recognize and comment favorably on his attendance at the end of a week during which he is at work every day. You might say something like: "John, I really appreciate your efforts. You know how important it is to our section to have everyone here. Keep up the good work." Chances are, John is now more likely to complete a second week with perfect attendance. His initial attempts at good attendance have been reinforced.

On the other hand, if you choose only to exert more controls, punishing John with more disciplinary measures the next time that he misses work, the results may be quite different. Punishment, although it has its place, normally has only short-term effects and seldom eliminates undesirable behavior permanently. Punishment typically only teaches the employee not to get caught the next time. Additionally, it often results in undesirable side effects, such as hostility toward the supervisor, grudge-holding, retaliation, subtle sabotage, and so on. In this case, John's long-term attendance record may not improve at all. In fact, John may increasingly avoid coming to work because of what he sees as a punishing, hostile work climate.

Using Reinforcement to
Maintain Performance

Not only can positive reinforcement *improve* performance; it is also necessary in *maintaining* good performance. Positive feedback about things that are going well can be a powerful force in *keeping* them that way. To illustrate, let's assume that you have another employee—Helen. In contrast to John, Helen has a good attendance record. She never misses a day of work unless a real emergency comes up. But unless her good performance is in some way recognized and reinforced, there's a definite chance her good attendance may drop off after a while. She may get the message that her efforts aren't really appreciated or don't really matter that much to her supervisor; so why bother? Again, the required reinforcement can be as simple as an occasional word of recognition and appreciation from the boss.

If good performance is reinforced, it generally continues; if it is *ignored*—or has no positive consequences when it occurs—it becomes *extinct*. [11]

Many supervisors and their organizations spend countless hours addressing the poor performers—the "problem employees." All sorts of procedures for discipline, punishment, and other negative controls are administered with the hope of salvaging such employees and improving their performance. Yet, employees who perform well are frequently taken for granted. All the attention is seemingly focused on the "bad apples."

Reinforcement Isn't Easy
for Most Supervisors

Some supervisors, upon examining this idea of positive reinforcement for the first time, have some definite doubts. For example: "They know I'm proud of the job they did; I don't have to tell them." Others will say that employees really "oughta wanna" do their jobs right in the first place. "Why should I give them any special recognition? They're *expected* to do outstanding work."

"You mean I should reward people for doing the job they're already being paid to do?" The answer to that question is, of course, a definite *yes*—because it works. To repeat, if you want high levels of performance from your people, reinforce them when they perform well.

Admittedly, though, during a supervisor's hectic days, it's much easier to devote more attention to things that are going badly and ignore the things that are being done right. Consistently recognizing and reinforcing good performance is harder for many of us than criticizing faults or weaknesses in performance. It's like the all-too-typical conversation that goes on between some wives and husbands: The wife complains, "I work for hours trying to make myself look good—makeup, hair, clothes—and you can't even make one comment about it; all you ever do is make critical remarks when you don't like how I look or what I'm wearing." At which point, the husband responds, "When I don't say anything, you can assume I like the way you look."

Reinforce Gradual Improvements, Too

When attempting to improve an employee's low performance, a supervisor cannot expect drastic changes overnight. You shouldn't wait for perfection before offering positive reinforcement. Even small degrees of progress should be recognized as a change in the right direction and should be reinforced as soon as possible. This will increase the chances of continued successive improvements.[12]

In our previous example of John—the absence-prone employee—it would be inadvisable to wait until John's attendance record was perfect before administering reinforcement. The slightest first indication of improvement in John's attendance should be recognized, as should each successive improvement—no matter how small the progress.

The Importance of Timely Reinforcement

For the greatest effect, positive reinforcement should take place as close as possible to the behavior you are trying to reinforce. The longer the delay between the employee's performance and your delivery of reinforcement, the less chance there will be for improving or maintaining performance.[13]

A well-meaning supervisor might say, "I've got to remember to tell Mary about the customer compliments she's been getting during the last month." But a month is probably much too long to wait to reinforce her efforts.

Or, in another situation, a supervisor might comment: "George is really producing more than anybody else. I'll be sure to write that down on his performance appraisal" (which, unfortunately, isn't due for another three months). Although it is certainly important to summarize specific examples of good performance during a yearly performance appraisal session, true reinforcement of the specific behaviors will be weakened by such a delay.

Reinforcement Must
Be Sincere

Of course, the idea of positive reinforcement can be turned into a manipulative "technique" by a supervisor who is not sincere in using it. This will only make things worse.

If you don't appreciate people's good performance, there's no point in faking it. What you *are* speaks so loudly that people have a hard time hearing what you *say*. And that thought is going to be running through an employee's mind every time a supervisor tries to fake genuine interest. Obviously, if *unwarranted* praise and recognition is heaped on everyone—and they know it isn't deserved or linked directly to their accomplishments—it becomes phony.

You are especially likely to have problems if you haven't been known to make many positive comments about people's performance in the past. In fact, a sudden increase in reinforcing comments will probably—at least initially—result in your employees being quite suspicious of your intent. "Does the boss have ulterior motives?" "Why is the boss doing this?" "When does the other shoe fall?"[14]

MOTIVATION IN
PERSPECTIVE

"How do I go about motivating my employees?" The answer to this frequently asked question is obviously of great importance to supervisors who view their primary function as getting work done through people. Ultimately, getting the work accomplished is entirely dependent upon the *behavior* of the employees comprising the work group. Thus, supervisors must have insight and knowledge about why people are motivated to behave as they do.

We have defined motivation as *goal-seeking behavior;* from a supervisory viewpoint, it is the stimulus for directing the behavior of employees toward the goals and objectives of the organization. It is every supervisor's responsibility to consider how a more motivating environment can be provided for employees. The supervisor's task is to create a work climate that will get employees to accomplish the organization's goals enthusiastically and *because they want to.*

The theories and concepts of the motivation process that we have discussed in this chapter may appear confusing and somewhat difficult to understand at times. Admittedly, their practical application on the job can often be even more difficult.

Nevertheless, the supervisor who has a basic understanding of human needs, who has the ability to estimate which need is predominant in an individual employee at a particular time, and who is able to supply a work environment that attempts to satisfy these needs will be far more effective in releasing the full potential of employees than will a counterpart who lacks these abilities. In essence, to understand what motivates people to want to perform well on the job is, in large part, to understand how to be a good supervisor.

Certainly, we still have much to learn about human motivation and the practical application of motivation theories to the work place; but there are productivity gains waiting for the supervisor who, even in a small way, can put to work our present supply of knowledge.

QUESTIONS FOR REVIEW AND DISCUSSION

1. a. What is *motivation*?
   b. From your experience, what factors distinguish a motivated worker from an unmotivated worker?
   c. Can supervisors actually "motivate" anyone? Explain.
2. Employers are often heard to say, "Why do we have to worry about motivating people? We pay them a good salary, provide good working conditions, and have excellent fringe benefits—and yet, people don't seem to be willing to put forth more than a minimum of effort. They *ought* to be motivated to do a good job for us, shouldn't they?" How would you respond to such a comment?
3. a. Explain the basic needs stated by Maslow in the sequence in which they normally occur. Is it necessary for a supervisor to be familiar with these basic needs in order to motivate employees successfully? Explain.
   b. Explain what is meant by the "hierarchical" nature of these needs. How can a supervisor make use of the need hierarchy concept?
4. "Virtually any social group or clique that forms and functions during working hours is a potential threat to satisfaction of an organization's goals." How would you respond to this comment?
5. a. It is often said that supervisors are frequently uninformed about their employees' needs for esteem and recognition. Do you agree? Why?
   b. Discuss various ways of helping employees satisfy these needs on the job.
6. a. "You can say what you want to about psychological needs. I still say money is the best motivator. In the final analysis, if you give employees a raise or promise to give them one, you'll motivate them." How would you reply to this statement?
   b. When you received your last pay increase, did you work harder? If so, for how long? How long were you satisfied with your new salary before you started actively desiring another raise?
7. What are some of the possible reasons other than salary or fringe benefits that might affect your decision to accept one employment offer over another? Would these reasons outweigh a difference in salary of $100 per month? Relate your reasons to Maslow's need hierarchy.

8. Many changes are occurring in our society today that are seemingly responsible for a shift in motivational emphasis from the "primary" needs to the "secondary" needs. What factors do you believe account for this?

9. A middle-level manager, whose future success seemed assured, quit her job four years ago at the age of thirty-one to become a writer. Since then she has sold very few stories and suffered a considerable financial loss. She maintains, however, that she is optimistic, happy, and satisfied with her work. How do you reconcile this situation with Maslow's hierarchy of needs?

10. a. What motivates *you* to do a good job?
    b. What is motivating you to take this course? Specifically, what needs are you attempting to satisfy?

11. Is a proper program of employee training and development a necessary requirement for effective employee motivation? Explain.

12. a. Repeated efforts to unionize engineers have largely met with failure. Many engineers agree that as a group they would likely be helped by the unions, but they don't want to join. How would you explain this?
    b. What motivates an employee to join a labor union (irrespective of the "closed shop")? In other words, what basic needs are typically fulfilled by union membership?

13. a. Discuss how *level of aspiration* affects an employee's needs.
    b. What effect might level of education have on a person's aspirations?

14. How does a supervisor go about identifying the individual needs and aspiration levels of his or her employees? How can this knowledge be used profitably?

15. a. When does *frustration* occur?
    b. "Employees are not disagreeable and uncooperative simply because they want to be; more likely, such behavior is caused by the lack of fulfillment of certain basic needs on the job." Evaluate this statement.

16. a. In what three basic ways can a person react in order to escape frustration? What is the primary purpose of these reactions? What can supervisors accomplish in utilizing their knowledge of the various defense mechanisms?
    b. Recall a recent experience that proved to be quite frustrating to you. How did you react? What *defense mechanisms* did you employ?

17. a. In McGregor's "Theory X," what are the assumptions a supervisor makes about his or her workers? Are these assumptions basically correct? Why?
    b. Do you believe that most organizations are based upon "Theory X" or "Theory Y" assumptions? Explain.

18. "The needs of employees are not only different from, but often in direct conflict with, the needs of the organization that the supervisor must satisfy." Do you agree? Explain.

19. a. What are the fundamental differences between "Theory X" and "Theory Y"? Which set of assumptions would you like your boss to make about you?
    b. Recall the approaches to motivating students used by different instructors

under whom you have studied. Which approaches were the most effective in motivating you to exert extra effort? Relate these approaches to McGregor's "Theories X and Y."

20. In your opinion, why do some supervisors persistently resist changing their traditional concepts of motivation?

REFERENCES

1. Herzberg, Frederick, "One More Time: How Do You Motivate Employees?" *Harvard Business Review,* Jan.–Feb. 1968, pp. 55.

2. Maslow, A. H., "A Theory of Human Motivation," *Human Relations in Management,* S. G. Huneryager and I. L. Heckmann, eds., 2nd ed. Cincinnati: South-Western Publishing Company, 1967, p. 343.

3. Newman, William H., Charles E. Summer, and E. Kirby Warren, *The Process of Management,* 2nd ed. Englewood Cliffs, N. J.: Prentice-Hall, Inc., 1967, p. 198.

4. Huneryager, S. G., and I. L. Heckmann, Eds., *Human Relations in Management,* 2nd ed. Cincinnati: South-Western Publishing Company, 1967, pp. 326-7.

5. Herzberg, *op. cit.*

6. McGregor, Douglas, *The Human Side of Enterprise.* New York: McGraw-Hill Book Company, 1960.

7. Levinson, Harry, "Asinine Attitudes Toward Motivation," *Harvard Business Review,* Jan.–Feb. 1973, p. 73.

8. Livingston, J. Sterling, "Pygmalion In Management," *Harvard Business Review,* July-August, 1969, pp. 81-84.

9. Hill, Norman C., *Increasing Managerial Effectiveness: Keys to Management and Motivation.* Reading, Mass.: Addison-Wesley Publishing Company, 1979, pp. 63-69.

10. Livingston, *op. cit.,* p. 84.

11. Miller, Lawrence M., *Behavior Management.* New York: John Wiley and Sons, 1978, pp. 10-11.

12. Hersey, Paul, and Kenneth H. Blanchard, *Management of Organizational Behavior: Utilizing Human Resources.* Englewood Cliffs, N. J.: Prentice-Hall, Inc., 1977, p. 208.

13. *Ibid.,* p. 207.

14. Miller, *op. cit.,* pp. 367-8.

Suggested Additional Readings

Because of the similarity of subject matter, suggested additional readings for this chapter are combined with those listed at the end of Chapter 3.

3

MOTIVATION THROUGH MEANINGFUL JOB DESIGN

In today's highly regimented, increasingly automated and deeply impersonal industrial society, the human being who has found fulfilling work is indeed among the blessed.[1]

Harold L. Sheppard
and Neal Q. Herrick

The employer's task is not to motivate his people to get them to achieve; he should provide opportunities for people to achieve, so they will become motivated.[2]

Frederick Herzberg

Although it may not be fashionable to admit it, most people actually like to work. Have you ever noticed how much mental and physical work people will do without getting paid for it? Consider those employees who put in their 40 hours doing highly repetitive jobs. The work is monotonous and they hate it and do only the bare minimum required, maintaining that the only reason they work at all is to make a decent living. Yet when their time is up each day, they can be seen rushing home to work in their gardens, mow their lawns, paint their houses, work on their cars, pursue a variety of time-consuming hobbies, serve as school board members, go bowling, take their families camping on weekends, and so on. Why do they put so much effort and enthusiasm into these tasks while lacking interest in their jobs? The probable answer is that they like these activities—something they can't say for their jobs.

It is unfortunate but true that a substantial gap often exists between the needs that employees bring to their work and the satisfactions they derive from the jobs. Certainly, in many jobs this gap is small or inconsequential, however, there are many where the gap is wide and seemingly unbridgeable. Typically these jobs are characterized by highly repetitive, monotonous activities that offer few opportunities for a motivating environment. One danger of the type of job in which workers find no challenge and little pride of accomplishment is that—even though they may show up every day—the organization has for all intents and purposes lost them.

THE MOTIVATION-
MAINTENANCE
THEORY

A logical starting point for discovering ways to narrow this gap and making work more motivating and meaningful is an examination of the work of Frederick Herzberg and his now famous Motivation-Maintenance Theory.

In extensive studies, Herzberg concluded that motivation is essentially a *two-dimensional* problem. He found that some factors of a job, when not present, primarily *dissatisfy* employees. However, the presence of these factors does not build strong motivation. Herzberg called these factors *maintenance* or *hygiene* factors because they are necessary to prevent dissatisfaction.*

On the other hand, other factors were found which, if present, build high degrees of job *satisfaction* and thus motivation. If not present, however, they do not prove highly dissatisfying. These satisfying factors were labeled *motivators*.

Thus, Herzberg determined that the factors involved in producing job *satisfaction* are separate and distinct from those leading to job *dissatisfaction*. He came to use the term "motivation" in a restricted sense, applying it only to job factors or experiences that produce high levels of satisfaction, rather than in its more general sense.

Because the Motivation-Maintenance Theory is admittedly difficult to understand at first glance, let us examine it in more detail.

The Motivators

When the subjects of Herzberg's studies said they were satisfied with their jobs, they most often described factors related directly to the job itself, i.e., *job content*. These job-centered *motivator* factors are:

1. **Achievement**: a feeling of personal accomplishment; meeting success in solving a problem; seeing good results from one's work; or completing a challenging job.
2. **Recognition for achievement**: being recognized for doing one's work well; receiving praise or acknowledgment from superiors, the organization, fellow workers, or the public.

*The term "hygiene" was originally used in a suggested analogy to the term used in preventive medicine.

3. **The work itself**: performing creative or challenging work; liking the work one does.
4. **Responsibility**: having some responsibility for making decisions affecting one's own work; being permitted to work without close supervision.
5. **Growth**: The opportunity to learn new skills and knowledge; personal development.
6. **Advancement**: the opportunity for promotion.

Again, these motivator factors lead to strong satisfaction when they are present but do not cause much dissatisfaction when they are absent. In other words, the employee does not seem to miss them when they are not around. For example, if recognition led to a good feeling about the job, the lack of recognition was seldom indicated as a cause of bad feelings.

Not only do these factors tend to satisfy and, in turn, motivate employees, they also serve to *develop* employees rather than merely maintaining them at a constant level of competence.

The Maintainers

In contrast to the motivators derived from the content of the job itself, Herzberg's subjects reported that the job factors that were most often dissatisfying were related to conditions that *surround* the job itself, i.e., the *job environment*. These *maintainers* include:

1. **Salary**: anything involving compensation and fringe benefits.
2. **Working conditions**: things such as lighting, tools, air conditioning or heating, or parking facilities.
3. **Security**: feeling certain about the future; financial contentment.
4. **Company policy and administration**: the competence of management; the effectiveness of personnel policies.
5. **Behavior of supervision**: the supervisor's competence, ability to provide guidance, and fairness.
6. **Interpersonal relationships**: social interaction with fellow workers and the supervisor.
7. **Status**: job titles and classifications, special privileges, furnishings, relationships, and image of the organization.

When any of these factors are deficient, employees are likely to become dissatisfied and to express this dissatisfaction in ways detrimental to the organization's goals. Thus, the supervisor must always be concerned with maintaining, in Herzberg's words, "a good hygienic environment." Just like machinery and buildings, people have to be maintained. However, the improvement of the maintenance factors is not likely to provide satisfaction or "genuine" motivation.

Relationship of
Motivators and
Maintainers

It is important to reiterate that the factors involved in producing job *satisfaction* (and, thus, motivation) are separate and distinct from the factors leading to job *dissatisfaction*. Satisfaction and dissatisfaction, in this sense, should not be viewed as extremes on a single scale; they are *not* opposites. Rather, it is helpful to visualize the Motivation-Maintenance Theory in terms of two separate scales, one running from "satisfaction" to "no satisfaction," and the other from "dissatisfaction" to "no dissatisfaction," as indicated in Figure 3-1.

The opposite of job satisfaction is not job dissatisfaction but, rather, *no* job satisfaction. Similarly, the opposite of job dissatisfaction is not job satisfaction but *no* job dissatisfaction. This relationship can be further seen in Figure 3-2.

As an example, when wages are considered to be inadequate, the principal effect is dissatisfaction. However, the principal effect of a wage increase is to remove dissatisfaction, not to create satisfaction. At best, employees can be brought only to a *neutral point* by such maintainers.

Satisfaction (and thus motivation), then, is a function of the *content* of the job done by the employee; dissatisfaction, of the *environment* in which the job exists. To increase motivation, the focus must be on the actual work that the employee performs—in other words, on how the employee is *utilized* on the job, not on how he or she is *treated* by the various maintenance factors.

As a further illustration, let's assume that one of your employees, Ken, seems to be working at only about 70 percent of his abilities—what is commonly referred to as "a fair day's work for a fair day's pay." When compared to others, his productivity is con-

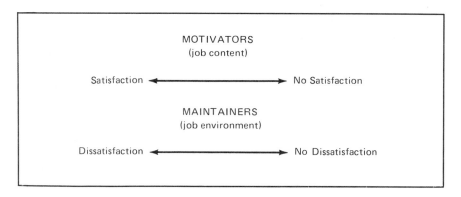

FIGURE 3-1.   The Motivation-Maintenance Theory

	MOTIVATORS	MAINTAINERS
If Present	Job Satisfaction	No Job Dissatisfaction
If Not Present	No Job Satisfaction	Job Dissatisfaction

FIGURE 3–2. Relationship between Maintenance and Motivation Factors

sidered just "average." Ken does just enough, you guess, to keep you "off his back," and you accept this because you have other employees who don't even come up to Ken's standards. You are also aware that Ken has never seemed to particularly enjoy the work he does. In fact, he told you once that "any idiot could do my job."

Now let's suppose that Ken learns through the grapevine that one of his fellow workers, who recently left to take a similar position with another organization, received a considerable pay increase—plus better fringe benefits and his own private parking space. How might this affect Ken's behavior and overall job performance?

There is little doubt that Ken would become increasingly dissatisfied with his pay and working conditions. This dissatisfaction with maintenance factors would most likely lead, in some degree, to a restriction of output and a decline in Ken's productivity. This might be intentional or he may not even be consciously aware that he's holding back.

Consider what would happen if it is within your power to give Ken his desired salary increase and to improve his working conditions. Can you expect Ken's motivation and productivity to increase? If so, how much?

Even if these improvements in Ken's working environment are above his expectations, his productivity will probably increase only to its former "average" level, and is unlikely to rise above that level—except, perhaps, for an initial short period of time. Attention to Ken's maintenance factors will probably reduce or eliminate his dissatisfaction with his job environment and may even make the work he does more tolerable, but he still won't like what he is being paid to do any more than before. In other words, he will move closer to the "no dissatisfaction" end of the "dissatisfaction" scale. But, since the content of his job remains the same, you can't really expect him to derive any more satisfaction from his work—or to be motivated or commited to working harder and producing more than what he considers "a fair day's work for a fair day's pay." He just can't be *bribed* into higher productivity.

(It is important to remember that Herzberg uses the term "motivation" in a restricted sense, applying it only to factors that normally produce high levels of job satisfaction, which are necessary for *sustained, superior productivity,* rather than merely normal or average efforts.)

On the other hand, let's take the same employee and suppose that dissatisfaction with pay and working conditions never occurred. Ken is still working at an "average" productivity level. This time, however, changes of some sort are made in the *content* of the job so that Ken is encouraged to take on more responsibility, make more decisions about how to do the job, is able to experience more of a sense of accomplishment from his efforts, and is learning new skills that may be useful for advancement. What effects might these changes have on Ken?

There is a good chance that Ken would become more "turned on" by the work, more motivated perhaps to perform at a better-than-average level. This isn't to say that he wouldn't be interested in better pay and working conditions, too, but such desires probably wouldn't be the overwhelming driving forces that they were in the first situation.

Do You Know Any "Maintenance Seekers"?

Herzberg's studies have indicated that when people are denied motivation opportunities through the work itself, they may become preoccupied with obtaining more and more "shots" of the maintenance factors. In other words, they become "maintenance seekers." Not being able to find any real satisfaction in their jobs, these employees continually strive to reach that neutral point of an absence of job dissatisfaction. In so doing, they are likely to continually find fault with the maintenance factors provided them.

One of the problems with meaningless, "nothing" jobs that provide no motivation is that it gives employees just that much more time to think about their feelings of dissatisfaction—no matter how insignificant and minor those dissatisfactions may be. When employees are motivated, however, they seem to have an increased tolerance for dissatisfaction arising from deficient maintenance factors.

Short-Term Nature of Maintenance

According to Herzberg, any job satisfaction—or desire to work harder or more efficiently—associated with the maintenance factors is short-lived, and, with the passage of time, a feeling of deficiency recurs. Just as eating a meal doesn't prevent one from becoming hungry later, a salary increase has only a temporary effect; it doesn't prevent an employee from becoming dissatisfied eventually with the new wage level. The second paycheck after a salary increase is the same as the first, and the employee starts moving back toward the negative end of the "dissatisfaction" scale. Herzberg says that wages motivate only in the sense that employees are motivated "to seek the next wage increase." Higher pay may temporarily buy more productivity, but it cannot buy commitment.[3]

Both the short-term nature of maintenance factors and their ability to dissatisfy is illustrated by the following story, related by Scott Myers of the Center for Applied Management:

When a plant manager surprised his employees one Christmas by giving each of them a frozen turkey, it seemed, at first, that the investment bought employee good will. Employees and their families expressed warm sentiments about their employer.

But as the year went by and the next Christmas approached, people began talking about last year's turkey and wondering if they would receive one this year. When the plant manager heard over the grapevine that people were expecting a turkey and would be disappointed if they received none, there seemed no choice but to give them a turkey. The manager noted that the enthusiasm was less on the second Christmas than it was on the first.

When the third Christmas approached, they began asking, "When will we get our turkey?" Moreover, when they received them, they began comparing the weights printed on the boxes—and persons receiving a turkey that weighed a few ounces less than their co-worker's turkey registered disappointment.

When supplemental benefits are perceived as a form of compensation, they may legitimately become an issue for collective bargaining. This being a unionized plant, the union leaders made the turkeys an issue of collective bargaining and, as a result, employees were now given a choice of a turkey or ham at Christmas time. Ham spoilage resulted in a changed procedure of issuing specially printed punch cards authorizing employees to pick up their turkeys or hams at a designated local supermarket.

But the supermarket manager permitted the employees to exchange the cards for other merchandise of comparable value. Hence, the intended symbolism of a friendly (though paternalistic) gift to employees became transformed into what became, in effect, an $8 grocery coupon.

When this organization expanded to 20,000 employees, the annual "turkey bill" was $160,000. It resulted in no increase in productivity or good will. However, its withdrawal now would certainly precipitate union intervention.[4] *

So we can say that the maintenance factors are usually subject to the "what-have-you-done-for-me-*lately*" syndrome. Or, as Herzberg describes it: "No matter how many times you have told your wife you love her, if you fail to tell her you love her, she says, 'You never tell me you love me.'"[5]

Motivators, on the other hand, tend to have a longer-term effect on employees' attitudes and job performance. They are more continuous in nature. For example, unlike the pleasures of a raise in pay or a larger office that soon lose their impact, the satisfaction derived from doing meaningful, interesting work is a daily occurrence as long as it lasts.

In our previous case of Ken, there would be little chance of his experiencing satisfaction with the work he was doing as long as he was actively dissatisfied with his pay and working conditions. Only when these blockages were removed could we begin thinking about Ken's motivation. But then again, Ken could never experience true motivation by obtaining better maintenance factors by themselves.

Think of it this way: "Motivators hoist the sail. Maintainers pull up the anchor so that the boat will move at all."[6]

*Myers, MANAGING WITHOUT UNIONS, © 1976, Addison-Wesley Publishing Company, Inc., Chapter 3, pages 29–30. Reprinted with permission.

Relationship to Maslow's
Need Hierarchy

Herzberg's Motivation-Maintenance Theory differs from Maslow's need hierarchy in that it is more specifically related to motivation on the job. However, there is also much similarity, enabling us roughly to interpret Herzberg's findings within Maslow's framework (see Figure 3–3).

Herzberg's maintenance factors roughly parallel the lower-order needs listed by Maslow, encompassing the *physiological, security,* and *social* needs. Herzberg views these lower-order needs as having little or no motivating force in today's work situation, only the ability to dissatisfy when absent.

The motivators roughly parallel Maslow's higher-order needs—*esteem* and *self-actualization.* Herzberg implies that most of our society's employees have achieved a level of economic and social progress such that these higher-order needs are the only genuine motivators.

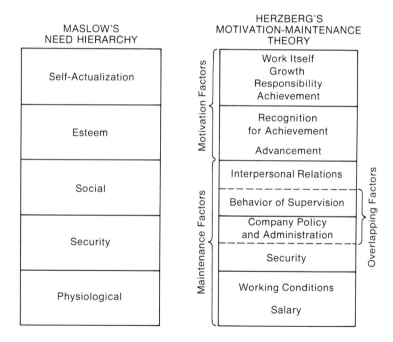

FIGURE 3–3. Relationship of Need Hierarchy to the Motivation-
Maintenance Theory [7]

Are Motivator Factors
More Important Than
Maintenance Factors?

Not at all. Both sets of factors must be considered. In fact, it is fair to say that the maximum motivation at work will occur when *both* maintenance factors and motivators are present in proper form in the employee's work situation.

As we have already seen, a deficiency in certain maintenance factors can make employees dissatisfied enough to affect their performance. Just as lower-order needs in Maslow's hierarchy must be reasonably satisfied before higher-order needs are activated, Herzberg concedes that the maintainers are a *prerequisite* for motivation even if they do not motivate in and of themselves. Put another way, dissatisfaction with the maintenance factors presents a *block* to bringing about motivation. Thus, concern with the factors that make up the work environment is always necessary to prevent active dissatisfaction.

Implications for
Supervision

The fundamental implications of Herzberg's work for the supervisor are that "maintaining" employees, while quite important, only avoids dissatisfactions; the absence of maintenance factors can make employees unhappy, but their presence seldom makes employees want to work harder or more efficiently. Making jobs truly motivating requires designing them to give the employees challenging work in which to assume responsibility and fulfill their higher-level needs. Maintainers simply meet people's expectations—motivators move them to *do* things.

Thus, supervisors who traditionally approach motivation from a solely maintenance angle are seriously handicapping themselves. Instead, they might better concern themselves with the nature of the work itself and making it more challenging and meaningful; in other words, more attention should be given to making jobs *intrinsically satisfying*. Expenditures beyond that needed to provide a basic maintenance level might better be spent on programs to increase the responsibility and development of the individual employee. In the long run, this could well be less expensive than sole reliance on maintenance.

The basic question for the supervisor then becomes: What can be done to increase the presence of such motivator factors as achievement, recognition, satisfaction from the work itself, responsibility, advancement, and growth? For the answer, the *design* of the job itself must first be closely examined, for this defines the satisfactions that employees can derive from it and sets definite limits on the degree that Herzberg's motivators can be provided by the supervisor.

THE TRADITIONAL
APPROACH TO JOB
DESIGN

The *traditional* approach to job design is based upon five general rules:

1. Skills should be specialized.
2. Skill requirements should be minimized.
3. Training time should be minimized.
4. The number and variety of tasks in a job should be limited.
5. The job should be made as repetitive as possible.

Thus, the most common way to design jobs has been to simplify them—to make them "idiot-proof." Work is divided into smaller parts with each employee producing one very small portion of it over and over again. The object is to permit the hiring of minimally qualified employees at lower wage rates, to reduce the chance of errors, and to avoid placing employees in a situation where they might be forced to make a decision. Training costs per employee are reduced, and, not coincidentally, the employee becomes fairly easy to replace. Scott Myers describes it this way:

> Work systems are characteristically designed on the assumption that the people who operate them are not competent or trustworthy. Systems designers admonish one another to "design the system on the assumption that the operators can't think." And, of course, it becomes a self-fulfilling prophecy when the operators fail to interact intelligently with their "idiot-proof" work systems. The systems designers point scornfully to the operators, saying, "See how stupid they are; they never think!"
>
> However, the operators do think—in retaliatory terms or about things away from the job or how to get away from the job, unfortunately. Hence they make more trips to the water fountain, rest room, first aid center, personnel department, and use up their sick leave. At work they think and talk about their bowling games, camping trips, school board memberships, church activities, do-it-yourself projects, avocational pursuits, job-hopping plans, and miscellaneous fantasies. Or, their thoughts find creative expression in counterproductive activities such as product sabotage, defiance of authority, concerted slowdowns, pilferage, complaints about working conditions, and preoccupation with real or imaginary grievances.[8] *

We are not questioning the basic advantages of specialization; no organization could possibly function without it. In fact, our entire mass-production economy is based on the concept of specialization. It is *over-specialization* that is now being questioned by many management experts who feel that we have carried the original concept to extremes, at the expense of the employees' need satisfaction and their job performance.

*Myers, MANAGING WITH UNIONS, © 1978, Addison-Wesley Publishing Company, Inc., Chapter 1, page 17. Reprinted with permission.

Negative Effects of
Over-Specialization

Specialization, when carried to extremes, has brought disadvantages in recent years along with its hoped-for advantages. In many cases, it has generated boredom, fatigue, apathy, higher turnover, absenteeism, more grievances, reduced productivity, and work stoppages, just to name a few. By slicing a worker's job into what is only a piece of a job, imagination has been stifled and any interest and challenge eliminated; any satisfaction to be derived from performing a whole job has been smothered.

Many studies have shown that hourly paid workers frequently report that their work has little meaning and just seems to go on endlessly and monotonously. Repetitiveness, when it leads to boredom, has also been shown to reduce quality rather than to increase it. In the long run, these negative effects of over-specialization seem to outweigh the cost savings that specialization is intended to bring about.

Current social trends in our country tend to indicate that over-specialization of jobs may cause even greater problems in the future. In the first place, as was noted in Chapter 1, today's employee is typically much better educated and more independent than the typical worker of only a generation ago. Organizations that once employed elementary school dropouts now often hire men and women with two or more years of college, people whose entire education has encouraged them to think for themselves. This better-educated work force wants more meaningful and challenging jobs. Faced with the tedium of specialization, many workers expend their excess mental energy in creating problems for the supervisor.

Michael Maccoby, a prominent behavioral scientist, accurately sums up the situation this way:

> . . . In general, workers want to avoid jobs that are monotonous, repetitive, over-controlled, and isolated from interaction with others. In contrast, they seek jobs that require activeness—planning and judgment—autonomy on the job, variety, and that are demanding enough to stimulate learning. Beyond these psychological factors, workers are also concerned with the dignity associated with the job and with opportunities for career development. They are also increasingly concerned that the work be "meaningful," that it involve clearly useful tasks and require sufficient skills to be worthy of respect.

> Taken together, these requirements move in the direction of humanizing work. In contrast, dehumanized work is a job which makes the worker into a machine part, totally controlled, fully predictable, and easily replaceable. . . .[9]

Although industrial jobs offer the best examples of jobs that are often not intrinsically satisfying, there are others equally guilty. Many retail and clerical workers, for instance, experience the same frustrations. Retailers, who have come to depend a great deal on minimally trained, low-paid personnel, seldom offer meaningful or motivating jobs at the lower levels, which undoubtedly partially explains why most two-year or four-year college graduates tend to ignore retail careers; experiences derived through part-time retail employment have led many to believe that this is not "where it's at." In return for meaningless jobs, retailers are increasingly plagued by higher sales costs, higher turnover, employee theft, and persistent efforts to unionize retail sales personnel.

"Healthy Reactions to an Unhealthy Environment"

Chris Argyris, a noted authority on human relations in organizations, has long been critical of excessive specialization, commenting that:

> From an employee's point of view this means that he is asked to be more passive than active; more submissive than responsible; to use his shallow, surface abilities and ignore his more complex and deeper abilities. Such conditions are better suited to the world of infants than the world of adults. This is why, in several instances, where work has been highly simplified, the mentally retarded and insane have outproduced healthy human beings by wide margins.[10]

Employee apathy and lack of effort are not, according to Argyris, simply a matter of laziness. Rather, they are often healthy reactions of normal people to an unhealthy environment. Herzberg puts it more bluntly when he says, "The proper attitude for a man in a Mickey Mouse job is a Mickey Mouse attitude."[11]

Argyris contends that the typical organization places most of its employees in roles that provide little opportunity for responsibility, self-reliance, or independence. On the contrary, too many jobs are designed to make only minimal demands on the individual's abilities.

To the extent that employees are relatively mature adults, they feel frustrated under such conditions; work becomes a necessary evil rather than a source of need satisfaction. As we have seen in Chapter 2, frustration arises when employees are unable to obtain need satisfaction. Argyris says that the common reaction of the employee's withdrawing his or her interest from the job—treating it with indifference or even a certain amount of contempt—is a necessary defense maneuver to protect one's self-respect. Obviously, the costs of such reactions to the organization are high.

The costly strikes that have recently been so prevalent in our economy may well be, in large measure, a spontaneous expression of the bitterness workers hold toward their jobs. Their frustrations may not reflect their low incomes so much as their inability to utilize their abilities in a significant way. In other words, they need a sense of pride and accomplishment; instead, they find their work neither stimulating nor dignifying.

In fact, Argyris feels that many workers view higher wages as a "penalty payment" —a sort of "fine" that they can periodically levy against employers to compensate them for the frustrating elements of the work situation. The employees say, "O.K., if you want us to work under these conditions, pay us!" They feel that the answer to any job dissatisfaction is more and more money.

JOB ENRICHMENT

Job enrichment is an approach that attempts to solve some of the motivational dilemmas created by over-specialization by making employees' work more meaningful. It seeks to get from employees not the least they are capable of doing, but the best they are capable of doing.

Job enrichment can be simply defined as **the enlargement of a job's responsibility, scope, and challenge.** In the context of Herzberg's Motivation-Maintenance Theory, we can view an enriched job as including the factors of achievement, recognition, satisfaction from the work itself, responsibility, growth, and advancement.

Focusing primarily on job redesign, job enrichment has the central objective of creating a job situation where workers can obtain internal motivation from the content of their work. In accomplishing this objective, jobs are generally designed so that workers: (1) are given responsibilities and challenge more in keeping with their skills, abilities, and expectations; (2) become aware of a completeness, or wholeness, to their work; (3) can more easily identify their contributions to the organization's objectives and experience a sense of achievement; (4) have the opportunity to participate in decision making that affects the jobs they perform; (5) control larger portions of their own work; and (6) are able to learn and develop to the extent that they are better prepared for future assignments.

Under a job enrichment effort, the design of jobs takes into account the human needs of employees as well as the technical production requirements and economic needs of the organization. Thus, attention is directed to the prescribed tasks to be performed, plus those aspects of the tasks that can heighten the motivation of employees.

Horizontal versus Vertical Expansion

Enrichment of a job can be brought about through *horizontal* or *vertical* expansion or, preferably, both. *Horizontal expansion* of a job is characterized by the addition of a variety of similar functions or activities. *Vertical expansion,* on the other hand, is achieved by providing employees with increased opportunities for planning and controlling their own work.

Horizontal expansion. Often termed "job enlargement," horizontal expansion of a job is characterized by the addition of a variety of similar tasks or activities. By expanding the scope of a job, previously specialized tasks are combined into a larger, more natural unit of work. For example, the job of a machine operator might be expanded to include sharpening the tools, setting up the machine, and inspecting the finished product, as well as performing the actual machining operation.

Or, as one more illustration, instead of ten workers each performing only one of ten steps in an assembly process, each worker might perform all ten steps, while working on a smaller total number of products.

Another common method of horizontal expansion is *job rotation,* in which employees are regularly switched from one job to another to provide variety in what they are doing and to prevent boredom; this also permits employees some physical movement and helps to reduce the psychological fatigue of repetitive work. Although the actual content of the various jobs is unchanged, job rotation provides a way to share unexciting tasks that must be done by somebody. Frequently, it can serve as a training and development tool by creating a broad base of highly skilled employees within the work group.

Although useful in reducing the negative effects of an over-specialized, repetitive job, horizontal expansion seldom offers the motivational opportunities provided through vertical expansion. Often, the worker is inclined to view horizontal expansion merely as a speedup. In many applications, it involves little more than adding meaningless additions to an already meaningless job. Job rotation, for example, accomplishes little in terms of added meaning if an employee is rotated from one inconsequential job to another of no greater consequence; as Herzberg has warned, this can be likened to "washing dishes for a while, then washing silverware."[12] For change to be really effective, meaningful activities and responsibilities must be added.

Vertical expansion. The key idea of vertical expansion is that employees (at least *some* employees) are capable of managing themselves to a much greater degree than they currently do. Thus, jobs are expanded to allow workers to participate in some of the normal managerial functions of *planning* and *controlling,* as well as the actual *doing* of the work.

Whereas horizontal expansion only adds more *doing* activities to the job's content, vertical expansion encourages the employees to exercise their own judgment and discretion in making decisions about their work, to participate with the supervisor in problem solving and goal setting, and to offer ideas, suggestions, and opinions. They are, therefore, encouraged to contribute with their minds as well as their skills.[13]

Completely compatible with McGregor's "Theory Y," discussed in Chapter 2, vertical expansion attempts to broaden the areas in which workers can exercise *self-direction* and *self-control,* as they develop greater insights and abilities.

Not only is employees' work made more meaningful and intrinsically motivating, but the supervisor is also freed from many time-consuming routine "checking" and "prodding" activities, allowing more time to be devoted to higher-level planning and decision making. The supervisor is given, in a real sense, the opportunity to *manage.* In fact, one of the most fertile sources of enrichment for employees' jobs is work done by the supervisor, much of which can be pushed down. Most of us have known a supervisor who goes around moaning that there is never enough time to attend to really important matters and projects because of mounds of paperwork and other inconsequential activities. Chances are this is a supervisor who also has some employees who are bored to death with their jobs.

Of course, the idea that workers can, to a greater degree, become their own managers may sound a bit radical to some supervisors. Traditionally, *planning* (which includes problem solving, decision making, goal setting, and planning the use of manpower and materials) and *controlling* (obtaining feedback for measuring results against planned goals and taking necessary corrective action) have been the exclusive property of managers. Workers have been excluded from these functions and allowed only the function of *doing* (the implementation of the plan). This point of view is consistent with "Theory X" assumptions—i.e., unintelligent, irresponsible, immature, uncreative people need to be directed and controlled. In job enrichment—specifically in vertical expansion—the functions of management are increasingly shared with or delegated to employees with the contention that work, to be meaningful and motivating, should include some aspects of planning and controlling, as well as doing.[14]

Characteristics of a "Good" Job

As mentioned earlier, an enriched job would, to a greater degree, include Herzberg's motivator factors. But, in addition to having these factors present in a job's content, job enrichment designs typically rely on several other concepts. It is generally agreed by most job redesign authorities that the following characteristics—or conditions—also need to be present for a job to be considered really meaningful to the jobholder:

Natural units of work. This means that employees are able to see a beginning and an end to the work for which they are responsible. Appropriate tasks are logically grouped together in order to increase employees' feelings of "ownership" for the complete unit of work. For example, in one department of an electronics assembly plant, employees assembled a number of different models of electronic apparatus called "hot plates," using a normal assembly line operation. Without making any changes in the department or its personnel, jobs were redesigned so that each employee assembled an entire hot plate, rather than its individual parts. Marking a positive reaction to the change, employees made such comments as, "Now it's *my* hot plate." To further demonstrate the positive aspects of the change, controllable rejects dropped from 23 per cent to 1 per cent in the next six months while absenteeism dropped from 8 per cent to less than 1 per cent, and productivity increased 84 per cent.[15]

This also adds *skill variety* to the job by avoiding the monotony of repeatedly performing the same task.[16]

Meaningful goals. Clear and moderately difficult goals provide the employee with something to shoot for. Goals not only give guidance, but are also a major part of providing a job with a sense of challenge and achievement. Generally, people most vigorously pursue goals that they have participated in setting for themselves. On the other hand, most employees don't particularly like it when the supervisor sets goals for them. Participation and involvement in goal setting encourages *commitment* rather than just *compliance.* Compliance means "doing it because I have to." Commitment means "doing it because I believe in it."[17]

Although goals should be set high enough to represent a challenge, they must also be realistic and attainable. If they are too high, they will discourage any effort. When employees are frustrated over their inability to reach goals, they often lose their desire to work well at anything. They figure that if they're going to fail anyway (and they've convinced themselves they will), why bother?

At the other extreme, any time a goal is set too low, it's robbed of its challenge. When it's met, employees have no sense of achievement because they knew they could do it all the time.

Direct feedback. A third ingredient is the ability of employees to get information on a regular basis about the effectiveness of their efforts. A goal or target is meaningful only to the extent that employees can obtain prompt and direct information about their success in achieving it.

Although feedback from the supervisor is important, such information about results ideally should come directly from the job itself—as the job is being done. In this way, employees have continuous data with which to "keep score" on their own performance and correct their own errors. This feedback serves two purposes—continued learning and motivation.[18]

Client relationship. Another ingredient necessary for a meaningful job is that employees are able to establish direct contact with the ultimate users of their products or services—i.e., their "clients," who may be internal or external to the organization.[19] In some companies, for example, customer complaints about quality are referred for response directly to the employee who completed that unit of work. The employee then becomes *accountable* to the client.

Feedback also increases, since employees have increased opportunities to receive praise or criticism of their work directly from the users.[20]

Autonomy (decision-making discretion). Closely related to the prior discussion of *vertical expansion* of jobs, this refers to the opportunity for increased decision making, planning, and controlling by the workers. The objective is to redesign jobs so that the jobholders are more involved in such activities as setting their own schedules, deciding on work methods, troubleshooting, checking on quality, training other workers, and seeking solutions to problems.[21]

As job redesign authority J. Richard Hackman and his associates summarize it:

When these. . .conditions are present, a person tends to feel very good about himself when he performs well. And those good feelings will prompt him to try to continue to do well—so he can continue to earn the positive feelings in the future. That is what is meant by "internal motivation"—being turned on to one's work because of the positive internal feelings that are generated by doing well, rather than being dependent on external factors. . . .[22]

JOB REDESIGN CHECKLIST

	YES	NO

DOES THE JOB IN QUESTION—

—— Utilize employees' skills effectively and provide a challenge worthy of attention?

—— Make a visible and understandable contribution to the overall value of the product or service?

—— Lend itself to being combined with some other job to save time and effort and to make the two more meaningful or complete?

—— Provide boredom-reducing variety for employees?

—— Give employees adequate and timely feedback so that they can evaluate their performance and correct their own errors?

—— Include any routine functions that could be eliminated?

—— Provide continuing opportunity to learn something worthwhile?

—— Give employees reasonable opportunities for individual recognition?

—— Allow employees to participate in problem solving and goal setting?

—— Provide access to all information employees need to do the work?

CAN THE EMPLOYEES—

—— Do things that are currently being done for them by their supervisor?

—— Make certain decisions concerning their work that are now made by others?

—— Suggest ways to make the job more efficient?

—— Operate better with less direct supervision?

—— Set their own performance goals and priorities?

—— Take on additional training to prepare them to operate at a higher level of competence?

—— Check their own work for accuracy?

—— Be given more freedom to plan and schedule their work?

—— Be given more information about how they are doing their work to allow them to correct errors and control their own work?

—— Keep their own records of quality and quantity?

Motivation and the Games
We Play

Can we learn anything about job satisfaction and motivation *at work* by analyzing why we like some of the games we play *away from work?* We can indeed, according to William H. Mobley, a University of South Carolina professor.

In analyzing the game of golf, Mobley identifies five specific characteristics of the game that motivate people to continue playing it. You'll probably recognize a definite similarity between them and the "characteristics of a 'good' job," above. (If you're not a golfer, by all means feel free to substitute most any other game—bowling, tennis, handball, and so on.)

Goals. There are a number of clear goals in the game of golf. You know the pin you are shooting for; you know par of the hole and for the course; you know your previous score. Clear goals give you something to shoot at, literally and figuratively. Goals give not only guidance but also are a major component of what we commonly call "challenge." Note that the goals in golf are neither too easy nor unattainable. Note also that goals provide the basis for the competition, with par, with self, with others, that so many of us enjoy.

Recall occasions when you had to hit a blind shot. If the entire game of golf were nothing but blind shots, would it continue to be interesting? How long would you be motivated to play golf if there were no pins, no pars, no scorecard—i.e., no goals?

Feedback . . . Feedback serves two purposes, instruction and motivation. Practice and repetition make for neither perfection nor interest in the absence of knowing what one is shooting for (the goal) and how one is doing (feedback).

For feedback to be most effective, it should be immediate, direct, and related to a goal. Golf provides feedback after every shot, after every hole, after every round. The feedback comes directly to you, is immediate, and is goal related.

How long will you be motivated to play golf if feedback were removed or significantly delayed? If you could not see where your shots landed, could not keep score, and could not see or did not know the pin placements or par, would you continue to be motivated to play and improve your game?

Completeness, Skill-variety, Judgment. These last three components . . . , while clearly identifiable, are interrelated and will be discussed together.

In golf there are 18 units or cycles. Each unit is complete from placing the ball on the tee to picking the ball from the cup. Each hole gives you intermediate goals, intermediate feedback, and the total 18 holes provides a complete round. Most humans seek a sense of completeness, a sense of what the Gestalt psychologists call closure, in what we do. We like to see the beginning and end of that for which we are responsible, to complete what we begin.

Golf possesses variety, not only in terms of terrain, distances, and conditions, but, more fundamentally, variety in the mental and physical skills utilized over a complete round. The game of golf requires judgment, discretion, and self control. You must judge distances, read greens, judge wind, select clubs, select and adjust stances and grips, choose strategies and, yes, be accountable for the consequences.

Excerpted with permission from William H. Mobley, "Where Have All the Golfers Gone?" *Personnel Journal,* July 1977, pp. 339-341.

Would you continue to be motivated to play golf if it involved playing only one hole or part of a hole, using only one club, under constant conditions and required no judgment or decisions?

By removing clear goals, by removing direct and immediate feedback, and by specializing to the extent that completeness, skill-variety, and judgment are minimized, we have effectively removed much of the motivational value of golf. Do you know of any jobs to which this analogy applies?

Like most analogies, the analogy we were developing between golf and work is an oversimplification. It is true that some people would not be motivated to play golf under any circumstances . . . . It is also true that the characteristics we have been discussing are not substitutes for equitable wages, equitable treatment, decent working conditions, etc. However, many jobs possess the latter, but don't seem to be eliciting employee motivation. . . .[24]

For employees who are really enjoying their jobs, work becomes very much like play. In the case of both play and work, people's motivation and satisfaction increase when the activity being performed is meaningful to them.

Limitations of Job Enrichment

It is easy to paint pretty pictures of the potential advantages to be derived from enriching work. We must recognize, however, that in many cases the road to actual practical application of job enrichment is not an easy one. Not all jobs *can* be enriched, nor do all jobs *need* to be enriched.

Certainly there are many lower-level jobs that simply do not lend themselves to job enrichment. There are few jobs more lacking in potential motivators than the production worker on a typical assembly line, for example. To suggest that an assembly-line supervisor develop in workers a sense of achievement, responsibility, and satisfaction in the work itself may be unrealistic at best.

It is also reasonable to assume that there are many employees (fewer than popularly supposed) who would not respond to additional responsibility, scope, and challenge. When we talk about a "meaningful" job, we need to ask: "Meaningful for whom?" We cannot generalize that the worker with a routine, repetitive job is of necessity bored and frustrated; there are doubtless many people who actually prefer to work under conditions of routinized small jobs. We must remember that what may be monotonous for one individual can be interesting and absorbing to another; "the beauty of the job is in the eye of the beholder."

So, when we talk of trying to design enriching jobs that will fulfill people's higher-order needs, we hopefully are not speaking of an organizational utopia. We fully recognize that every organization has a certain amount of routine, dirty (but, necessary) work to do. Most employees realistically expect to do some unattractive work as part of their jobs; life requires learning to mix the bitter with the sweet. Job enrichment merely seeks to devise a more satisfying mixture.

The Importance of Each
Employee's Contribution

Regardless of whether a job can or cannot be enriched in the true sense, it can often be made more meaningful by simply letting employees know the importance of their individual contributions to the success of the organization as a whole and the results of inadequately done work.

Many employees seldom see the total operations of the organization; they see only the small and often uninteresting part to which they are assigned. It is, therefore, not surprising to discover how many workers are actually unaware of the importance of their work to the finished product or of how their own work affects the work of others in the same organization. If employees don't know where they fit, they cannot have a sense of importance or identification.

Essentially, any means of communication that acquaints employees with the organization's various operations, how their individual jobs contribute to the organization's or department's success and affect the work of others, the end use of the product or service by the customer, and the results of inadequately done work are helpful.

Other than ongoing two-way communications by the supervisor, ways for accomplishing this might include: training programs, tours of the organization, orientation programs emphasizing a "team approach" to organizational effectiveness, brief periods of rotation in other departments, features in the organization's newsletter, and any kind of feedback—both good and bad—from customers or top management about the performance and quality of the product or service.

Does this constitute true job enrichment? Technically, no, since the content of the job remains the same. But it can provide workers with a sense of importance and *identity*. Even a monotonous job can often be made more interesting if the employee understands how it relates to other jobs and to the success of the organization as a whole.

JOB ENRICHMENT—
A FEASIBLE SOLUTION
TO MEANINGLESS
WORK

There is little doubt that the majority of employees comprising today's work force is capable of exercising more initiative, creativity, and responsibility than is presently required or allowed by most lower-level jobs. In his best-seller, *Up the Organization,* Robert Townsend remarked:

All you have to do is look around you to see that modern organizations are only getting people to use about 20 percent—the lower fifth—of their capacities. And the painful part is that God didn't design the human animal to function at 20 percent. At that pace it develops enough malfunctions to cause a permanent shortage of psychoanalysts and hospital beds.[25]

One solution for tapping the potential of employees may be found in *job enrichment*, where the supervisor's basic task is to create wherever possible an environment in which workers can contribute the full scope of their talents. Entirely consistent with our previous discussions of McGregor's "Theory Y" and the Herzberg theory, job enrichment attempts to expand the areas in which workers can exercise *self-direction* and *self-control* as they develop greater insight and ability.

Fortunately, many routine meaningless jobs have already been eliminated by automation, and certainly more will be—but these jobs are only a small part of the problem. The concept of job design must be changed if the challenges of a better-educated work force and a rapidly changing business world are to be met.

QUESTIONS FOR REVIEW AND DISCUSSION

1. What role of importance does work play in a person's life? Analyze this question in relation to your own work experiences and what you have read in this chapter and Chapter 2.

2. Older employees are often heard to say, "People today just don't care about putting forth the effort on their jobs like they used to." Do you agree? Why?

3. a. Explain Herzberg's motivation-maintenance theory and the extent that you feel it applies in actual work situations.
   b. Do you feel that the motivation-maintenance theory is equally applicable to blue-collar workers as to managerial and professional workers?
   c. What factors do you personally believe cause satisfaction or dissatisfaction in working at a job?

4. a. Are the motivator factors more important than the maintenance factors? Why?
   b. Herzberg contends that a wage increase provides only a temporary decrease in dissatisfaction, not a long-term increase in motivation. Is this true in your experience?
   c. When truly motivated by the content of the work, might employees be more tolerant of deficient maintenance factors?
   d. What causes some people to become "maintenance seekers"?

5. "Negative motivators can be dissatisfiers too, but not so frequently as the maintainers. For example, while *achievement* is a motivator, *failure to achieve* can be a dissatisfier." Evaluate this statement.

6. "We supervisors give a great deal of lip service to the importance of developing our employees and really helping them to grow. Yet, most of us tend to keep our people in a dependency relationship with respect to us. We prefer individuals who turn to us for the answers—individuals who can't make a move until we call the shots for them." Do you agree with this statement? Why?

7. a. How important is job design in employee motivation?
   b. Comment on the statement: "Job design in industry is strictly an engineering problem."
8. What is the usual effect of excessive job specialization on an employee's motivation and productivity? Explain fully.
9. Experiments have shown the feasibility of using employees with less than average intelligence in very routine jobs. Handicapped workers have also been successful in routine jobs. Does this constitute manipulation of these people? Is there any implication from these experiments for the very common policy of hiring nothing less than a high school graduate?
10. The number of people suffering from mental illness has increased at an alarming rate during the time that most job content has been reduced in significance. Is it unrealistic to attribute at least part of this increase to the traditional approach to job design?
11. The quality control manager of a company blames the high rates of waste and rejects on poor training. What factors other than training might be at fault?
12. a. Explain in detail what is meant by *job enrichment.*
    b. Distinguish between *horizontal expansion* and *vertical expansion.*
    c. How do you feel your own job could be enriched in the sense of making it more intrinsically satisfying? Consider both horizontal and vertical means of expansion.
13. Proponents of job enrichment say that it is a common management error to underestimate the level of work that employees are capable of attaining. Do you agree? Have you ever felt that your job underutilized your abilities?
14. a. The chapter states: "Not all jobs *can* be enriched, nor do all jobs *need* to be enriched." Can you give some examples from your own organization of jobs that cannot be enriched?
    b. Why might a particular job be satisfying to one individual but not to another?
15. a. Do you feel that retail jobs lend themselves to job enrichment concepts as readily as industrial jobs?
    b. In what ways could a typical department store salesperson's job be enriched? That of a checker in a supermarket?
16. Should individuals participate in determining how their jobs should be enriched?
17. a. How would you predict that union leaders would react to the concept of job enrichment?
    b. What problems might be encountered in implementing a job enrichment program in a unionized organization? What might be done to overcome these problems?
18. Is the concept of "work simplification" the natural enemy of the concept of job enrichment? Are the two in direct conflict or can they peacefully coexist?
19. How can a supervisor best go about letting each employee know the importance of his or her individual function to the success of the organiztion as a whole?

20. This chapter presented a pretty strong case for job enrichment. Can you visualize any potential pitfalls in this approach to motivation?

REFERENCES

1. Sheppard, Harold L., and Neal Q. Herrick, *Where Have All the Robots Gone?* New York: The Free Press, 1972, p. xi.

2. Herzberg, Frederick, "The Human Need to Work," *Industry Week*, July 24, 1978, p. 49.

3. Herzberg, Frederick, "One More Time: How Do You Motivate Employees? *Harvard Business Review*, Jan–Feb. 1968, p. 55.

4. Myers, M. Scott, *Managing Without Unions*. Reading, Mass.: Addison-Wesley Publishing Company, Inc., 1976, Chapter 3, pp. 29–30. Reprinted with permission.

5. Dowling, William F., "Managers or Animal Trainers? An Interview with Frederick Herzberg," *Management Review*, July, 1971. Also in: Herzberg, Frederick, *The Managerial Choice*, Homewood, Ill.: Dow Jones-Irwin, 1976, pp. 301–314.

6. *This Matter of Motivation*. Chicago: The Dartnell Corporation, 16 mm. motion picture film.

7. Adapted from: Davis, Keith, *Human Behavior at Work*. New York: McGraw-Hill Book Company, 1972, p. 59.

8. Myers, M. Scott, *Managing With Unions*. Reading, Mass.: Addison-Wesley Publishing Company, Inc., 1978, Chapter 1, p. 17. Reprinted with permission.

9. Sheppard and Herrick, *op. cit.*, p. xxv.

10. Argyris, Chris, "We Must Make Work Worthwhile," *Life*, May 5, 1967, p. 56.

11. Dowling, *op. cit.*

12. Herzberg, *op. cit.*, p. 59.

13. Myers, M. Scott, *Every Employee A Manager*. New York: McGraw-Hill Book Company, 1970, pp. 62–74.

14. *Ibid.*

15. Huse, Edgar, F., and Michael Beer, "Eclectic Approach to Organizational Development," *Harvard Business Review*, Sept.–Oct. 1971, pp. 103–7.

16. Hackman, J. Richard, Greg Oldham, Robert Janson, and Kenneth Purdy, "A New Strategy for Job Enrichment," *California Management Review*, Summer 1975, p. 59.

17. Morrisey, George, "Making M.B.O. Work—The Missing Link," *Training and Development Journal*, Feb., 1976, pp. 3–4.

18. Herzberg, Frederick, "The Wise Old Turk," *Harvard Business Review*, Sept.–Oct. 1974, p. 72.

19. *Ibid.*, p. 73.

20. Hackman, *et. al.*, *op. cit.*, p. 64.

21. *Ibid.*, pp. 64–65.

22. *Ibid.*

23. Adapted from a framework provided in: Myers, M. Scott, *Every Employee a Manager.* New York: McGraw-Hill Book Company, 1970, pp. 74–75.

24. Excerpted with permission from: Mobley, William H., "Where Have All the Golfers Gone?" *Personnel Journal,* July, 1977, pp. 339–351.

25. Townsend, Robert, *Up the Organization.* New York: Alfred A. Knopf, 1970, p. 140.

Suggested Additional Readings

Cooper, M. R., B. S. Morgan, P. M. Foley, and L. B. Kaplan, "Changing Employee Values: Deepening Discontent?" *Harvard Business Review,* Jan.–Feb. 1979, pp. 117–125.

Grote, Richard C., "Implementing Job Enrichment," *California Management Review,* Fall 1972, pp. 16–21.

Hackman, J. Richard, "Is Job Enrichment A Fad?" *Harvard Business Review,* Sept.–Oct. 1975, pp. 129–138.

Hackman, J. Richard, Greg Oldham, Robert Janson, and Kenneth Purdy, "A New Strategy for Job Enrichment," *California Management Review,* Summer 1975, pp. 57–71.

Herzberg, Frederick, "One More Time: How Do You Motivate Employees?" *Harvard Business Review,* Jan.–Feb, 1968, pp. 53–62.

——,"The Wise Old Turk," *Harvard Business Review,* Sept.–Oct. 1974, pp. 70–80.

Levinson, Harry, "Asinine Attitudes Toward Motivation," *Harvard Business Review,* January–February, 1973, pp. 70–76.

Livingston, J. Sterling, "Pygmalion In Management," *Harvard Business Review,* July–August, pp. 81–89.

Mager, Robert F., and Peter Pipe, *Analyzing Performance Problems.* Belmont, Calif.: Fearon-Pitman Publishers, Inc., 1970. lllpp.

Myers, M. Scott, "Every Employee A Manager," *California Management Review,* Spring 1968, pp. 9–20.

——, "Overcoming Union Opposition to Job Enrichment," *Harvard Business Review,* May–June, 1971, pp. 37–48.

Paul, William J., Jr., Keith B. Robertson, and Frederick Herzberg, "Job Enrichment Pays Off," *Harvard Business Review,* March–April, 1969, pp. 61–78.

Woodman, Richard W., and John J. Sherwood, "A Comprehensive Look at Job Design," *Personnel Journal,* Aug. 1977, pp. 384–390, 418.

4

EMPLOYEE PARTICIPATION IN DECISION MAKING

> *One of the most misunderstood concepts in management is participation. Some managers equate it with permissiveness. Others believe it to be a sign of weakness. Still others do not see its application to management functions. This is ironic in a democratic society since the process of participation forms the basis for our political system. Somehow the transfer of this concept from our political system to the management of our organizations has yet to take place.*[1]
>
> William P. Anthony

> *None of us is as smart as all of us.*
>
> Anon.

Pick up almost any business-related periodical today—or even the general press—and you are likely to find someone pleading the cause of employee "participation" and "involvement." Organizations are increasingly accused of being too closed and undemocratic, and participation in decision making is proposed as *the* way to improve both employee job satisfaction and productivity.

Actually, this current interest in participation isn't anything very new. The basic concept of "participative management" has been around in one form or another since at least the early 1950s. For various reasons, though, it has never really achieved widespread popularity in organizations.

At first glance, the concept of participation can be very appealing. After all, it's certainly more popular to be viewed today as being a "participative" or "democratic" super-

---

[1] Anthony, William P., *Participative Management.* © 1978, Addison-Wesley Publishing Company Inc., Chapter 1, p. 3. Reprinted with permission.

visor than to be labeled "autocratic" or "authoritarian." Unfortunately, translating the theory of participation into practice hasn't always been easy, and many who have joined the participation bandwagon—thinking that it is a magic formula that can be applied by any supervisor in any situation—have met with considerable disillusionment and failure.

Insightful supervisors who have had a chance to carefully think through the idea of employee participation in decision making typically come up with questions like these:

"If I'm being paid to make decisions, doesn't participation mean I'm 'passing the buck' to my people?"

"If I share decision making with my employees, won't I lose authority and control?"

"Aren't there times when I alone have to make the decisions—and be pretty arbitrary about it?"

"Why should I waste time getting suggestions from employees when the solution is already a foregone conclusion?"

"What is the best 'style' of supervision? Is a participative style the best?"

"How can I get people to participate when they don't want to accept any responsibility?"

"How can I be expected to find time to meet with all my employees every time a decision has to be made?"

Those are all legitimate and difficult questions to answer. They also illustrate that there are differences of opinion and considerable confusion over just what is meant by the concept of participation. This chapter may help to clear up some of the "fuzziness."

THE PARTICIPATIVE
APPROACH TO
SUPERVISION

The participative approach to supervision is based on the premise that **many employees want to participate in decision making and, furthermore, that they very often have the ability to help shape better, more meaningful decisions.**

Thus, the supervisor draws on the ideas of those employees who will be affected by the decision. An attempt is made to get the employees to think about issues of the problem; their comments and suggestions are actively sought before the decision is made. The supervisor obviously cannot consult with employees on every problem, but a *climate of consultation* can be set by being genuinely receptive to people's ideas and providing them with a voice in the affairs that directly concern them. In many cases, this may prove to be highly motivating and contribute to the meaningfulness and enrichment of the individual's job.

Autocratic versus Participative Styles of Supervision

Participative supervision can generally be considered the opposite of autocratic or authoritarian styles of supervision.

Autocratic supervisors *centralize* all authority and decision making within themselves. In this style of supervision, all planning, goal setting, work standards, organization, and information dispersion are highly structured and are exclusively within the province of the supervisor; he or she assumes full authority and responsibility for the complete work situation. Employees are simply informed of the supervisor's decisions and expected to carry them out and do what they are told.

In contrast, the use of participation *decentralizes* managerial authority. Whenever appropriate, decisions affecting the group are not made unilaterally by the supervisor, as by the autocrat, but individual members of the group are brought in and encouraged to offer ideas and suggestions on current problems facing the supervisor.

As we shall see, however, there is seldom one "pure" style of supervision. Rather, there are degrees between these two extremes.

Dispelling Some Common Misconceptions About Participation

Now that we have a working concept of what participative supervision is, let us at this point also mention what it is not, in order to avoid confusion later. Many supervisors, at the mere mention of the word "participation," immediately reject the concept because of oversimplified notions of what it really is.

It is not to be thought of as "pure democracy" in the political sense, with every employee having the right to vote on all major decisions, with the majority ruling; pure political democracy can rarely be equated with participative or democratic supervision within a business organization. Keep in mind that when we refer to participation by employees in planning and decision making we are referring not to direct democracy but rather to individual or group participation in making *some* (but not all) decisions that affect the way things are to be done in the group. As supervisor, you still reserve the right to make the final decision and are accountable for it. But before doing so, you take into consideration the needs and opinions of those working for you, actively soliciting rather than merely tolerating or attempting to squelch their contributions.

Neither is participation synonymous with holding group meetings or forming committees or task forces, as is commonly believed. Participative decision making can involve only *two people*—the supervisor and one employee. Participation does not mean that you have to call your entire work group together—unless, of course, you decide that is desirable.

Still others have the mistaken notion that participative supervision is too permissive and that it results in the supervisor losing authority and control. Participation is confused with "laissez-faire," "country-club," or "leaderless" management or "group-think." This is far from the real intent. In using participation, you still must retain the ultimate responsibility for your unit's operation; when using participation, you are *sharing* (not surrendering) some of this responsibility with those who actually perform the work. Yes, you loosen some control, but you do so based on confidence in your employees' abilities to assume additional responsibility.

Formal authority isn't weakened because you still retain the right to make the final decision and are accountable for the performance of the decision.

Ultimately, the source of any supervisor's authority lies in its *acceptance* by employees. And the use of participation may actually enhance the supervisor's authority by reducing the amount of resistance to the exercise of formal authority.

THE PROCESS OF DECISION MAKING

Before continuing our discussion of allowing employee participation in decision making, perhaps we should take a quick look at what the decision-making process really involves. Wise decisions are crucial to supervisory success; but we often fail to understand all the things involved in arriving at an intelligent, rational decision.

Decision making of any kind involves **a choice or selection of one alternative solution from among a group of two or more alternative solutions to a particular problem.** In its simplest form, the decision-making process involves these four steps:

1. **Identification and diagnosis of the basic problem**: Decision making is never an isolated activity; it is always related to a problem, a difficulty, or a conflict. Decisions bring about an answer to the problem or a resolution of the conflict.

2. **Identification of all alternative courses of action available for resolving the problem**: True decision making necessitates that a choice be made from two or more alternatives. Obviously, if there is only one choice, there is no decision to be made. Several possibilities are available for resolving a problem from which the ultimate selection must be made.

3. **Evaluation and comparison of alternative courses of action**: This involves weighing the *advantages* and *disadvantages* of each possible alternative, and considering the *probability of success* and the *risks* of complications inherent in each alternative. Naturally, all pertinent data that can be tracked down should be assembled and related to the alternatives at this stage.

4. **Selection of the final solution from among the available alternatives**: Decide which

course of action promises to be most successful, recognizing the strengths and weaknesses of your chosen solution.*

POTENTIAL BENEFITS
OF PARTICIPATION

Although there are several potential benefits to be obtained from participative supervision, **the primary purpose of practicing participation—and the primary benefit to be
derived from it—should always be to improve the quality of supervisory decision making
and the total performance of the supervisor's work unit.**

Other benefits that we will discuss—*raising the level of employee motivation* and *increasing the acceptability of decisions*—are best viewed as by-products of the primary
purpose of achieving improved decision making.

Improving the Quality
of Decision Making

As you begin to utilize the full range of experiences, insights, and creative abilities
of your employees, the overall quality of your decision making is likely to improve. People working together may be able to generate a greater quantity of information and
variety of approaches than can any single individual. Group decision making can, in fact,
unleash a *synergistic effect:* that is, the final decision emerges as a product much better
than the sum of its individual inputs. The premise is that, "None of us is as smart as all of
us."

Frequently, employees are able to point out factors of problem situations that you
might overlook when you make certain decisions solely on your own. In soliciting the
ideas of those employees directly involved in the problem and affected by the decision,
decisions can many times be made more efficiently. For example, it is seldom if ever
possible for you to have knowledge of all aspects of a problem, all alternative courses of
action, or all consequences and risks related to all the decisions you must make.

Employees often can shed practical ideas on the problem from an *operative stand-
point;* by discussing certain problems with them and drawing upon their practical experiences, you may actually find that you have not completely explored the problem. The
interchange of ideas and different views of the problem can often give you a much
broader view of the situation.

Thus, you may find a ready reservoir of technical expertise that can be easily tapped
through participation.

---

*You may argue that, in reality, a supervisor does not always *consciously* go through these four
steps in making all decisions—especially in making simple routine decisions. The point may be argued,
however, that, regardless of the routineness or complexity of the decision to be made, any intelligent,
rationally made decision requires the supervisor to go through the four steps, on either a conscious or
an unconscious level. Many poor decisions are the direct result of neglecting to devote adequate consideration to one or more of the steps.

Overgeneralizations can get us into trouble, though. As we'll see, the use of participation is certainly *not always* the most effective way to make decisions. Whether a decision reached by an individual or through involvement by a group of people is better ultimately depends on the variables of the particular problem, situation, and people with whom you are dealing.

Importance of supervisor's attitude. To utilize participation in this manner effectively, you must project to your employees an attitude reflecting the fact that you recognize that they have talents and abilities that can enhance the quality of decisions—that they have the ability to think and come up with new ideas. You must be *genuinely* receptive to employees' ideas, perceiving their ideas as useful. In fact, in order to work properly, participation requires that both you and your employees sincerely believe that the final decision can be better because the ideas of two or more people have been integrated into it.

Furthermore, you must admit that you don't always know everything about every problem, which of course requires a certain degree of humility—something that many supervisors seem to lack (!). However, if this attitude is not displayed when using participation, employees will usually quickly perceive your participative efforts as being a superficial facade, interpreting it merely as a *manipulative tactic* rather than a genuine desire for their ideas.

Freeing the upward flow of communication. Because of the barriers often existing in the upward flow of communication from workers to management in most organizations (discussed fully in Chapter 6), valuable information and ideas that can be vital to a decision are often withheld and never reach the supervisor. Ideas go unrecognized and untapped in most organizations in enormous numbers.

A climate of participation within your work unit is one tool that can help to break down some of these barriers to upward communication, making information available to you that may improve the quality of your decisions. Involving employees in problem solving allows them to voice attitudes and feelings that may go unheard in any other way.

Raising the Level of Employee Motivation

Although participation should be used to achieve improved supervisory decision making primarily, a welcome by-product is that it often improves the level of employee motivation and morale. Not only can participation be a source of many practical suggestions that can improve the effectiveness of the work group, it can also be highly motivating and intrinsically satisfying to the employee who comes to feel a sense of involvement in the group's goals.

Intrinsic job satisfaction. If employees are invited to participate in various steps in the decision-making process, they can find an important source of satisfaction and meaning in their work.

People who play a meaningful role in decision making can become ego-involved in their jobs instead of merely task-involved. This can motivate them to contribute more fully to the organization's goals and to accept a greater degree of responsibility. By means of participation, the needs of employees to feel important and to contribute are recognized and utilized.

Additionally, most employees derive a sense of personal satisfaction from being able to solve problems. Challenging employees with a problem and then having them report back their ideas and possible courses of action can be a positive motivating factor in supplying employees with a sense of achievement and recognition. For employees to know that they can freely express their ideas and that they can help shape the final decision can be a definite source of intrinsic job satisfaction.

Teamwork and commitment to group goals. Participation can also motivate employees to develop *teamwork.* Teamwork results when individual employees form a closely knit work group that has a unity of purpose to which each employee becomes dedicated. Employees come to feel that they are an integral and important part of the group; this feeling of belonging and being needed not only helps to satisfy their social needs but also encourages employees to accept responsibility in their work group's activities.

Employees who can become ego-involved in their jobs as a result of the participation process tend to have a much greater feeling of identification with the organization and its goals. In a sense, participation helps to bring about a coincidence of individual employees' personal goals and the organization's goals. Employees come to recognize that helping the organization to attain its goals will, in turn, enhance the satisfaction of their own needs. When employees feel a personal stake in the organization's goals, they will usually be more willing to do what is needed to achieve them; job problems then become "ours," not "theirs."

Furthering the individual development of employees. In motivating employees to contribute through participation, you are also providing the opportunity for them to release their own resources of initiative, creativity, and ingenuity. You are creating a climate in your work group conducive to individual employee growth and development, where new skills and knowledge can be learned. When employees are given the opportunity to suggest and question instead of the traditional pattern of following rigid sets of instructions, they usually can develop into more mature and responsible individuals.

In contrast, totally autocratic supervision may well pay off in terms of dollar profits, but it seldom offers a climate for human growth and development. Thus, in the choice of a supervisory style, "human costs" should be considered together with a desire for high productivity and profits; in the final analysis, the two usually complement each other.

Increasing the Acceptability
of Decisions

Decisions that employees have been involved in making are generally more acceptable to them than those decisions that are arbitrarily forced upon them by the supervisor. Employees are more likely to support what they help to create. When they take an active part in the decision-making process, they develop a greater "ownership" in the outcome and are less inclined to find fault with the decision. As the old saying goes,"The fellow in the boat with you never bores a hole in it."

Of course, it is often argued that it may actually be easier and more efficient for the supervisor to make departmental decisions without bothering to involve employees; as we shall see later, in many instances this is true. However, we need to keep in mind that your job as a problem solver does not end with the making of the decision; you also are responsible for the *implementation* of the decision. Thus, in reality, you have two things that must be accomplished: (1) **the making of the decision itself** and (2) **the activities required to carry out the decision.** The latter usually requires cooperation and acceptance on the part of employees.

As a result, in many cases you may well do better by taking the extra time to discuss problems with your employees and, on occasion, perhaps even to accept suggestions that you believe may be somewhat less efficient than your own in order to obtain employee acceptance and cooperation in carrying out the decision. In other words, **solutions of lesser quality accompanied by a high degree of employee acceptance might be more effective in some cases than solutions of higher quality without employee acceptance.**[2]

Such a choice should not be interpreted as "buying" cooperation or manipulating employees by letting them participate. Again, we emphasize that, in using participation, the supervisor's first concern is **improving the quality of the decision.** You by no means have to accept solutions that you consider to be poor or incompatible with the objectives of the organization; acceptance of a poor solution certainly accomplishes nothing in the way of improving the group's performance. If you believe you have a substantially better course of action than has been offered by employees, you should present your reasoning and evidence to support your viewpoint.

Even if employee's suggestions are not accepted, the mere fact that they have been consulted can make the final decision more understandable to the employees, less likely to be misinterpreted, and generally more acceptable. As decisions arrived at through participation are more likely to take into account the needs and interests of all parties, supervisory control is less likely to seem arbitrary and threatening.

Overcoming resistance to change. Participation has proven to be especially useful in overcoming resistance to the introduction of change. (The topic of "change" is fully discussed in Chapter 5.) Employees tend to react adversely to decisions that impose changes upon them. You can often minimize this resistance by drawing the employees affected by the change into participating in the planning and implementation stages of the change. Employees who are consulted and allowed to participate in the decisions about the change are normally able to more easily adjust to it.

DETERMINING WHEN TO USE PARTICIPATION

It is necessary to emphasize that the benefits of participative supervision that we have discussed are merely potential benefits and can be successfully derived only in the proper situations and circumstances. Thus, we must guard against the tendency to overgeneralize about these benefits, because they by no means automatically follow from the use of participation. Their success is entirely dependent upon the manner and conditions under which participation is applied. In fact, there is much evidence that participation in many situations may not be desirable at all.

Choice of a Style of Supervision to Fit the Situation

You cannot simply choose to use or not to use participation in making all your decisions. The essential question that you must ask is: "Under what conditions is participation likely to be beneficial or not beneficial?"

As seen in Figure 4-1, Robert Tannenbaum and Warren Schmidt describe the use of participation as existing on a continuum, ranging from little or no participation under a highly autocratic style of supervision at one end of the continuum to almost complete democratic participation with a minimum of imposed authority at the other end. In other words, the use participation on any specific problem may fall anywhere between two extremes. On the left side of the continuum, the supervisor maintains a high degree of control and complete centralization of decision-making authority, merely announcing his or her conclusion and attempting to get employees to carry out the plan. At the other extreme, on the right side of the continuum, the supervisor completely delegates decision-making authority to the employees.

As the continuum illustrates, a number of supervisory styles can be employed between the two extremes; within a period of time, an effective supervisor may well practice varying degrees of participation along the continuum: [3]

1. *Manager makes decision and announces it.* Here, the boss identifies the problem, considers alternative solutions, selects one of them, reports the decision to employees, and expects the decision to be accepted and implemented without question. There is clearly no opportunity for participation in the decision-making process.

2. *Manager "sells" the decision.* Next in line on the continuum is when the manager, as before, identifies the problem and makes the decision independent of the group's

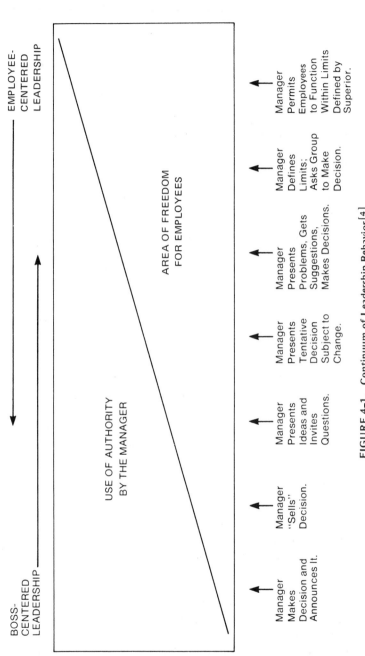

FIGURE 4-1. Continuum of Leadership Behavior[4]

involvement. But, instead of just announcing the decision, an attempt is made to persuade the employees to accept it by showing them what they have to gain by going along with it.

3. *Manager presents ideas and invites questions.* Here again, the boss independently makes the decision. However, an extra step is taken by allowing employees to discuss and question the decision and to get a more complete understanding of the boss's thinking and the intent of the decision.

4. *Manager presents tentative decision subject to change.* This point on the continuum allows the group to exert some influence, although minimal, on the decision. After identifying the problem, the boss reaches a tentative decision. But, before finalizing it, it is tested out on the group by asking for their reactions. Although the decision might be changed if there are serious objections to it, the boss clearly reserves the right to make the final decision.

5. *Manager presents problems, gets suggestions, makes decision.* Until this point, the boss's own solution to the problem has been presented. Here the employees get their first opportunity to suggest solutions. The boss defines and presents the problem and asks the group to offer alternative solutions for consideration. The solution that seems best to the boss is then selected.

6. *Manager defines limits; asks group to make decision.* The boss defines the problem and asks the group to make the decision. However, before doing this, the boundaries within which the decision must be made are prescribed. The boss may or may not join in the discussion as a member of the group.

7. *Manager permits employees to function within limits defined by superior.* At this extreme of the continuum, the group has complete freedom to define and diagnose the problem, develop alternative solutions, and reach a decision, as long as it is within prescribed limits. The boss agrees in advance to carry out whatever decision the group makes.

Factors to Be Considered

In reality, supervisors can seldom be totally autocratic or totally participative in all circumstances. There are different *degrees* of participation, and the appropriate degree chosen to fit a particular situation depends on the interaction of the five factors that follow.

Supervisor's expectations about employees. In deciding on the appropriate degree of participation to use, a major consideration should be your own assumptions and expectations about your employees.

Should you possess predominantly "Theory X" assumptions (as discussed in Chapter 2), effective use of participation will be limited and uncomfortable for you. Consciously or unconsciously, you will use participation as a manipulative device for getting people to do what you want, rather than as a means for improving decision making and developing your people. You may go through the motions of asking for employee comments and suggestions, but rarely pay much real attention to them.

A "Theory Y" supervisor, on the other hand, would likely be more comfortable using participation. In this case, your expectations about people's abilities and desire to contribute would be higher.

Supervisor's confidence in employees. Similarly, do you have enough trust in your employees' knowledge and abilities to think that their involvement could improve the decision? Or, do you feel that they're really not qualified to deal with such a problem? You may, justifiably or not, have more confidence in your own abilities to deal with the problem than in those of your employees.

The important question to ask, of course, is whether this is really a valid assessment of your people.

Nature and complexity of the problem. The problem itself should be interesting and challenging to the employees. Otherwise, they will only regard it as busywork. On the other hand, it should not be so complex as to exceed their abilities and knowledge. Some problems are so complex and specialized that only one or two people in the entire organization may be qualified to deal with them.[5]

Time constraints. This is probably the reason most commonly cited for not delegating or involving employees in the making of decisions. And it is frequently a legitimate reason. It normally takes a group more time to make a decision than it does for an individual. Situations can arise when there is no time to talk to anyone—action is needed *now*.

So the more pressure there is to reach an immediate decision, the more difficult it is to involve people. This especially becomes a constraint in organizations where there is a constant climate of "crises" and "firefighting." It's important, however, to make sure "lack of time" is not just a convenient rationalization for continuing to "do it yourself."

Employees' readiness to participate. Before considering an increased use of participation, you'll want to ask yourself, "How strongly have my employees come to expect being involved in decisions that affect them?"

Not all employees expect or want to be involved in decision making. Some may view participation positively, coming to expect to be involved. Others may see it as "passing the buck." Their attitude may be: "You're paid to be the boss, we're paid to do the work; so don't ask us to make *your* decisions." Many employees have an "authoritarian set" to their personalities, deriving a sense of security and dependency from working within a strong authority structure. They prefer to have clear-cut directives given to them, and have come to expect strong autocratic supervision. When suddenly confronted by a supervisor who asks them to participate in decision making, they are often bewildered, reacting quite adversely to this new experience.[6]

On the other hand, if their expectations about their supervisor's role can be gradually changed and their perceptions about the degree that they should participate can be raised, participation may in time become more acceptable to them.

All these and other factors must be taken into account in determining the appropriate degree of participation to be used at any one time. Each factor can place restrictions on the value and desirability of participation. Collectively, they permit participation to work better in some situations than in others; in certain situations, it doesn't work at all. As the restrictions become greater, the value and desirability of participation become less.[7]

In a case where there are restrictions and participation cannot really add to the quality of the decision, there is no point in trying to fool your employees into believing they are helping to reach what is already a foregone conclusion. On the other hand, you do not have to be "tied" to such restrictions forever. As you look to the future, it may be possible to change and improve some of the factors. For example, you can gain new insights and skills for yourself, better train your employees to accept new responsibilities, and gradually provide them with participative experiences.[8]

Maintaining Flexibility in Supervisory Style

Hence, the "ideal" style of supervision on the continuum is nonexistent. The uniqueness of each work group and situation prevents prescribing a "one best way" to supervise people that will be appropriate in all circumstances. Style *flexibility*—not rigidity—is the key. A participative style is no more effective than an autocratic style if it isn't adaptable to the demands of the situation.

The most effective supervisors are those who are adaptable, maintaining a sense of flexibility so that they can cope with different situations. They may have a typical style that lies somewhere between the two extremes on the continuum, but their flexibility allows them to "tailor-make" a style for each particular situation.[9]

As in all attempts at motivating and working with employees, this requires that you be *empathetic*—knowing your employees, their needs, attitudes, and aspirations—in order to judge effectively the degree of participation that will be appropriate.

PROBLEMS TYPICALLY ENCOUNTERED IN IMPLEMENTATION

Even though the basic concept of participative supervision has been around since early in the human relations movement, great difficulty is often still encountered by supervisors in understanding and applying the concept. In addition to the factors we've already looked at that limit its use, there are other problems.

Application Within a "Theory X" Framework

Undoubtedly, the not infrequent failures encountered by supervisors in implementing participation can be partially attributed to the fact that they have "bought the idea" but have applied it within the traditional "Theory X" framework and its assumptions. Consciously or unconsciously, they consider participation mainly as a way of manipulating their employees rather than as a means of improving decision making and developing their people. The goal often becomes to handle people skillfully so that they come up with the answer the supervisor had in mind in the first place, but believe it is their own. This attempt to "make 'em think it was their idea in the first place" can be quite risky. It may succeed in giving employees a "sense of participation," but it cannot provide the results derived through participation in the true sense.

Obviously, a change from a strictly autocratic style of supervision to a more participative style necessitates a change in attitudes on the part of the individual supervisor; namely, from those attitudes about people associated with McGregor's "Theory X" to those supporting "Theory Y" (see Chapter 2). For many supervisors, such a change can be quite difficult to justify or accept, as attitudes that have been formed over years of experience are always difficult to change. Nevertheless, the change is a requirement for the success of any participative attempts.

Moving Too Fast

There is also much evidence that participative supervision can get into trouble if it is implemented too fast. Participation simply can't be put into full-scale practice overnight. This is particularly true where employees have been conditioned throughout their entire work experience to expect traditional autocratic styles of supervision.

Yet, many supervisors decide one morning that they're going to be more participative with their work group, only to conclude by the afternoon that it doesn't work. Participants in supervision seminars can be seen rushing out and trying to use their newly-learned participative techniques immediately—and, a week later, woefully and disappointedly complain to the class that it was a complete failure. Their employees typically have reactions ranging from feelings of manipulation and distrust to contentions that the supervisor was becoming mentally ill (!), or to feelings of "that's what supervisors are paid for—to make decisions—so don't bug me with your problems!" Such reactions are common when you move too fast; many employees aren't as ready for participation as one might think. Unfortunately, when supervisors feel their participative efforts have failed, their frustrations usually erupt into an immediate revival of their former autocratic approaches to any problem.

You simply can't abruptly order employees to start participating and taking on more responsibility. Where participation is suddenly imposed on all group members, it may well create as much resentment as highly autocratic methods.

Thus, the solution is simple: *Move slowly;* begin in a small way. You should gradually expose your employees to participative experiences. This requires a continuing effort to *condition* them to participate in decisions that affect them in their work. As their abilities expand and they become accustomed to their new role, you can then expand their participation and responsibilities step-by-step.

In reality, it is not uncommon to find that a complete transformation to a participative climate may take several years. Thus, an evaluation of participation's success too early in the game will not necessarily give an accurate indication of its ability to produce the desired results.

Miscellaneous Pitfalls

There are other inevitable pitfalls and shortcomings that you must be prepared to encounter in your early participative efforts. For example, employees whose ideas and suggestions have been rejected may become alienated. In attempting to be more participative, you may well meet resistance from your more apathetic and dependent workers who prefer to let you do all the thinking and take all the responsibility. Some employees may never wish to participate, nor can it be assumed that all are capable of contributing to problem solving. Other employees will be able to take on only *limited* responsibilities, regardless of how much you try to give them. Participation may actually lead to greater group cohesiveness *against* management if the goals of the group are contrary to the goals of management. Employees may expect further increased participation that you are restricted from providing. Finally, union leaders are sometimes antagonistic toward participation, fearing that it will draw the loyalty of workers away from the union and closer to management.

IN PERSPECTIVE—
A MODEL OF
PARTICIPATIVE
SUPERVISION

Although management experts have not yet agreed on any one consistent concept of participative leadership, the following model offered by R. E. Miles may be helpful as a summary of the subject:

Attitudes Toward People

1. In addition to sharing common needs for belonging and respect, most people in our culture desire to contribute effectively and creatively to the accomplishment of worthwhile objectives.

2. The majority of our work force are capable of exercising far more initiative, responsibility, and creativity than their present jobs require or allow.

3. These capabilities represent untapped resources that are presently being wasted.

Kind and Amount of Participation

1. The supervisor's basic task is to create an environment in which his subordinates can contribute their full range of talents to the accomplishment of organizational goals. He must attempt to uncover and tap the creative resources of his subordinates.

2. The supervisor should allow, and encourage, his subordinates to participate not only in routine decisions but in important matters as well. In fact, the more important a decision is to the supervisor's department, the greater should be his effort to tap the department's resources.

3. The supervisor should attempt to continually expand the areas over which his subordinates exercise self-direction and self-control as they develop and demonstrate greater insight and ability.

Expectations of Participation

1. The over-all quality of decision-making and performance will improve as the supervisor makes use of the full range of experience, insight, and creative ability in his department.

2. Subordinates will exercise responsible self-direction and self-control in the accomplishment of worthwhile objectives that they understand and have helped establish.

3. Subordinates' satisfaction will increase as a by-product of improved performance and the opportunity to contribute creatively to this improvement.[10]

As we have seen, participation has its limitations, as well as its often cited advantages. When applied in inappropriate situations or by those who naively view it as a magic formula, it may not achieve any gains at all. In fact, improperly applied participation can be worse for productivity and employee satisfaction than simply doing nothing. Unrealistic expectations of its benefits are sure to meet with disillusionment and premature condemnation.

In spite of these cautions, there is also enough evidence to indicate that properly implemented participation offers some real benefits for any supervisor interested in: (1) improving the quality of decision making; (2) raising the level of employee motivation; and (3) increasing the acceptability of decisions.

QUESTIONS FOR REVIEW AND DISCUSSION

1. What is meant by the concept of *participation?*
2. "It is fine to talk about the 'rational process of decision making,' but how often do supervisors have the time for such luxuries? Something happens and you have to act fast. This is where supervisors earns their salaries—making fast, intuitive decisions under pressure." How would you respond to this statement?

3. a. Recall a decision that you recently made. Did you go through the four steps in the decision-making process cited in this chapter? Trace your decision through the four steps, explaining each.
    b. Which of these four steps could an employee, friend, or associate have contributed to that might have improved the overall quality of your final solution?
4. Which style of supervision—autocratic or participative—is generally the easiest for the supervisor to practice? Why?
5. Discuss the major potential benefits of participative supervision.
6. "Solutions of lesser quality accompanied by a high degree of employee acceptance might be more effective in some cases than solutions of higher quality without employee acceptance." Do you agree or disagree with this statement? Explain.
7. As you see it, which is better—a decision reached by an individual or one reached by a group? Explain.
8. Many organizations utilize *committees, departmental meetings,* and *suggestion systems* as devices for obtaining employee participation. How would you evaluate the desirability and benefits of these techniques? If you have had experiences with any of these techniques, relate to the class how they have been implemented and if they have been successful; if they have not been successful, how do you account for this?
9. a. What factors determine the degree of participation that should be used in a given situation?
    b. What are some of the "realities of life" in an organization that can restrict the use of participation?
    c. Are supervisors "tied" to these variables or do they have some control over them?
10. What are the major implications for supervision of the "leadership continuum" discussed in this chapter?
11. Can the points on the leadership continuum be related to the degree that employees are allowed to participate in the four steps in the decision-making process? Explain.
12. Does the leadership continuum basically represent McGregor's "Theory X" at one end and "Theory Y" (discussed in Chapter 2) at the other end? Explain.
13. As you see yourself as a supervisor, what style of supervision do you (or would you) use most of the time? Why? Where does your style fall on the leadership continuum?
14. *Supervisor A:* "I always give my people directions in a few words, telling them clearly what is expected of them. When possible, I do this in writing to give them a permanent statement of what is required. If they have questions on what is expected they may raise them, but I don't encourage questions dealing with why a decision was made as it was. This way they are clear as to precisely what I want."
    Supervisor B: "I usually talk over my decisions with the people who carry them out to be sure they not only understand what is expected of them but why, and

how what they do fits into the total picture. This way they see the reasons for my requests, and they can carry them out with higher motivation and greater perspective."

   a. Which points on the leadership continuum do you feel would typically represent each supervisor's style of leadership?

   b. Under what conditions might A be better? When would B be better?

   c. If you were receiving orders, which approach would you prefer?

15. In what ways can the use of participation by the supervisor aid in supplying the employee's job with Herzberg's *motivator* and *maintenance* factors, discussed in Chapter 3?

16. How does the concept of participation by employees in the decision-making process relate to (a) *horizontal expansion* and (b) *vertical expansion* of jobs, as presented in Chapter 3?

17. The basic concept of participation has been with us since early in the human relations movement. However, it has never attained great popularity with management and has apparently not been successful in all applications. How would you attempt to explain this failure to gain universal acceptance?

18. "Often I will consult with employees who lack the interest or ability to make constructive suggestions. They don't really add anything to the quality of the decision, but it gives them a sense of importance. Besides, who knows? Someday, somebody might come up with a good idea." Do you believe that the supervisor making this statement will get the results he or she expects from the use of participation? Why?

19. Can you tell how "participative" a supervisor is by the number of decisions his or her employees make? Explain.

20. Do supervisors lose a certain degree of authority, control, and influence when they allow their employees to influence decisions through participation?

REFERENCES

1. Anthony, William P., *Participative Management.* Reading, Massachusetts: Addison-Wesley Publishing Company, 1978, p. 3.

2. Miles, Raymond E., "Human Relations or Human Resources?" *Harvard Business Review,* July–August, 1965, p. 150.

3. Tannenbaum, Robert, and Warren H. Schmidt, "How to Choose a Leadership Pattern," *Harvard Business Review,* May–June, 1973, pp. 162–170.

4. *Ibid.,* p. 164.

5. Anthony, *op. cit.,* pp. 44–45.

6. Davis, Keith, *Human Behavior at Work.* New York: McGraw-Hill Book Company, 1972, pp. 149–50.

7. Davis, Keith, "The Case for Participative Management," *Business Horizons,* Fall 1963, p. 60.

8. Tannenbaum and Schmidt, *op. cit.,* p. 179.

9. *Ibid.,* pp. 173–180.

10. Miles, *op. cit.,* p. 151.

Suggested Additional Readings

Albrook, Robert C., "Participative Management: Time for a Second Look," *Fortune,* May, 1967, pp. 166–70, 197–200.

Anthony, William P., *Participative Management.* Reading, Mass.: Addison-Wesley Publishing Company, 1978, 214 pp.

Davis, Keith, "The Case for Participative Management," *Business Horizons,* Fall 1963, pp. 55–60.

Greiner, Larry E., "What Managers Think of Participative Leadership," *Harvard Business Review,* March–April, 1973, pp. 111–117.

McMurry, Robert N., "The Case for Benevolent Autocracy," *Harvard Business Review,* Jan.–Feb. 1958, pp. 82–90.

Miles, Raymond E., "Human Relations or Human Resources?" *Harvard Business Review,* July–August, 1965, pp. 148–163.

Sherwood, John J., and Florence M. Hoylman, "Individual versus Group Approaches to Decision Making," *Supervisory Management,* April, 1978, pp. 2–9.

Tannenbaum, Robert, and Warren H. Schmidt, "How to Choose a Leadership Pattern," *Harvard Business Review,* May–June, 1973, pp. 162–175, 178–180.

5

EFFECTIVE INTRODUCTION
OF CHANGE

All changes are irksome to the human mind, especially those which are attended with great dangers and uncertain effects.

John Adams

The basic fact of today is the tremendous pace of change in human life.

Jawaharlal Nehru

"Too radical."

"But, we've never tried that before."

"We tried that before and it didn't work."

"Not practical; too 'ivory tower.' "

"You can't teach an old dog new tricks."

"But we've always done it this way."

"That would never work in *our* company."

"Why rock the boat?"

Sound familiar? Each of those statements expresses common reactions of people who are suddenly confronted with "change."

Have *you* ever made similar remarks yourself? Is the introduction of change a problem in your organization? Are you often puzzled when people in your organization actually resist changes that are, in your opinion, obviously beneficial and in their own best interest?

If you've been a supervisor for any length of time at all, you no doubt answered each of these questions with an emphatic *yes*.

Few would disagree that sociological and technological change is taking place around us at an unprecedented pace. Of necessity, change has become a way of life for competitive organizations. Those that have survived and will continue to be competitive are the organizations that have learned to cope effectively with this accelerated rate of change.

Change is inevitable for us all. Things can never be kept exactly as they are or as many of us might like them to be. There is no such thing today as standing still; we either move ahead or we slip back. Even though we know this is true, we also have a definite tendency to highly resent certain changes; at times we strongly *resist* them. The mere word "change" produces emotional reactions; it is certainly not a neutral word. To many people, it very often carries a threatening connotation.

Supervisors can be viewed as "change agents," responsible for the effective implementation of various changes in such a way that there will be satisfactory acceptance and a minimum of resistance within the work group. As such, successful supervisors must be equipped to understand the nature of change and to diagnose and deal with the normal tendency of their employees to resist change.

In this chapter, we shall first look at what resistance is and then examine some means whereby resistance can be prevented or decreased by the supervisor. We should keep in mind, however, that our discussion of resistance to change is applicable equally to managerial and supervisory personnel and to rank-and-file employees. Resistance can be just as pronounced and stubborn in a white collar as in a blue collar.

THE NATURE OF RESISTANCE TO CHANGE

Human beings are creatures of habit and like to settle into a routine, especially on the job. Even if the way they are presently doing things is not the best, it's at least familiar and comfortable, and they're adjusted to it; there are no unknowns. Therefore, **people tend to resist any ideas that threaten to change their established way of doing things.** The fact that a change is even suggested seems to imply a criticism that the old way was not good enough. This often evokes the familiar question, "What's wrong with the way we've always done it?"

To give up well-established and therefore easy habits and to experience the possible threats of new work conditions are upsetting. Unless there is more to be gained than lost and unless the gain is made clearly apparent, people naturally resist having to change.

Of course, not all changes are resisted by employees. Some are actually wanted. The tendency to resist change is somewhat offset by a desire for new experiences and for the rewards that may come from certain changes—for example, promotions, more interesting work, better working conditions, and so on. More specifically, people may actually *seek* change when:

1. It is apparent *to them* that there is more to be gained than lost through the change;

2. It is seen as adding to their level of need satisfaction;
3. The change occurs through *their own* efforts and involvement.

In this sense, people are curious creatures. They seek many changes and find change resulting from their own efforts to be highly rewarding. But, almost paradoxically, they also seek stability and predictability in their environment. It is when change is perceived as *imposed* upon them and is seen as a threat that they begin to resist. The *way* the change is introduced may create more resistance than the change itself.

So, instead of saying "people naturally resist change," it is far more accurate for us to say "people naturally resist *being* changed."

Resistance Not Always Undesirable

We should also realize that all behavior representing resistance to change isn't necessarily undesirable. Some opposition on the part of employees may be perfectly logical and grounded on well-supported reasons. Resistance may also force management to more sharply clarify the reasoning for the change and the possible consequences of it.

Management tends to fall into the trap of assuming that change is always "good" and should be accepted without question, while those who oppose it are the "bad guys." However, we can all probably recall experiences where changes were introduced (for example, by politicians!) that proved to be unwise changes, and people were perfectly right in resisting them. Thus, there are actually two kinds of resistance to change—one based on *logical, rational analysis* and another based on *emotional reactions* to fear and real or imagined threats.[1] Although it is admittedly difficult to distinguish between them, it is to the latter that we shall direct our interest.

Perceived Threats to Need-Satisfaction

Any form of imposed change disturbs the stability and predictability of the person's environment which causes an *imbalance in need-satisfaction.*

This simply means that, before the change, the degree of satisfaction of the person's basic needs—physiological, security, social, esteem, and self-actualization (discussed in Chapter 2)—is relatively stable. The change is perceived as a threat to this stability; this threat, of course, can be real or imagined. In either case, the person becomes fearful that the change will decrease the level of satisfaction of one's various basic needs.

Therefore, resistance to change can be viewed as **a reaction intended to protect the individual from a perceived threat to need-satisfaction.** Anything that threatens such fundamental needs as job security, social relationships, self-esteem, status, level of achievement, or responsibility may be desperately feared and resisted.[2]

Fears Underlying
Resistance to Change

The threat of change to the individual's need-satisfaction is evidenced through various job-related *fears*. Typical of these deep-seated fears underlying resistance to change are:

1. Fear of unemployment, displacement, or demotion.
2. Fear of reduction in earnings.
3. Fear of a "speed-up" or of being forced to work harder in order to maintain existing rate of earnings.
4. Fear of having to break or alter established social relationships and/or having to establish new relationships.
5. Fear that the change implies criticism of the individual's or group's past performance.
6. Fear of losing power over an area that the individual formerly controlled.
7. Fear of impaired status and/or recognition within the group.
8. Fear of inability to learn new methods.
9. Fear of greater specialization, resulting in a boring, meaningless job and a decreased sense of achievement.
10. Fear of *any unknown* which the individual does not understand.

It is important to recognize that the same change may elicit different fears within individual members of the group, simply because **different people often perceive different meanings in the change**.

Furthermore, in those organizations where employee fears, insecurities, and frustrations are already present, even relatively minor changes in policies or procedures may evoke profound reactions of resentment and hostility. In other words, any added fears only reinforce and accentuate the existing ones.

Of course, as with almost any effort at effectively dealing with human behavior, empathy on the part of the supervisor—the ability to put oneself in the employee's shoes—is essential in determining the probable fears existing in the group.

Forms of Resistance

People resist change for highly personal and unique reasons—sometimes reasons buried so deeply that the individuals themselves do not know what they are. Thus, the behavior used by the resister can be expected to take many forms, depending on the individual, the nature of the change, and the particular situation.

The ingenuity of workers in devising various overt and subtle resistances is often astonishing and almost limitless. The form of resistance can range from direct or indirect aggression against the change itself, or against the supervisor, to such reactions as withdrawal or apathy. Efforts may be made to block the introduction of new methods or to discredit them and force their removal after their implementation. In extreme cases, outright sabotage of the change may occur. Resistance can also be reflected in such things as decreased quantity and quality of production, absenteeism, tardiness, turnover, grievances, accidents, strikes, and so on.[3]

PREVENTING AND DECREASING RESISTANCE TO CHANGE

Though the supervisor typically has the role of "change agent," we must keep in mind that it is really the employees who ultimately control the decision to *accept* the change, and they are the ones who determine the eventual success of the change. Therefore, employee support of the change is essential.

In order to obtain this support, employee resistance to change must be either prevented or decreased. Thus, we shall now turn our attention to some procedures and techniques by which this may be accomplished. Most of these are little more than common sense; all of them have been well tested and proven useful.

Prevent Excessive and Unnecessary Changes

Although it may seem quite obvious, one of the most important ways to prevent resistance is to determine first if a proposed change is really necessary and advantageous. Any modification in policies or procedures that may be interpreted as a threat to employee need-satisfaction should be carefully considered, anticipating and identifying all probable consequences of the change.

Change merely for the sake of change serves little purpose and frequently produces adverse reactions that far outweigh any supposed advantages. In the long run, therefore, it is sometimes better not to make trivial, moderately needed changes because the disturbances they cause may be more costly than will a continuance of current methods. Even "little" changes can create big conflicts.

Move Slowly

If it is finally decided that a change is necessary and must be made, it is wise, whenever possible, to move slowly.

A sudden proposal to change things typically arouses fear of the unknown and the unfamiliar. Many good ideas for change that ought to work fail simply because they are put into effect too abruptly and rapidly. The same plan introduced more gradually in a step-by-step manner, with time for employees to adjust their thinking and get rid of some of their fears and objections, will normally meet with greater success.

Disrupting surprises can be avoided if you *prepare* and *inform* your employees (and yourself) well in advance of any changes that will affect them. This can do much to allay the fears that sudden change typically arouses. Some remaining anxiety about the change may remain, but advance preparation can help to minimize it.

Of course, how much preparation you are able to provide depends to a great extent on where the plan for the change originates. For example, if the change is *your* idea and affects only your work group, you can usually prepare everyone in plenty of time to ensure a smooth transition. On the other hand, if a proposed change comes from higher-level management, the time for adequate preparation may be greatly restricted.

Adequate Preparation through Effective Communication

Once a change has been announced, the maximum possible information should be communicated to employees about it in order to allay as many of their potential fears and anxieties as possible.

Resistance can be expected when the change is not made understandable to those who will be influenced by the change; **what employees don't fully understand, they typically suspect, fear, and resist.**

On the other hand, resistance is almost always lower if the nature, goals, benefits, and drawbacks of the change are made completely clear. In general, **the greater the degree of effective communication, the greater the employees' willingness to accept and support the change.**

Complete explanation of the change. A full statement must be given, explaining the need and reasons for the change and indicating how the organization, the department, and, especially, the employees themselves will benefit from the contemplated change.

Employees are much more likely to accept change if they can see the immediate or the long-range benefits. If they can be made to see that the proposed change will make their jobs easier, faster, more challenging, safer, more productive, or better in some other way, there is that much more chance that they will accept it with only minimal resistance.

In the explanation, you should make every effort to relate the needs for the change as closely as possible to the employees' own personal needs and interests. In a very real sense, you must use the same approach in "selling" a change that successful salespeople use in selling goods and services: **Tell the users what's in it for them.** If employees perceive the change as primarily benefitting only the organization, rather than themselves and their fellow workers, greater resistance is likely to be encountered.

Additionally, you yourself need to understand the change fully before attempting to explain it to your group, so your presentation must be planned with care. For example, let's assume that top management decides on a new cost-reduction program. Before you can help fulfill the organization's new goal, you must understand (1) why the new program was initiated and (2) exactly what is expected of you and your work group.

Also, in the case of an organization-wide change or one instituted by higher-level management, you may find *yourself* resisting the change. Nevertheless, it is your responsibility to present the new policy or procedure to your workers in a favorable light, whether or not you completely agree with the change. You cannot afford to communicate a "them" (higher authorities) versus "us" attitude. If you do not feel personally responsible for the change, then neither will your employees. This does not imply that you cannot communicate your own dissatisfaction with the proposed change upwardly—if you feel free to do so. It can even be argued that you have a responsibility to question the change if you have logically thought through your reasoning. Nevertheless, in your role as a change agent, you have the responsibility to implement the change effectively. In fact, your performance will be evaluated in large part on your ability to accomplish this.

Establishing a continuing dialogue. To this point in our discussion of effective communication as an aid in preventing and decreasing resistance, we may have inadvertently given the impression that the *direction* that such communication takes is only one-way—*downward* from supervisor to employees. Nothing could be less desirable.

Because of the emotional nature of resistance to change, a direct, logical, one-way presentation of the merits of the change is seldom enough. What is really needed is an explanation of the change followed by a *two-way* dialogue or discussion whereby members of the work group can become highly involved in expressing and discussing their ideas, attitudes, opinions, and suggestions about any aspect of the change with each other and their supervisor. In fact, this feedback from employees is the only means the supervisor has to determine if the information transmitted about the change has been properly understood and accepted; in addition, it can often allow employee fears and anxieties to be expressed and perhaps dealt with on the spot.

Yet, all too often, supervisors, along with staff personnel (especially technical specialists such as engineers, personnel specialists, and accountants), become so convinced that the change is logical, technically correct, and beneficial that they see no need to *discuss.* They simple *tell,* and they consider any opposition to "their" change as coming from obviously bullheaded and ignorant people. Anyone who feels this way should keep in mind that, regardless of the "facts," employees still may perceive them as a threat and respond accordingly; complete information about a change can be distorted just as readily as incomplete information.[4]

Through discussion, freedom to ask questions, and the sharing of ideas, the group's level of resistance to change tends to decrease, while their understanding and "trust" of the change increases. Obviously, face-to-face communication is much more desirable in accomplishing this than any form of written announcements.

Furthermore, effective communication in the change process cannot be viewed as a "one-shot" presentation or discussion. Rather, it should be looked upon as a continuing dialogue taking place as needed up to the time of the actual implementation of the change —and frequently continuing even after the implementation.

Tensions and hostilities will almost invariably arise both before and after the change is put into effect. Thus, it is advisable to provide employees with ready outlets; for example, periodic informal meetings or "gripe sessions" (either on an individual or group basis) for "talking out" and relieving their accumulated anxieties, fears, and resentments from time to time. Complaints and grievances should actually be invited during the transitional period of the change.

There is definite value in being able to "blow off steam" without fearing reprisal from the supervisor. (Psychologists call this "catharsis.") A good gripe session often clears the air, and employees are then able to return to a reasonable discussion of how they can best adjust to the requirements of the change.

The desirability of establishing a continuing dialogue after the change is put into effect is also illustrated by the need to keep employees fully informed of the results and progress of the change and of how well they are doing in terms of the change. Good performance by employees should be rewarded and recognized. Additionally, you need to continue to express your confidence that all employees will be able to adjust to and benefit from the new methods.

Employee Participation
in the Change Process

Employee participation is another effective means for building support for change. People who are consulted and allowed to participate in making decisions about a proposed change are normally more receptive and able to adjust better to the change.

Therefore, whenever possible, give those affected by change an opportunity to have some degree of influence on such decisions as the *nature, direction, rate,* and *method of introduction* of the change.*

As a general rule, **resistance to change increases when change is arbitrarily introduced from above and pressure is put on employees to accept it, and it decreases when employees are allowed to have some "say" in the planning and implementation of the change.** The use of force in dealing with human behavior, as in physics, breeds counter-force— often aimed at discrediting or sabotaging the new methods; but when employees are able to offer suggestions, ideas, and comments concerning the change, they at least feel that they are involved and have had an opportunity to be heard.

Even when employees' contributions are negligible or their suggestions are not practical, the chance to participate in the early stages of change can alleviate many fears and misunderstandings, while giving workers a sense of having some control over their own destinies. Employees are more likely to support any change of which they are, even to a minor degree, the co-architects.

Ideally, employees should be involved as early as practicable in the planning stages of the change; in so doing, they can often aid in making a diagnosis of what needs to be changed and why. This process of diagnosing the existing situation and discovering problem areas for themselves can lead to a definite "unfreezing" of employees' present attitudes, thus increasing their recognition of the need for new methods of operation.

*The relative *degree* of employee participation used in effecting decisions about a change depends on the variables present in each individual situation, as discussed in Chapter 4.

If employees are able to develop their own understanding of the need for change and the benefits that can be derived from it, they are in a much better position to develop their own internal motivation to achieve the change. Voluntary steps are taken to change the existing situation instead of having the boss order that the change be made.

Through group participation, employees also tend to become more *committed* to seeing that the change is carried out successfully. If they are involved in the change right from the start, it is possible for the new methods to become "their" new methods, and suspicions and resistance can, to a great extent, be eliminated. Furthermore, commitment to take part in a program for change is much more meaningful when expressed by an individual in a group setting, rather than in private with one's supervisor; commitment expressed in a group usually means that the employee intends to carry that commitment into action.

Although early employee involvement in the planning stages of the change is usually preferable, participation can be useful even if you say, "This much about the change has already been decided; I now would like your thoughts and suggestions on the rest; although I can't guarantee to accept all of your proposals, I will certainly consider them." In other words, you can establish broad guidelines for the objectives to be achieved in the change and then leave the details of implementing the proposed change to be worked out by the group.

Preventing and decreasing resistance to change should certainly not be considered the only reason for soliciting employee participation, however. Adding the contributions of those who will be directly affected by the change can also improve the overall *quality* and *success* of the change. Employee participation can prove to be invaluable in spotting potential difficulties in the change that haven't been anticipated. Those who actually perform the work often see problems from a completely different perspective than their superiors do and frequently spot bugs and oversights that may otherwise go undetected. Even the most appealing and obviously beneficial idea for change can have something wrong with it that hasn't occurred to its initiator. So why "bull" ahead when it is so easy to utilize employees as a "sounding board" for evaluating a proposed change and to tap the group's ideas and suggestions for improvement?

Of course, as was discussed in Chapter 4, the success of any of your participative efforts rests on the extent that employees view them as legitimate and honest; the group must be convinced that their ideas and suggestions are sincerely wanted and will be given serious consideration. "Pseudo-participation" is a waste of time for everyone. Nothing communicates itself as rapidly as involving employees in decision-making when, in fact, nothing that they offer will be incorporated into the final decision.

Participation, therefore, should not be asked for if there is no flexibility in the plans for the change and a course of action has already been settled on; if all decisions about the change have, by necessity, been determined, then there is no need for participation. In this case, you must depend on other methods for gaining employee support for the change.

Don't Expect Miracles

Lastly, **be patient**. Getting people to accept change is difficult and frequently takes a great deal of time.

A mistake made by many supervisors—and one that can be fatal to the introduction of change—is the belief that, once the change has been put into practice and the employees have seemingly adapted themselves to it, the supervisor can then relax his or her efforts.

The supervisor who does this forgets how powerful a force habit is. A high level of contact must be made until you're certain, on the basis of frequent observation, that there is no danger of employees reverting to their former habits.

IN PERSPECTIVE—
HOW TO INTRODUCE
CHANGE

Every imposed change in operations, even a relatively minor one, is almost certain to face some degree of resistance. Change disturbs complacency—that comfortable feeling that all's right with the world. When this comfortable state is threatened, people naturally resist. Even changes that are obviously advantageous to employees are often objects of attack.

Even though employee resistance may appear to you as irrational and illogical behavior, there are definite causes of it. Therefore, you would be wise to first concentrate on the reasons why resistance to change occurs. If you recognize that the normal reactions to change are not the result of mere stubbornness or stupidity but are caused by basic fears, anxieties, and perceived threats to need satisfaction, a much more understanding and empathic view can be taken of the phenomenon. With this background, you can effectively concentrate your efforts on preventing or decreasing the resistance.

Just as we have argued in the previous chapter that there is no one "best" style of supervision, neither is there one best strategy for introducing a change that will ensure employee adjustment with a minimum of resistance. For any specific situation, there are likely to be several approaches that would be equally effective. If forced to choose one universally useful technique, however, effective communication of the change through complete explanation and the establishment of an ongoing dialogue concerning the change is normally always important.

Can resistance to change be totally eliminated? Realistically, no. But supervisors who realize the causes of resistance, understand their employees, and lay the groundwork for properly implementing needed changes can go a long way toward reducing employees' negative attitudes.

1. a. Explain why people resist change.
    b. Under what circumstances do people *seek* change?
    c. Is resistance to change always undesirable?
2. Using examples from your own experience, discuss some of the ways in which employees typically resist change.
3. How does resistance to change differ from *reactions to frustration* (discussed in Chapter 2)?
4. Explain the difference between *technological* and *social* changes. Which has the greatest influence on employees? Why?
5. Would a supervisor who has recently taken over a department be in a better position than his or her predecessor, who was supervisor for three years, to install a new operating procedure?
6. "The successful supervisor is one who knows how to play the role of a change agent." Evaluate this statement.
7. Discuss the various methods for preventing or decreasing resistance to change. Which do you feel are the most useful?
8. Is it sometimes better not to make a change? Explain.
9. "By reducing unnecessary or trivial changes, employees' receptivity to future needed changes may be increased." Do you agree with this statement? Why?
10. Discuss the role of communication in the change process.
11. Why is a direct, logical presentation of the merits of a change often futile in overcoming resistance?
12. Because supervisors must "sell" a change to their work groups, must *they* be "sold" on the change before presenting it? If so, what should supervisors do if they must implement a change that they do not completely support? Explain.
13. Some employees may have had good things happen to them after a change; others may have experienced hardship or unhappiness following previous changes. How might these past experiences affect responses to future imposed changes?
14. Because today's youth have been brought up in an environment of rapid technological and social change, are members of this younger generation generally more receptive to change? Explain.
15. The implementation of a job enrichment program (discussed in Chapter 3) necessarily involves change. If such a program were installed in your organization, what degree of employee resistance would you predict? How would you suggest reducing this resistance?

REFERENCES

1. Davis, Keith, *Human Behavior at Work,* 4th ed. New York: McGraw-Hill Book Company, 1972), pp. 162–163.
2. Huneryager, S. G., and I. L. Heckmann, *Human Relations in Management.* Cincinnati: South-Western Publishing Company, 1967, pp. 656–67.
3. *Ibid.,* pp. 661.
4. Davis, *op. cit.,* pp. 164–65.

Suggested Additional Readings

Lawrence, Paul R., "How to Deal With Resistance to Change," *Harvard Business Review,* Jan.-Feb. 1969, pp. 4–12.

Mealiea, Laird W., "Employee Resistance to Change: A Learned Response Management Can Prevent," *Supervisory Management,* Jan. 1978, pp. 16–22.

Reddin, W. J., "How to Change Things," *Executive,* June, 1969, pp. 22–6.

Wickes, Thomas A., "Techniques for Managing Change," *Automation,* May, 1967.

6

COMMUNICATION–THE AVENUE
TO UNDERSTANDING

The normal result of any attempt to communicate is at least *partial misunderstanding.*

Anon.

It is often charged that communication is an overworked subject. An ailment called "lack of communication" has become a general explanation for all an organization's problems in interpersonal relationships; "better communication" is offered as a universal panacea for any ill. We may be tired of hearing this, but its validity is difficult to deny. Certainly, one of the greatest problems of all segments of our society (as well as the rest of the world) is the lack of adequate understanding among people.

From the first time people found it necessary to join others in achieving common goals, they have faced the necessity of communicating. An organization is made up of a scattering of people; these people become an organization when they work intelligently together as a team to reach common goals. This teamwork, however, is attained only when they understand one another and communicate clearly. Coordinated effort toward common goals is impossible without effective communication of information and ideas, attitudes, and feelings among individuals and groups throughout the organization. Communication can be looked upon as a *network* that binds all the members of an organization together, making it possible for members to influence and react to one another.

Initiation and maintenance of a successful organization-wide communication program are primarily dependent on top management. If higher-level management establishes a sound climate of information exchange with its associates and insists that they do likewise with others, this climate tends to permeate the whole organization. This, however, does not relieve any other level of management of its responsibility for effective communication. In fact, although important at all levels of an organization, communication between supervisors and their employees represents perhaps the most critical area in the organization because of the direct influence of supervisors on employees' behavior and motivation.

Communication is the heart of supervisory activities. It encompasses all activities by which supervisors influence and interact with others. Communication is the process by which all orders, instructions, praise, criticism, discipline, requests, and reports are exchanged.

As a supervisor, you exert influence only by conveying ideas, feelings, and decisions to your employees. They, in turn, must communicate with you if you are to appreciate their responses to your actions and their own personal ideas, opinions, and problems.

Of course, all the topics that we have previously examined–motivation, participation, and change–directly involve communication. Every aspect of human behavior is related in some way to the process of sending and receiving information. Communication, therefore, should be viewed not as an independent activity but as an essential adjunct to everything a supervisor does.

Are most managers and supervisors effective communicators? Unfortunately, in the majority of cases they seemingly are not. It is estimated that as much as 75 to 90 per cent of the average manager's or supervisor's time is spent in some form of communication– writing, speaking, listening, and observing. Yet available research indicates that as much as 70 per cent of all business communications fail to achieve their intended purpose. In fact, of all the abilities required for successful supervision, the ability to communicate effectively is commonly the one in which most supervisors seem to be deficient. Hence, is it any wonder that so many employees are unclear as to exactly what is expected of them, why certain policies are in effect, how their work ties in with the organization's goals, why changes are needed, and so on?

So perhaps, as charged, communication is an overworked subject; but then, it is an overworked problem.

ANALYSIS OF
THE COMMUNICATION
PROCESS

Although the term has different meanings for different people, for our purposes communication can be defined as **the passing of information and understanding from one person to another by an effective means**. The word "understanding" in this definition would ideally be printed in red because without understanding we have no effective communication. Communication seeks to *inform,* but transmission of facts must be followed by *understanding.*

Because we talk to each other constantly, write memos and letters by the dozens, and see the technical marvels of modern communication equipment all around us, we're inclined to take for granted the ability to communicate. This assumption of communication in large part explains why most of us experience so many instances of "lack of communication." As W. H. Whyte, Jr., aptly put it, "The great enemy of communication is the illusion of it." The *illusion of communication* is believing that understanding has taken place simply because one person has spoken to another or because what has been written by one has been read by another.

An example of this error concerns a true story you may recall reading in the newspaper several years ago. A woman whose car had stalled on the New Jersey Turnpike finally managed to flag down a passing motorist. "My car is stalled." she said. "Can you give me a push?" "Why sure," replied the motorist. Then she informed him that, "I have an automatic transmission and you'll have to get up to about 35 miles an hour." He responded, "Whatever you say." The woman got back in her car and waited. Nothing happened. She waited a little longer and still nothing happened. Finally she looked in her rear-view mirror and saw him bearing down on her at 35 miles an hour!

After the tempers and metal were untangled, the woman no doubt asked, "Why didn't he do what I *told* him?" The answer, of course, is that **what is expressed is not necessarily what is understood.**

Many supervisors ignore this fact. They think the mere act of telling someone something is sufficient. These are the ones who are constantly surprised that their employees have misinterpreted their communication. They typically react in a tone of astonishment, "It's written right there in black and white; how could you possibly misunderstand it?"

The most successful communicators, in contrast, are those who assume that communication is not automatic, that it takes work and must be approached with care. The process of communication is much less simple than we ordinarily realize, and the meaning that gets across is more than a matter of transmitting logical facts.

The goal of all communication should be complete understanding, which means that the receiver interprets or perceives the message exactly as the sender intended. Full communication occurs only when one person receives both the same *intellectual message* and the same *emotion* that the other person sent and felt. Understanding, of course, neither assures nor necessitates that the receiver agrees with the content of the message or has the same emotional response to it as the sender; but understanding is necessary in *seeking* agreement.

In reality, there are always a myriad of barriers standing in the way of this ideal state of complete understanding, basically because no two people ever perceive anything exactly the same way. However, as in all aspects of the study of human behavior, recognition of the *real* does not prevent us from continually striving for the *ideal*.

One-Way versus Two-Way Communication

Are you a one-way communicator or a two-way communicator? The answer to this question is of utmost importance to any supervisor. Picture a man stranded on a desert island crying at the top of his lungs for help. Is he communicating? Of course not. But how often are our business communications no more effective than this? Many people are conditioned to a *one-way* flow of words, believing if they speak enough words or send enough memos, the message will reach the right person and be understood.

In *one-way* communication, the sender presents an idea but there is no opportunity for the receiver to indicate a response to the sender, to express another idea, or to question the meaning of the sender's message.

In *two-way* communication, there is some form of interaction between the sender and the receiver. By having a two-way flow, the sender is able to check the clarity and effectiveness of the expression. In response to *feedback* from the receiver, a message can be modified if necessary to assure understanding. At the same time, the two-way interaction provides a rich opportunity for obtaining suggestions from the receiver on the subject of the discussion.

One-way communicators tend to think of the communication process as something akin to pouring water into a jug; in other words, you can communicate ideas by pouring them into someone's head. One-way communicators consider the subject solely from their own viewpoint and sincerely believe that if they describe their ideas and tell the receiver why their ideas should be accepted, the job is finished. If the receiver is unconvinced or misinterprets the message, this communicator is mystified.

On the other hand, two-way communicators realize that communication starts with the other person's needs; they concentrate more on the receiver than on themselves. Their presentations remain flexible, constantly guided by responses from the receiver. They keep trying until they are sure they have "gotten through" or resolved the receiver's difficulties in understanding.

In addition to one-way and two-way communication, there is another type worthy of mention. This is "phony two-way," usually labeled two-way by the sender and one-way by the receiver. The supervisor who says, "Let's have a meeting to let the employees voice their opinions before we tell them what we've decided," is a phony two-way communicator and will eventually be recognized as such by the receivers.

Until supervisors accept the necessity of genuine two-way communication and become skilled in both transmitting and receiving information, they face problems in leading and motivating people to work efficiently.

Steps in the Communication Process

To improve our communication, we must first have a basic understanding of what actually happens in the communication process. The entire process of one person communicating with another involves six steps, regardless of whether they talk, send written messages, use facial expressions or hand signals, or use any other form of communication. The accompanying figure illustrates this sequence of steps.

Familiarity with these steps is valuable in analyzing and comprehending the barriers to understanding that typically occur.

Ideation.   The first step in the sequence is ideation—the creation of an idea—by the

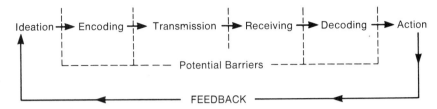

FIGURE 6-1. A Model of the Communication Process [1]

sender. This step forms the content or basis of the message. Obviously, you need to fully understand the idea that you want to communicate; for example, if you wish to effectively explain the operation of computers, you must know the subject thoroughly. Yet, one of the most common causes of communication breakdown is that the sender is unclear in his or her own thinking about the subject. A message that is not clearly formulated or adequately planned in the mind of the sender is quite likely to be misunderstood by the receiver. Thus, the motto for this step might well be: "Don't start talking until you begin thinking."

Furthermore, because messages tend to become increasingly filtered, distorted, or diluted as they pass through each step in the process, this first step is crucial to the success of the entire process.

Encoding. In the encoding step, the ideas formulated in the first step are converted into a series of *symbols* that communicate the message to the receiver. Words, numbers, pictures, or gestures stand for something; they are symbolic. The key is to select a combination of symbols that have the same meaning for both the sender and the receiver and are appropriate for the situation.

At this stage, we often know what we want to express but are hampered in our ability to express it. How many times has the average teacher heard this excuse about an exam: "I knew the answer, but I just couldn't seem to put it into words"? This type of barrier is caused by various limitations—limited vocabulary, inability to write clearly, inability to precisely express ourselves, and the like.

In addition to picking the proper symbols in this step, the sender must also choose the *medium* for transmitting the symbols, whether it be face-to-face oral communication, written communication, the telephone, or some other form. Like symbols, the medium also must be appropriate for the receiver and the situation.

Transmission. Transmission is the actual sending of the encoded message through the medium selected. For example, in using verbal communication, the words are spoken; in writing a letter, the letter is mailed.

At this point in the process, the sender begins to lose control of the message. Such things as distractions, noise, interruptions, and breakdowns in mechanical means of communication can interfere with the transmission of the message. This interference must be minimized if the message is to have a chance to reach the receiver.

Receiving. In the fourth step, the receiver finally enters the picture. Essential here is getting the receiver's *attention* so that he or she will "tune in" on the message. The best message is of little use unless the receiver listens or reads and attempts to understand it. No matter how brilliant and informative you and your message may be, if the receiver is uncooperative, defensive, disinterested, or not perceptive, your message is lost.

Yet, how often do we speak without listeners or speak when we should be listening? And, how often does the avalanche of memoranda, letters, and reports common to the business world fail to find readers? A partial solution may be to speak less and say more and to write shorter, fewer, and better messages.

Decoding. In the decoding step, the receiver converts the symbols transmitted back into ideas, interpreting and evaluating the message. Encoding is message *creation,* while decoding is message *recreation.*

If understanding is to occur, the receiver must take from the message the meaning intended by the sender. However, as we shall discuss later, there are many subtle perceptual barriers that prevent this from happening; the receiver's perception of the message may never be exactly what the sender intended.

Action. Finally, the receiver acts or responds to the message in a certain way— ideally, in the manner intended by the sender. This action may take many forms; the receiver may simply file the information away for future reference, perform a specific function, ask for more information, or disagree (remember, there can be disagreement along with understanding). In any case, the receiver must do something in response to the message.[2]

The Desirability of Feedback

No communication is ever completed with certainty unless some type of *feedback* is available to determine the degree to which the message has been received and understood (see Figure 6-1). This reinforces the desirability of *two-way* communication. **Without feedback, there is no guarantee that the message was correctly interpreted and acted upon by the receiver.**

The normal result of any attempt to communicate is partial misunderstanding. Through feedback, the sender can make the necessary corrections and adjust the message to fit the responses of the receiver. For example, in face-to-face oral communication, if the receiver looks puzzled, the speaker can repeat what was originally said or try saying it differently.

Feedback in communication can be likened to the thermostat that regulates your home air conditioner on the basis of feedback—namely, the temperature of the room. In human communication, you need some way of "taking the temperature" of the people with whom you are communicating so that you can adjust your message to their needs.

As a supervisor, you must accept the fact that at least some of your workers are going to misunderstand your communication efforts at least some of the time. The most effective attitude is to take nothing for granted. Some supervisors are content to rely on a simple question after involved instructions or directives are given: "Have you got that?" "Do you understand?" Such questions invariably obtain affirmative responses such as, "Yes, I have it," when what the employee often really means is, "No, I don't understand, but I'm too afraid or too proud to admit it." Rather than ask for clarification, the employee will muddle along, trying to work things out alone, sometimes with disastrous results. Why? Perhaps because the individual simply wants to convince the supervisor that he or she is a good worker and can do the job.

In order to confirm that your communication has resulted in mutual understanding, you need to keep alert to *any* feedback available. As one useful means, feedback can be solicited simply by asking employees questions designed to get them to repeat or summarize the message. Many supervisors hesitate to try this approach, thinking that it may give the impression that they're "talking down" to the employee or don't trust the employee's abilities. By asking properly, such hesitation can be overcome. For example, you might say: "Harry, it's important to both of us that this be done correctly the first time. So, just to make sure I did a good job of communicating, could you tell me what you heard me ask you to do?" Few employees are likely to be offended by such an approach.

In addition to asking questions, you can tune in on puzzled expressions, tones of voice, and other gestures. You can observe whether the employee acts in accordance with your message. In fact, *everything* the receiver says and does can provide sources of feedback–*if* you're sensitive and observant. When direct observation isn't practical, you can watch various reports or other results that can serve as feedback cues.

Unfortunately, we frequently don't capitalize on available feedback simply because we're not alert to it. We get so wrapped up in concentrating on *our* thoughts and words that we ignore the receiver's signals. We may also tend to overlook feedback because it becomes threatening to us. Indications that the receiver isn't understanding us may make us feel inadequate as communicators–and, for most of us, that's difficult to accept. The feedback is taken as an "attack" on our communicative abilities and makes us a bit defensive and uncomfortable.

Yet, only feedback can tell you what you're communicating or, in fact, whether you're communicating at all.

Transmission Media

Although there are an endless number of specific media for transmitting information (telephone, letters, conferences, reports, gestures, and so on), all fall into three general classifications: *oral, written,* and *nonverbal.*

Oral communication. Oral communication is the most frequently used business communication medium. Generally speaking, it is the most effective medium as well, especially when the communication is intended to be persuasive rather than factual.

With the exception of the telephone, a public-address system, or other such me-chanical media, oral communication is face-to-face, allowing the advantage of *maximum feedback*. Because it encourages two-way communication, there is opportunity for im-mediate response from the receiver. Each party can question the other if the meaning is not clear, and different points of view can be voiced. The communicator's approach can be changed or varied according to the situation, thus making oral communication a very *flexible* medium. Added explanation and reassurance can be readily provided, and dis-agreements and misunderstandings can frequently be resolved on the spot.

In contrast with written communication, the spoken word is more natural, personal, and expressive. It is also usually more flattering to the receiver. By a smile, gestures, or the right tone of voice, you can communicate things orally—emotions, emphasis, and feelings —that could not be easily written.

Yet, day after day, people grind out letters, memos, and bulletins about subjects that could be better handled face-to-face. In some cases, people write memos to others whose desks or offices are located nearby! Before writing a memo or sending a message via a third party, stop and consider: Wouldn't it be smarter to do this in person? Or at least follow it up that way? If it is impractical to see someone, consider telephoning. It is quicker and more personal than a memo and still gives the person a chance to ask ques-tions and express opinions.

The major inherent disadvantage of oral communications is that it is usually filtered and distorted each time it is passed from one person to another. Whenever possible, tell your message to the person directly affected. As the number of intermediaries between the sender and the eventual receiver increases, the chances of distortion and dilution of the original message are also increased.

Written communication.   Although less personal than oral communication, written communication is essential in any organization and is more effective in transmitting cer-tain kinds of information than oral methods.

It can best be used when the message is lengthy, complex or technical, extremely important, has long-term significance and is needed for future reference (such as policies or procedures), or concerns many people and needs to be widely circulated. Written com-munication can be kept and referred to later as a guide for future action. It can be widely distributed so that everyone concerned gets the same story with a minimum of distortion. It can sometimes be more carefully thought through than spontaneous conversations or other oral communication and can be checked for accuracy before being issued.

Additionally, written messages are often used to supplement and reinforce orally transmitted information. On matters that are particularly important, easily forgotten, or subject to misinterpretation, you can confirm your oral communication with a written message. In a similar way, oral communication can be used effectively to accompany or follow up written communication to provide added explanation and clarification, meet objections, and head off misunderstandings before they occur.

The primary disadvantage of written communication is its limited ability to provide prompt feedback and encourage a two-way exchange of information. Furthermore, skill is usually required in conveying written ideas meaningfully, and, unless the writer is available for discussion, his or her intentions may not be understood by the receiver as intended. Because of its impersonal nature, it also tends to foster greater suspicion than oral communication.

Furthermore, written communication in business is typically expensive. *Needless* written communication is staggeringly expensive. One study done several years ago by a governmental agency discovered that a memo or letter of average length costs between $2 and $6, depending on the wage levels of the writer and the secretary, the time spent on each memo or letter, and the material costs. These figures take into account time spent in preparation, researching, dictation, proofing, signing, and the like by the writer and the secretary's time devoted to taking dictation, transcribing, proofing, mailing, filing, and so on. A more recent study claims that the cost ranges from about $6.50 all the way to $15 on some letters. Regardless of whose figures you choose to accept, written communication is obviously time-consuming and costly when used unnecessarily.

Such costs, of course, do not include reading and "translating" costs at the receiving end; if the communication is not understandable, the cost skyrockets, depending on the number of receivers. One writing-cost analyst figures that 15 per cent of all letters or memos are "fog-induced"–merely requests for clarification of a previous letter or memo. Obviously then, the extra time you devote to making your communication clear and readable the first time is economically spent, especially on a memo that takes thirty minutes to read and interpret when it should have taken only five![3]

Nonverbal communication. Of the three general media of transmission, oral, written, and nonverbal, the first two are always considered by communicators, while the latter is often dangerously overlooked. By our original definition of communication, "the passing of information and understanding from one person to another *by an effective means,*" it should be obvious that you are not restricted to the use of words alone, either spoken or written. You communicate through nonverbal means as well. Communication encompasses *all* human behavior that results in an exchange of meaning.

In fact, research has indicated that more than 90 per cent of the impact of what you communicate to others is conveyed by nonverbal means.[4] Even though it is such an important medium of transmission, many people seemingly don't realize that it even exists. An awareness of this type of communication is essential because, consciously or unconsciously, we all use it every day.

In its simplest form, nonverbal communication would assume the form of a child sticking out his tongue, or an irate person making an appropriate gesture. Neither of these actions is verbal, but both do a great deal of communicating.

In its more complex form and in relation to supervision, nonverbal communication includes such varied examples as the "look" in one's eyes, avoidance or maintenance of eye contact, a raised eyebrow, posture, a pointed finger, a shrug of the shoulders, the way a person walks, manner of dress, a man's buttoned or unbuttoned coat, a smile or a scowl, a firm or limp handshake, the manner in which a verbal message is conveyed, tone of voice, inflections, a slammed door, "noncommunication" (lack of explanation when it is needed or failure to give an employee recognition when it is expected or desired), signs, pictures, charts, or a demonstration. Any of these can communicate, either consciously or unconsciously, a message to others as surely as words can. Even silence can convey meaning and must be considered a part of communication.

Nonverbal communication is often quite effective in transmitting ideas, attitudes, and feelings. For instance, a supervisor pounding on the desk may communicate very clearly the action desired. Or, consider what usualiy happens when people want to terminate a conversation. They may shift their bodies, tap their fingers, divert their gazes from the speaker, or look at their wristwatches periodically. The more they fidget, the more they communicate their boredom or disinterest in further conversation.

As another illustration, George has an appointment to meet Jane at 10 o'clock; due to unknown reasons, he arrives at 10:30. Their conversation is friendly, but Jane retains a lingering hostility. Why? Because George, through his tardiness, has unconsciously communicated that he doesn't think the appointment is very important or that he has little respect for Jane.[5] In each case, you can see the subtle power of nonverbal communication.

As the well-worn saying goes, "Actions speak louder than words." This is particularly true in supervision. In the long run, employees are influenced not so much by what supervisors say but by what they do. When your actions, behavior, or attitudes contradict your words, employees tend to discount what you say; their past experiences lead them to know what is believable and what is not. Ralph Waldo Emerson put it this way:

> What you are stands over you the while, and thunders so that I cannot hear what you say to the contrary.

A supervisor who tells workers that he or she is interested in their problems, but ignores their requests for help or information, is communicating that he or she is *not* interested in them. Similarly, it is useless for a supervisor to announce an "open door" policy if employees don't feel comfortable once they go through the door.[6]

Every action of a supervisor has some influence on the people who observe it. Meaning is attached to your behavior, even if it is nothing more than a smile, patting an employee on the back, or closing your office door. Keep in mind that you are communicating almost all of the time—whether you intend to or not.

ORGANIZATIONAL NETWORKS FOR COMMUNICATION

You may have noticed by now that effective communication between members of this class is often difficult—at times seemingly impossible!—even though you are all students at the same level. It is easy to see then that when *hierarchical* relationships exist, as in a

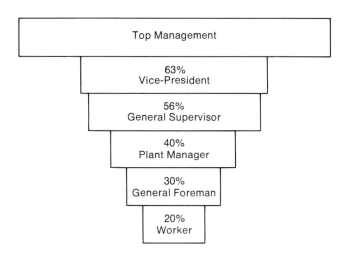

FIGURE 6-2. Loss of Information in Downward Communication

business organization, the process of communication requires even more attention and effort if it is to yield the degree of understanding necessary for efficient operations among the various levels of the organization.

Formal Communication Networks

Formal communication takes place between personnel on the basis of established lines of authority and according to established procedures and relationships.[7]

Formal communication is used in sending and receiving information between different organizational levels—to and from supervisors and employees—and between personnel at the same level; for example, between the production department and the marketing department. The type of communication flowing in this network is primarily *work-related;* it has a direct relationship to the operation of the work group or the organization.

Generally, formal communication follows the lines or networks indicated on the organization chart. It may flow in any of three directions—*downward, upward,* and *horizontally.*

Downward communication. In downward communication, information flows from the top to the bottom of the organization, or from a higher level of authority to a lower level of authority, until it reaches the intended receivers. This is the most frequently used channel for transmitting orders, instructions, objectives, policies, feedback to employees about their performance, and so forth.

There are a great many barriers to effective downward communication as it passes through the various levels in the organization. A study conducted by Pidgeon-Savage-

Lewis, Inc., of the communication efficiency of 100 representative business and industrial organizations reveals a tremendous loss of information as it passes from top management down to the rank-and-file worker. As shown in Figure 6-2, lower-level employees receive only about 20 per cent of the original content of a message. The validity of such findings is open to debate; however, there is little doubt that sizeable dilution and distortion of downward communication are realities in most organizations.

One difficulty is that personnel at certain levels are often not sure whether the communication is intended for their level alone or whether it should be passed on to a lower level. A second is that some people have a tendency to treat information as their personal property or to filter it according to what they think lower levels should or should not be told.

An effective system of downward communication is essential to any organization's success, but reliance on this channel alone allows little, if any, provision for feedback. It is strictly a one-way street.

Upward communication. In addition to downward communication, part of each supervisor's responsibilities includes having the needs, aspirations, ideas, attitudes, complaints, and problems of employees conveyed to him or her through an *upward* channel of communication. If employees are unable to freely communicate upwardly, the supervisor will not receive much of the information needed to supervise effectively.

Aside from being an excellent source of ideas, suggestions, and indicators of the work group's state of morale, upward communication is also a supervisor's most important source of *feedback.* As feedback, it can provide a check on employees' reception, understanding, and acceptance of downward communication, as well as whether the intended action has been taken. In other words, did the message get through without distortion or misunderstanding?

The value of upward communication does not end with its feedback potential, however. As a by-product, employees' motivation will generally be greater if they feel free to discuss problems with their supervisor and to participate in decisions affecting them. Upward communication is thus one of the means that individuals can gain satisfaction from their work, feeling that they "belong" and are important. If no means are available to assure that employees' ideas are heard, they always have recourse: They can simply close their minds to their superiors' ideas.[8]

Although "lip service" is frequently given to the desirability of upward communication, many organizations do not provide adequate outlets for such flow. We have already seen that communication efficiency *down* through the levels of an organization is often poor; but upward communication through the levels is apparently an even greater problem in many instances. In fact, one theory is that the major reason for the formation of unions and the willingness of workers to join them is the lack of effective upward communication channels within the organization. This theory holds that unions become the only medium by which employees can convey to management their ideas, opinions, and needs.

Why is upward communication often inadequate? Undoubtedly, part of the problem can be traced to poor listening habits on the part of the superior; far more attention is typically given to telling, informing, and commanding than to listening, asking, and interpreting. Additionally, upward communication can be poor if an atmosphere exists where employees' ideas and opinions are viewed by management as not being important or worthy of attention. In such a case, employees often decide there is no point in even trying to communicate upward.

As with downward communication, each successive level filters and distorts upward communication, and, as you go higher, the message is increasingly edited and garbled–or eliminated altogether. To make matters worse, because upward communication is "against the current" and normally doesn't benefit from top management's "seal of approval," the filters and distorters are generally even greater than those applied to messages transmitted downward.

The primary barrier, however, to the upward flow of communication is *fear of reprisal.* Fear of being criticized, disciplined, or denied promotion can often make even the strongest and most secure employees hesitate before presenting "all the facts" to their supervisor. Whether or not such fears have any basis in fact makes no difference; they are real in the eyes of the employees and cause upward communication to suffer. **Employees are reluctant to communicate anything that could have a negative effect on their relationship with the supervisor.** If they fear that a frank criticism, a voiced grievance, a suggestion, or a nonconformist opinion will be taken in the wrong way by the supervisor, they will ordinarily hold back, camouflage, or distort their upward communication. Good news is emphasized, while information that doesn't convey a rosy picture is withheld or distorted. The supervisor gets told only what the employees think he or she *wants* to hear, rather than what he or she may *need* to hear.[9]

Many things can be done to keep upward communication channels open. The policy of the "open door" is suggested by many as a solution to the problem. Effective upward communication, however, normally requires more from a supervisor than just a statement that "my door is always open." If employees feel that the person behind the door won't really listen to them, allow them to talk out their problems, or take any action regarding their suggestions or complaints, the door is in effect still "closed." Furthermore, many supervisors who proudly point to their open door often mistakenly conclude that when no one ventures in to complain or talk about problems, there are in fact no complaints or problems. Such is seldom the case.

The idea of the "open door" is admirable in theory, and a *genuine* open door may be an aid to upward communication. Perhaps, as Keith Davis has stated, "the way the open door can be most effective is for a manager to walk through it and get out among his people. The open door is for managers to walk through, not employees!"[10]

Suggestion systems are another frequently offered solution. In many organizations, employees' suggestions and ideas obtained through such systems have proven invaluable. When improperly used, they have also proven to be miserable flops in other organizations.

The best place to start in freeing upward communication is to eliminate fear on the part of employees. This, of course, isn't as simple as it may sound. Basically, it requires the building of a mutual trust relationship between employees and supervisor that encourages and rewards complete disclosure. Supervisors must continually encourage their employees to convey information upward, including information that is "bad news." Employees must have confidence that they can freely express their sentiments or "speak their minds" without the threat of direct or indirect reprisal by the supervisor. Upward communication will exist to the degree that it is *allowed* and *encouraged* by the supervisor.[11]

In summary, management at all levels needs an awareness that communication *up* is a subject equal in importance with communication *down*. In fact, *downward* communication is likely to improve when a better understanding of the attitudes, opinions, and problems of employees is acquired through *upward* communication.[12]

Horizontal communication. The horizontal channel is used for the sending and receiving of information between people at the same organizational level. For example, a supervisor in one department communicates directly to a fellow supervisor in another department.

Horizontal communication is essential to assure *coordination* of the organization's various activities–production, marketing, finance, credit, personnel, and so on. It establishes an overall atmosphere of cooperation, building rapport and understanding between personnel involved in diverse functions. It encourages communication about common problems.

Personal rivalries and ambitions can create barriers in these channels. Jealousy between functional areas or departments, infighting, and "empire building" often arise, blocking the exchange of ideas and the sharing of information that could be beneficial to all.

Informal Communication
Networks

In contrast to formal communication networks, **informal communication ignores formal lines of authority and established relationships,** existing outside the official networks. Whereas the formal network is deliberately planned and designed by management, the informal network is unplanned, unrestricted, and spontaneous.

Informal communication is basically an attempt by employees to interpret their environment and make it more understandable. Although the formal network carries messages that the senders want the receivers to believe, the informal network usually carries messages that the senders themselves want to believe.[13]

The informal network is perhaps more commonly known as the "grapevine." As the name suggests, the grapevine is intertwined throughout the organization, branching out in all directions–up, down, and across the organization. It carries non-work-related information as well as work-related information.

Although it frequently carries more accurate and reliable information than normally thought, a large proportion of the grapevine consists of *rumors, gossip, speculation,* and *partial or inaccurate information*–all spread with surprising speed. Even though it may lack access to official sources of information, its credibility among employees is usually quite high.

Contrary to popular opinion, the grapevine is not always "sinister" and undesirable. Properly understood and controlled, the informal network can be an effective part of an organization's communication system, serving as a useful adjunct to the formal network.

The nature of rumors. Rumors sent through informal channels are based on uncertainty and insecurity. They flourish most often where little reliable information is available to employees through the organization's formal communication network. If the organization neglects to provide adequate information about its plans, operations, and anticipated changes, employees will supply their own answers through speculation and rumors. Even if their speculation turns up the "true story," the message passed from person to person along the grapevine is subject to progressive filtration and distortion. Each person who takes part in transmitting a rumor has his or her own ideas and perception of the subject, and will thus tend to omit certain facts and exaggerate others. Before you know it, an initially accurate statement such as "I hear they're going to transfer and retrain 50 people because of the new automated equipment" becomes "I hear those new machines are going to put us all out of work."

Managers at any level can contribute to the rumor mill whenever they choose to withhold bad news for fear that it will be damaging to morale or when they decide not to comment on a problem in the naive hope that "maybe no one has noticed, so why call their attention to it?" Some perceptive employees most assuredly will notice, and not talking about the problem will start the grapevine buzzing, increasing their anxieties and stimulating speculation.

Information hunger. Rumors basically result from what Saul Gellerman has called "information hunger." According to Gellerman, "*information hunger* exists due to the tendency for people who already have information to assume that other people also have it."[14] We might also attribute it to the common assumption that others don't need the information.

Today's employees have an active desire to know more about their jobs and their organization. Matters that directly affect employees and their jobs, such as promotion possibilities, policies, working conditions, work methods, fringe benefits, and the importance and contribution of their individual jobs to the organization as a whole, are naturally always of interest to them. However, they also like being informed about many higher level issues—more so than is normally expected. For example, information concerning the general welfare of the organization, profits for the year, progress in attaining general objectives, sales forecasts, major expansion plans, and the organization's contribution to social improvements in the community is often of interest to lower-level employees. Unfortunately, such information is sometimes made public through press releases before giving any consideration to the need for informing lower-level workers directly through internal communication.

Employee newsletters or bulletins and organization-wide meetings for all employees can be useful in keeping workers informed. But the immediate link between employees and top management is the supervisor; part of his or her job is to keep the work group up to date on what is happening within the department and the organization. As an illustration of a simple "opening up" of communication, one company initiated a program whereby supervisors held monthly meetings with their production employees. The initial format was simply for the supervisors to fill in their employees on what was going on in the plant and in their department. They discussed the monthly objectives of the plant, how it was doing with regard to its objectives, and how departmental objectives fit in with plant objectives. At the beginning, the meetings were rather formal and stiff with little two-way communication. This soon changed, however, with employees becoming truly involved. The content of their questions, complaints, and comments also changed. Discussions of specific worker-related topics such as vacation and sick-leave policies evolved into discussions of broader concern such as: What is our product being used for? Who is using it and what do they think of it? Are our quality standards high enough? The program became quite successful, and it was soon evident that employees wanted even more information about their jobs, how their jobs related to the company, and how the company was doing.[15]

The question usually arises, "How *much* should employees be told about the organization's operations?" As much as might be of interest to them, so long as the information isn't of necessity confidential. Nevertheless, many supervisors firmly believe that such information is not really the employees' business; in other words, the rule is that employees should do their jobs and management will run the organization. Obviously, there will inevitably be an information gap under such circumstances.

Besides helping prevent needless fears and misunderstandings, sharing information with employees supports their sense of belonging. Employees come to believe that the organization cares enough to keep them informed. And when workers feel they are truly part of the organization—that management is honest and direct with them and that they know the facts they want to know—the rumor mill's level of activity is sharply reduced.

Guidelines for controlling the grapevine. The grapevine exists in every organization. As a result of the natural desire of people to communicate with one another and to make sense out of their situation, informal communication is sure to develop wherever a group of people interact.

The grapevine cannot be abolished or suppressed; the supervisor has to learn to live with it. But there are ways that the grapevine can be influenced and controlled. Here are eight guidelines and suggestions that can help reduce the number of rumors and keep employees supplied with reliable information:

1. Instead of ignoring the grapevine and hoping it will go away, *listen* to it and *study* it; learn what the grapevine is saying. Rumors not only reveal the hopes and fears of

employees, but also indicate the kind of information they need. However, you can analyze and prevent rumors from spreading only if you have *access* to the grapevine; you won't know what it is saying unless you have created an atmosphere encouraging upward communication, in which employees feel free to talk about anything that troubles them.

2. Encourage employees to ask about subjects they feel might be rumors. Then, play it straight. Answer questions honestly and thoroughly. When you don't know the answer, admit it, and tell the questioner you'll find out. Don't bluff an answer, and always follow through on getting the information.

3. Report any distortion of facts you hear circulating to your own superior. Rumors grow out of anxiety; the *cause* of the anxiety rather than the rumor itself must be discovered and corrected for effective rumor control.

4. Counter false rumors with a presentation of the correct facts. Rumors can be stopped or weakened only by getting out the full story as quickly as possible. In accomplishing this, face-to-face communication is generally more effective and believable.

5. Keep workers informed about what is going on concerning their jobs and the rest of the organization. Tell them everything that might be of interest, and be sure that what you tell them is correct. When explaining a directive or a change, make certain through feedback that employees understand it thoroughly.

6. Never consider a rumor "silly." Many times, people who know the true situation tend to dismiss an unfounded anxiety as only a "silly rumor." While false or exaggerated ideas may sound ridiculous to you, they are no laughing matter to the employee who is hungry for the facts.

7. Think twice before deciding that anything must be kept secret. Because of its ability to cut across organizational lines and deal directly with people "in the know," the grapevine often cracks even the most tightly-controlled "secrets" anyway.

8. Always remember: Rumors *start* when information *stops*.

QUESTIONS FOR REVIEW AND DISCUSSION

1. Diagram a model of the communication process. Briefly explain each of the steps in the process.
2. a. What is the difference between *one-way* and *two-way* communication?
   b. How would you describe the supervisor who is more likely to prefer one-way over two-way communication? What are the likely results of his or her practices in terms of employee satisfaction and performance?

    c. Is two-way communication always more effective than one-way communication? Why?

3.   a. What is a *symbol?*
    b. Name as many types of symbols as you can that are commonly used in communication.
    c. Can you think of any examples of communication breakdowns that have resulted from people's confusing the symbol with the thing or idea represented?

4.   a. What is *feedback?*
    b. Can effective communication take place without feedback? Explain.
    c. What are some of the means that a supervisor can use to obtain feedback from employees when communicating with them?
    d. Can you recall an instance where communication failed because you ignored or didn't use the feedback you were getting? If so, why do you think you didn't use the feedback?

5.   a. Name as many specific types of communication *media* as you can think of.
    b. Why is face-to-face communication usually more effective than other media? Under what circumstances would other media be more effective?

6.   "*Failure* to act is an important way of communicating." Evaluate this statement.

7.   Is the same nonverbal behavior perceived in the same manner by different societies, ethnic groups, and cultures? Discuss.

8.   What nonverbal connotations can written communication convey?

9.   a. What are the three directions in which formal communication may flow? Briefly explain each.
    b. Which of these directions is the most important to an organization's efficiency? Why?

10.   a. What are the benefits of *upward* communication?
    b. Discuss some of the typical barriers to upward communication.
    c. What are some of the means whereby upward communication can be improved?

11.   a. Do you feel that the organization you now work for encourages upward communication? Why?
    b. Could you freely communicate any message (good or bad news) to your supervisor without in any way diluting or distorting it?

12.   "Receiving only a few complaints or grievances is a good sign of high morale in the work group." Evaluate this statement.

13.   We sometimes find ourselves telling strangers things about ourselves that we don't tell those close to us. How would you explain this?

14.   a. Explain the difference between *formal* communication and *informal* communication.
    b. Why are informal communication networks usually formed?

15.   Under what circumstances are rumors most likely to arise? How can they be prevented?

16.   Discuss some of the ways that the grapevine can be influenced or controlled.

17. Would it ever be advisable for a supervisor to spread information informally via the grapevine? Explain.
18. To what extent is a supervisor the key person in an organization's communication network? Explain.
19. "As the complexities of an organization increase, so do the difficulties of efficient and accurate communication." Discuss this statement.
20. How can effective communication increase an employee's motivation?

REFERENCES

1. Adapted from: Chruden, Herbert J., and Arthur W. Sherman, Jr., *Personnel Management.* Cincinnati: South-Western Publishing Company, 1968, p. 327.
2. Davis, Keith, *Human Relations at Work,* 4th ed. New York: McGraw-Hill Book Company, 1972), pp. 368–87.
3. O'Hayre, John, *Gobbledygook Has Gotta Go.* Washington, D.C.: U. S. Government Printing Office, 1966, pp. 91–95.
4. Mehrabian, Albert, "Communication Without Words," *Psychology Today,* Sept. 1968, pp. 52–55.
5. Hall, Edward and Mildred, "The Sounds of Silence," *Playboy,* June, 1971, p. 139.
6. Fischer, Frank E., "A New Look at Management Communication," *Personnel,* May, 1955, p. 495.
7. Chruden and Sherman, *op. cit.,* pp. 330–31.
8. Gellerman, Saul W., *The Management of Human Relations.* New York: Holt, Rinehart and Winston, 1966, p. 65.
9. Stieglitz, Harold, "Barriers to Communication," *Management Record,* Jan. 1958, pp. 3–4.
10. Davis, *op. cit.,* p. 412.
11. Gemmill, Gary, "Managing Upward Communication," *Personnel Journal,* Feb. 1970, pp. 107–10.
12. Borman, Ernest G., *et. al., Interpersonal Communication in the Modern Organization.* Englewood Cliffs, N. J.: Prentice-Hall, Inc., 1969, p. 190.
13. Gellerman, *op. cit.,* p. 60.
14. *Ibid.,* p. 64.
15. Huse, Edgar F., and Michael Beer, "Eclectic Approach to Organizational Development," *Harvard Business Review,* Sept.–Oct., 1971, pp. 109–10.

Suggested Additional Readings

Because of the similarity of subject matter, suggested additional readings for this chapter are combined with those for Chapter 7.

ROADBLOCKS IN THE AVENUE
TO UNDERSTANDING

*I know you believe you understand what you think I said, but I
am not sure you realize that what you heard is not what I meant.*

Anon.

*Nature has given men one tongue, but two ears, that we may hear
from others twice as much as we speak.*

Epictetus

As discussed in the previous chapter, the ultimate goal of communication—complete understanding—is seldom achieved. Because of the countless barriers to communication that litter our avenue to understanding, we must often accept less than complete understanding. Perhaps, when we consider the magnitude of these barriers, we should not be dismayed that communication is frequently poor but wonder that it is as good as it is!

Fortunately, these barriers are usually not *absolute* blocks to communication. Rather, by screening and distorting the original meaning of the message, they reduce the *degree* of success in achieving understanding.

COMMON BARRIERS
TO EFFECTIVE
COMMUNICATION

Many of these barriers were necessarily examined in our prior discussion of the communication process and its relation to organizational structure. However, special attention is due four specific barriers that commonly create communication breakdowns. The fifth barrier presented—poor listening—is of such importance that a separate section is devoted to it. Hopefully, a basic understanding and awareness of these barriers will mean that you can start to win the battle of overcoming them.

Differences in Individual
Perception

As has been stressed, **no two people perceive or interpret the same event in exactly the same way.** This single fact constitutes the major obstacle to effective communication; in fact, all of the other psychological barriers to communication are directly related to this one principle.

Many problems and misunderstandings arise because of people's perceptual differences. An old World War II story provides a humorous example of this: On a train in Europe, an American grandmother, her young and attractive granddaughter, a Rumanian officer, and a Nazi officer occupied one of the train's compartments. As the train passed through a dark tunnel, a loud kiss, followed by a vigorous slap, was heard. After the train emerged from the tunnel, the grandmother thought to herself, "What a fine granddaughter I have. She can take care of herself. I am proud of her." At the same time, the granddaughter was saying to herself, "I am surprised what a hard wallop grandmother has; why should she get so upset over a little kiss?" The Nazi officer was meditating, "How clever these Rumanians are. They steal a kiss and have the other fellow slapped!" And the Rumanian officer sat chuckling to himself, "What a smart fellow I am. I kissed my own hand and slapped the Nazi."

Each individual brings to the communication process his or her own set of experiences, attitudes, values, interests, motives, assumptions, and expectations. Collectively, these components form the person's perceptual *frame of reference*—the key concept in communication because it determines how the individual perceives and interprets whatever is seen or heard.

Communication is, of course, best between people who have similar frames of reference. Unfortunately, such an ideal state seldom exists, since no two sets of experiences, attitudes, etc., are ever exactly the same. Whenever the frames of reference of the sender and receiver are not relatively homogeneous (as is more frequently the case), meaning will be difficult to convey between the two.

The obvious implication for supervision is to **accept and consider another's frame of reference and then communicate in terms of it.**[1] How often have you asked (or been tempted to ask) someone, "Why can't you see things *my* way?" Your concern might better be focused on how and why the other person perceives the situation as he or she does. What are his or her background, viewpoints, biases, current position on the subject, intelligence, educational level, age, race, occupation, and position in the organization? All of these things can affect the individual's perception of your message and should be taken into account if you are striving to achieve understanding with him or her. Thus, communication is influenced not only by how the *receiver* perceives the sender and the sender's message, but also by how the *sender* perceives the receiver and the receiver's frame of reference.

This, once again, points out the universal importance of *empathy* in everything a supervisor does in interacting with others. To be an effective communicator, you must attempt to put yourself in the frame of reference of the other person; i.e., to empathize and to sense the receiver's feelings about the matter. After considering the characteristics of the receiver, ask yourself: "How is this person likely to react to my message, and what can I do to make sure it is understood in the way I mean it?"

Although the field of psychology has offered a variety of individual factors that influence the complicated process of human perception, our limited space dictates that we examine only a few of the more significant ones:

Expectations. We tend to perceive what we *expect* to perceive. If a communication is not in keeping with what we expect, we may unconsciously reject or distort the objectionable part of the communication. There is truth in the often-quoted statement, "He hears only what he wants to hear."

Two people rarely meet with what is called an "open mind." Instead, each has preconceived ideas or expectations about the other person and the topic of their communication; any information that doesn't fit these expectations is filtered or distorted.

For example, if employees have had a bad relationship with a previous supervisor, they may perceive anything their present supervisor says or does with distrust and dislike. Their earlier experiences are used as a basis for their current expectations. In a similar way, teachers have been known to unconsciously grade a good student's test paper disproportionately higher than a poorer student's paper simply because they expect the better student to make a higher grade.

Mental set. Probably one of the most prevalent and difficult of the perceptual barriers to successful communication is known as *mental set*. Quite similar to expectation, mental set is a psychological term used to describe the tendency or readiness to react in a particular way. We tend to perceive something in the way that we have become accustomed—or set—to perceiving it. From early childhood, people begin absorbing attitudes, values, and ideas to which they continue to cling. When developed over a period of years, a mental set may become so rigid that it is often practically impossible to change.

Perceptual selectivity. Perception is *selective*. In other words, we seldom pay attention to everything that is communicated to us. Rather, we are inclined to select or focus on those things that particularly interest us. In a meeting with ten people, each will leave with a somewhat different view of what occurred; each of us filtered the communication that took place, sifting out those ideas that we agreed with or found important.

Emotional state. Our current emotional states or moods can greatly influence our perceptions. Just as the heavy drinker may view the world more cheerfully today than he or she will with tomorrow's hangover, you will perceive things differently when you are angry, emotionally upset, or simply have a bad headache from when you're reasonably calm, happy, and healthy.

Semantics

If words are to effectively communicate ideas between the sender and the receiver, they must have the same meaning to both people. The problem is that **words have varied meanings.** Because of different perceptions, the meaning intended by the sender may vary greatly from the meaning understood by the receiver.

It is difficult to believe, but the *Oxford Dictionary* lists an average of 28 separate meanings or definitions for each of the 500 most frequently used words in the English language. Is it any wonder that we encounter semantic problems in communication? To compound our difficulties, dictionaries are overflowing with definitions that are outmoded and seldom used anymore, and people are overflowing with definitions dictionaries have not yet chosen to include.[2]

A frequently overlooked principle is that **words do not convey meaning; only people convey meaning through their use of words.** Or, put another way, the meanings of words are in the minds of the sender and receiver, not in the words themselves. Words are simply *symbols* that represent something; they have meaning only because people in a particular society or culture *give* them meaning. As we grow up, we learn to associate words with their specific meanings.

Since people come from varying geographic, ethnic, social, educational, and occupational backgrounds, the same word (or, for that matter, nonverbal action) often has entirely different meanings to different people because of each individual's perceptual frame of reference. Each person interprets words according to past experiences; as no two sets of experiences are exactly the same, perceptions of words may be different.[3]

We have a tendency to assume that we are referring to exactly the same thing when we use words such as *small, tall, hard, cold, comfortable, fast, easy,* and so on, but more likely we aren't. For example, what may be "easy" to one person may be "impossible" for someone else. Ask ten people for their definitions of a "small town" or a "tall man," and you can assuredly expect to receive ten diverse answers.

Don Kirkpatrick in his book, *No-Nonsense Communication,* tells this tale of misunderstanding:

> The story is told about a plant in Racine, Wisconsin that makes tail pipes for automobiles. The pipes, of course, are of different shapes. Few of them are straight. A new worker came on the job. The foreman was too busy at the time to get the worker started on his assigned job. In order to keep him busy he told him, "I'll be with you in a few minutes to show you your regular job. For now, go on over and straighten out those pipes over there." The foreman came back about 15 minutes later and was astounded to find the new worker using a large hammer to try to knock the bends out of the pipes in order to make them straight. All the foreman wanted, of course, was a little housekeeping done. He blamed the new worker for

"not using his head". The new employee was embarrassed and mad at the foreman for not communicating clearly.[4]

Both people in this story assumed that they were using the same words—"straighten out"—to mean the same things.

Do the same words mean the same to the college graduate and the person who left school after completing the sixth grade? Frequently not. As another example, the language of a company vice-president is obviously different from that of the janitor, and communication between the two may not always be presented in terms that are understandable and familiar. This is not to imply, however, that you should "talk down" (or "write down") to someone. The vice-president talking to the janitor would be well advised not to talk like a janitor, but certainly shouldn't talk like a vice-president either.

A partial solution to the problem of semantic barriers is to use words in their proper *context*. Words do not stand alone; they are combined to form phrases and sentences. Every word occurs in a context of other words, and the meaning of a word depends on the pattern of these other words. Consider these two phrases: (1) the first man's house; (2) the man's first house. The difference in meaning clearly has to do with the same set of words existing in different contexts.

The only real solution, however, is to **communicate in terms of the receiver's background and frame of reference.** In encoding a message, we tend to use words that are familiar *to us*—words *we* use every day, and words that have specific meanings to *us*. But what about the receiver? In choosing language, we must ask ourselves what meanings the receiver will likely read into the words chosen and how the receiver will respond to them. As N. R. Diller has colorfully put it, "Words should be developed to shape, mold, and express thought. They are capsules of mental effort and must be projected toward the target in order to be effective. If this is not done, they are like so many blank shells or 'duds' which make a feeble sputter and fizzle out."[5]

"Gobbledygook"

Closely related to semantic barriers, but deserving of separate attention, is the use of "gobbledygook"—wordy and generally unintelligible language—in oral and written communication.

Occasionally, many of us use words or phrases that are really meant to *impress* more than *express*. As a supervisor, your job is to *inform,* not to impress others with your extensive vocabulary. Pretentious four- or five-syllable tongue-twisters may sound very eloquent; but, if they are not understood by the other person, they are useless. Simpler words that are more easily grasped by the receiver can be used to convey the same meaning.

This is illustrated by the old story of a plumber who wrote to a governmental agency, the Bureau of Standards, inquiring if his longtime practice of cleaning drains with hydrochloric acid was harmless.

The Washington bureau replied: "The efficacy of hydrochloric acid is indisputable, but the chlorine residue is incompatible with metallic permanence." In gratitude, the plumber wrote back saying that he was glad they agreed with him that it was harmless.

With a note of alarm, the Bureau rapidly replied: "We cannot assume responsibility for the production of toxic and noxious residues with hydrochloric acid and further suggest you use an alternate procedure." Flattered by Washington's interest, the plumber expressed in another letter that he was happy to find that the Bureau still agreed with him.

As the story goes, he received an immediate reply which very concisely read: "Don't use hydrochloric acid; it eats the hell out of the pipes!"

The point of the story is simply that *true* communication and understanding existed only at the end. It also illustrates the need to communicate in terms of the receiver and his or her frame of reference.

The use of gobbledygook is especially serious in *written* communication where the receiver is often unable to obtain additional clarification of the message. And let's face it —many of us don't know *how* to write simple, clear English. In fact, we are seldom even *exposed* to it. Many textbooks (perhaps even this one) are perfect examples of complicated, verbose, pompous, and often meaningless language. As E. A. Stauffen has said, "If you think good writing comes easy, then you either don't write, or if you do, you don't know how yet."[6]

Technical jargon, common to all trades and professions, is another frequent nemesis to understanding. Truck drivers, musicians, engineers, nurses, papermakers, prison inmates, various ethnic groups, and many others, all seem compelled to invent substitute words that say what has to be said, but in a more colorful and "private" way. At times, various trades and professions seem to be *competing* with each other to see who can come up with the most status-seeking, complex terminology! Only "members of the club" use these terms—and normally only with each other. This doesn't mean that technical jargon is "bad," for it certainly has its place. When used among people in the same technical area, it efficiently conveys meaning. But it is dangerous when used to communicate with people in other fields or with someone who hasn't been on the job long enough to learn the jargon. To make the point that technical jargon is understood only by those within a trade or profession, see if you can figure out this statement made by a printer: "I can't put her to bed; she pied when I picked her up." What is the printer trying to communicate? Simply that the job couldn't be put on the press because the type fell out when the form was picked up. To another printer the statement would be quite clear, but to an outsider it is sheer gobbledygook.[7]

In summary, the aim of communication is *not* to test the receiver's literacy; it is to reach mutual understanding.

Facts versus Inferences

Inferences—conclusions drawn from observation of facts—are an essential part of our communication. However, it is wise to recognize that there is a distinct difference between inferences and facts. At times, inferences may prove to be correct; at other times they give a wrong signal that can result in misunderstanding.

As an illustration, consider the hypothetical case of Frank Cain, an accounting clerk for the XYZ Company. For years, Frank has dressed in a casual, unassuming manner, usually wearing a sport shirt or sweater. Today, Frank arrives at work attired in a dress shirt, a flashy tie, and a sports coat. In this situation, the only available *fact* is that Frank is indeed dressed differently from usual. However, a variety of *inferences* can be made from this single fact. His boss may *infer* that Frank's "new look" is an attempt to impress him. A fellow accounting clerk might infer that the change is a result of the boss berating Frank about his previous sloppy dressing habits. The guard at the plant entrance may infer that Frank has received a promotion. The office secretary may decide that Frank is making a play for her attentions. Perhaps *one* of the inferences may be correct; then again, *none* of them may be correct. In each case, Frank's nonverbal behavior (which may or may not have been a conscious attempt to communicate anything) would be misinterpreted. Who knows? Further investigation of the facts might simply reveal that all of Frank's sport shirts and sweaters were dirty!

What are the implications for your job as a supervisor? First, many of us jump to conclusions before all of the facts are in. And when inferences are mistaken for facts, we can get in a lot of trouble. For example, suppose one of your employees, Janet, has come to work fifteen minutes late for the last four days. This is an observable fact. You, as her supervisor, might infer that Janet has become apathetic and irresponsible and has lost all interest in her work. Your inference may impulsively lead you to take immediate disciplinary action against her. Would your inference and action be correct? You can't be sure unless you make an attempt to discover additional facts about why the employee has been tardy.

Secondly, you need to remember that people will make inferences from *your* words and actions which could possibly lead to misunderstanding of the facts you intend to communicate. By anticipating probable inferences that employees may make, you can furnish them with sufficient factual information to lessen the possibility of unwarranted inferences.

LISTENING—
THE NEGLECTED AVENUE
TO UNDERSTANDING

Listening is one of the most important—and most neglected—skills in communication. Few people really give much thought to the time they spend listening. Generally speaking, a breakdown of the total time supervisors spend in communication during a normal day shows that 9 per cent of their time is spent writing, 14 per cent reading, 32 per cent speaking, and *45 per cent listening.* In other words, supervisors do more listening than anything else. This is obvious when you stop to consider all of the instructions, information, advice, criticism, complaints, and so on, that the average supervisor is confronted with each day. And as the supervisor rises on the management hierarchy, the time devoted to listening is apt to increase even more.

How well do most of us listen? Is there any need to improve listening skills? We can answer both questions by citing the findings of research conducted by Dr. Ralph Nichols of the University of Minnesota. Nichols' studies of the listening aspect of communication indicate that most people retain only about *half* of what they hear immediately after listening to a short talk. After a few weeks, the same people will recall *only about 25 per cent* of what was said. Put another way, the majority of us operate at a 25 per cent efficiency level when listening. This finding is a bit unnerving when applied to business and industry, where management likes to talk in terms of 90 per cent or higher efficiency in the organization's operations!

The poor listening ability of the average person was pointed out by one of the students in a salesmanship class. We are discussing the importance of promptly recognizing customers in a retail store. One student who was a salesperson in a large department store told the class that all of her store's personnel had been instructed to greet customers with a friendly "Hello, how are you today?" Another student, who frequently shopped in this same store, told us that he always smiled back at the salesperson and answered, "I have ten days to live, thank you." His weird sense of humor rarely received any reaction from the salesperson, who probably expected to hear the usual "Fine, thank you."

Although Mother Nature has wired us for sound, most of us evidently transmit better than we receive. And yet no communication is ever complete until there is understanding on the part of the receiver. Our problems in communication are not solved by seeking only to be *understood;* equally important, we must seek to *understand* others— i.e., to be a good listener.

Nichols has suggested that our country's educational system has overlooked an important subject—refining our ability to listen. Our schools teach writing and reading skills (even though the average high school graduate still reads at the eighth-grade level) and offer courses in speech, but relatively little attention is given to listening, the form of communication that occupies the greatest amount of our time.

Advantages of Effective Listening

The biggest plus for effective listening by supervisors is that it encourages beneficial interpersonal relationships with employees. Of all the sources of information available to you for knowing and accurately "sizing up" the people in your work group, listening to the employee is the most important. Additionally, it indicates a willingness to understand and respect the other person; that person, in turn, will be more willing to understand and respect you.

If you want to stimulate upward communication and a two-way flow of ideas, you must learn to be a good listener; the only way you will get a person to be willing to talk is to be willing to listen.

Yet, too often in a discussion about listening, a supervisor will exclaim, "I don't have time to listen carefully." The obvious response is, "You don't have time *not* to listen carefully!" Effective listening *is* a difficult, time-consuming process, but the return justifies the investment by paying handsome dividends. Failing to listen to the people in you work group invites many problems that might otherwise never develop.

The Difference Between
Listening and Hearing

Don't fall into the trap of confusing *listening* with *hearing*. Many of us who consider ourselves good listeners might be better described as good hearers. Hearing is merely a physical act and is almost impossible to avoid. Listening, however, requires more than just remaining passive and silent while the other person speaks; it involves more than just hearing words. Listening is an *active, conscious* act, requiring as much, if not more, mental effort and concentration than speaking.

Hearing is with our ears; listening is with our minds. If you only hear people, you're probably missing valuable information, suggestions, and ideas.

Common Bad Listening
Habits

No one is born with the ability to listen effectively. Just like all other communication skills, good listening must be *learned*. To a great extent, this involves forming good listening habits and breaking bad habits. Here is a short test that, *if answered honestly* will give you an idea of whether you have any bad listening habits:

1. You think about four times faster than a person usually talks. Do you use this excess time to think about other things while you're keeping track of the conversation? . . . . Yes   No
2. Do you listen primarily for facts, rather than ideas, when someone is speaking? . . . . Yes   No
3. Do you avoid listening to things you feel will be too difficult to understand? . . . . Yes   No
4. Can you tell from people's appearance and delivery that they won't have anything worthwhile to say? . . . . Yes   No
5. When somebody is talking to you, do you try to make the person think you're paying attention when you're not? . . . . Yes   No
6. Do certain words or phrases prejudice you so that you cannot listen objectively? . . . . Yes   No
7. Do you turn your thoughts to other subjects when you believe a speaker will have nothing particularly interesting to say? . . . . Yes   No
8. When you're listening to someone, are you easily distracted by outside sights and sounds? . . . . Yes   No
9. When you are puzzled or annoyed by what someone says, do you try to get the question straightened out immediately, either in your own mind or by interrupting the speaker? . . . . Yes   No

10. Do you catch yourself concentrating in a conversation more on what you are going to say when it's your turn to speak than on what the speaker is saying?
   . . . . Yes   No

If you truthfully answered "No" to all the questions, you are a rare individual—perhaps a perfect listener. (You may also be kidding yourself!) Every "Yes" means you are guilty of one of the ten bad listening habits that we shall now examine.[8]

Wasting thought power. We listen and absorb ideas at a much faster rate than most people talk. On the average, most of us *talk* at a rate of 125 words per minute. Yet, we can easily *think* in terms of 400 or 500 words per minute. Unfortunately, this difference between speech speed and thought speed is responsible for many *mental tangents;* in other words, instead of concentrating on the speaker's message, your mind frequently uses its excess capacity for thinking about some other subject. At the same time you are listening to a conversation or speech, you can periodically ponder your plans for the weekend, your hobby, last night's party, or Sunday's football game. Before you know it, your mind wanders too far away and "tunes out" the speaker altogether.

What is the solution? Obviously, if you have the ability to think four times faster than a person can talk to you, this can be turned into a listening asset. By disciplining your thoughts, your spare thinking time can be used to think about the speaker's subject and improve your listening comprehension. How? By anticipating the speaker's next point, reviewing or summarizing the points the speaker has made, and listening "between the lines" to get any hidden messages that may go unspoken.

Listening only for facts. One common mistake made by poor listeners is attempting to remember all the facts. Instead of memorizing a series of facts, try to get the gist or main ideas of the speaker's message. Facts are understood and retained only when they are tied together to support a concept, principle, or generalization.

"Throw-in-the-towel" listening. Many people quit listening if they think the speaker is going to talk about something that is technical or difficult to understand. And little wonder; we are *conditioned* to evade difficult material. You only need to watch a night of TV—"the vast wasteland"—to recognize the widespread tendency in our society to listen only to light, recreational, unchallenging material. Many of us are simply inexperienced in listening to difficult material; others are just out of practice and in a rut.

Don't shy away from tough subjects or those outside your field. As you continue to listen, you may find that the subject isn't so hard to understand after all.

Criticizing the speaker's appearance or delivery. It is easy to criticize a speaker's appearance, delivery, dress, mannerisms, or eccentricities. However, when you react in this manner, you are not listening effectively and are short-changing yourself by closing the door on what might be useful information.

If a male employee stops to offer a suggestion, but he has long hair, do you think you might say to yourself: "Anybody who has long hair can't have much to say"? Be careful, the employee may have a good idea that can solve one of your biggest problems. Dr. Nichols provides another illustration:

> Suppose that right now a janitor interrupted you, yelling in broken, profane English, "Get the hell out of here! The building is on fire!" You wouldn't lean backward and say, "Please, sir, will you not couch that admonition in better rhetoric?" You would rush pell-mell out of the room, as you know. That is my point. The message is ten times as important as the clothing in which it comes.[9]

Concentrate on the *content* of the message, not the speaker's dress or mannerisms. The speaker must have something worthwhile to say, so why not dig it out? Give the person the benefit of the doubt; in the long run, you'll pick up some excellent ideas from "dull" or "eccentric" speakers.

Faking attention. Many people only go through the motions of listening; they figure that if they pretend to listen, no one will notice the difference. They are wrong in two ways. First, you seldom can fool the speaker. Even though you appear to be listening intently, the speaker can tell from your reactions that you haven't heard a thing; and, when employees brand their supervisor as a phony listener, they will cut off upward communication. Second, you are shutting yourself off from a potentially good source of ideas and information.

Reacting to "red-flag" words. Another bad listening habit is allowing emotional words—often called "red-flag" words—to block rational listening. We react emotionally to certain words because of past experiences and attitudes connected to those words. Examples of words that may be emotion-laden to some people are *automation, taxes, discipline, unions, women's lib, welfare, documentation, computer, inflation, bussing,* and *mother-in-law.* The mere mention of such words often has the power to cause a listener to "see red" and miss or distort the entire message; i.e., it can cause an emotional "deaf spot."

You can probably think of many words that personally turn *you* off. But remember, words are only *symbols* of something; so why let a simple word disrupt your listening efficiency?

Calling the subject uninteresting. A seventh bad listening habit is to immediately declare a speaker's subject uninteresting. Naturally, the most attention-getting subjects are those you are personally interested in; because of your personal interest, you *want* to listen. If, however, the subject doesn't appear to directly involve you or seems boring, you may go off on a mental tangent, feeling that there is no reason to listen.

Nichols suggests that, inasmuch as you're "trapped" and can't gracefully walk away in such a situation, you should concentrate on sifting, screening, and hunting for *something*—even if only a few words—the speaker says that is meaningful and useful to you.

This can be a very profitable activity. Actually, there is no such thing as a talk completely lacking in useful information.

As G. K. Chesterton said long ago, "In all the world there is no such thing as an uninteresting subject. There are only uninterested people."[10]

Tolerating or creating distractions. Poor listeners are easily distracted by other sounds or sights going on around them. A good example is the supervisor who is always willing to see an employee but who allows the conversation to be interrupted time and again. The supervisor talks to everybody who sticks their heads in the office and answers a continuous stream of phone calls.

The author once attempted a conversation with an administrator who prided himself on being able both to listen to someone and open and read his mail at the same time! Perhaps there are some people who are able to pull off such amazing feats successfully. However, such persons are likely to convince those talking to them that they really have no interest in listening attentively.

"I-can't-buy-that" listening. When you find yourself disagreeing with people, do you start mentally planning a rebuttal before they are finished talking? Do you tend to prejudge or make assumptions about what is said before your comprehension is complete? To do so is to allow your emotions to affect your objectivity and reduce your listening effectiveness. And, if you jump to a conclusion about what people are getting at before they actually make their points, you may find yourself embarrassingly wrong.

We all have certain sensitive topics and prejudices that can cause us to get emotionally involved with the speaker's message. But this is no excuse for becoming over-emotional and argumentative. Wait for the speaker to finish talking before judging and evaluating ideas. Hear the speaker out; if you still disagree, then offer your opinion in a calm and rational manner.

Similarly, we sometimes find ourselves not listening to someone because we don't like the individual personally. In other words, we don't like the person, and therefore we don't like his or her ideas. Here again, when you react in this emotional manner, you are closing the door on what might be useful information.

"Open-mouth" listening. One of the most prevalent causes of poor listening is impatience to have our "say." Silence is difficult for many of us. We like to speak more than we like to listen. Thinking that we must say something each time the speaker takes a breath, we often concentrate more on what *we* are going to say next than on what the speaker is saying. Obviously, this is part-time listening, at best.

Choke off the temptation to "butt in" or dominate the conversation. Let people know they have your full attention. An occasional nod or a comment like "that's interesting" or "I see" will work wonders.

Perhaps we should keep in mind the warning of an old proverb: "Nature gave us two ears and only one mouth so that we could listen twice as much as we speak."

General Suggestions for
Improved Listening

Aside from becoming sensitized to the bad listening habits discussed above, here are some suggestions that will improve your listening and help you discover a world of useful information:

Listen empathetically. The key to effective listening is *empathy* (there's that word again!) You must attempt to get yourself into the speaker's frame of reference and sense his or her feelings about the topic of discussion; try earnestly to see the other person's point of view in light of individual backgrounds, attitudes, and needs.

When listening empathetically, listen *nonevaluatively,* without passing judgment on what is being said at the time. This opens the way for people to talk freely about their ideas and feelings without worrying about justifying every statement they make.

A supervisor's empathetic listening can actually be therapeutic for employees. Very often the mere act of listening to employees' problems and letting them "get it off their chests" helps them to work things out for themselves.

The ability to listen with genuine empathy and understanding is rare, but it can be acquired through desire and practice.

Listen between the lines. Listen to what *is* said, and then try to hear what is *not* said. Consider this illustration. One of your employees, Peggy, has just approached you to report:

"Well, I finally finished up the order for the Ace Publishing Company. What a mess! But you said it was an emergency job, so I saw to it that it went out today. You know, I've been here every night this week to finish that darned thing. My husband may throw me out tonight! Ace's specifications were rediculous, but the order is on its way. And let me tell you, if I never see another job as tough as that, I'll be happy. That one was blood, sweat and tears!"

If you should answer, "Great, Peggy; now let's get back to work on the Wilson order," you haven't really been listening, have you? What was Peggy really trying to get across to you? We can't be sure, of course, but it's doubtful that she was simply saying the Ace order was difficult. More likely she was saying, "How about a little recognition for a job well done?"

Sensitive supervisors look beyond the words for the meaning and emotions the speaker is attempting to convey; they hear what the other person is often inhibited from saying directly.[11]

In order to better analyze the speaker and his or her message, you should also note any change in tone of voice, gestures, facial expressions, and body movements. Such things can be important clues to the real meaning of the message. Be careful to evaluate these visual signs only in connection with what is being said, however; otherwise, they may only become distractions to your listening.

Anticipate the speaker's next point. Good listeners try to think ahead of the speaker, anticipating the speaker's next point or line of reasoning. If you guess correctly, learning is reinforced. Even if you guess wrongly, you have forced yourself to concentrate on the subject.

Make mental summaries. Periodically make quick mental summaries of what has been said to that point. Not only does this reinforce learning, it helps utilize the differential between thought speed and speech speed.

Provide feedback to the speaker. During a conversation, try to rephrase or summarize in your own words the content and feeling of what the speaker is saying, to the speaker's satisfaction.

This helps to verify your understanding to both yourself and to the speaker. It can also help in further drawing out and encouraging the speaker to continue. Such feedback might begin with: "Now, what I've heard you saying is that . . ." or "Mary, as I understand you, you feel that . . . ."

COMMUNICATION IN PERSPECTIVE

Further pleading the cause for communication following our lengthy discussion of the topic in these last two chapters is surely superfluous. Little shrewdness is needed to realize that the job of supervision—getting work accomplished through others—requires effective communication. Communication is a basic skill of supervision and the foundation upon which all cooperative group activity rests.

However, every communication situation poses a challenge to those involved in it. Effective communication requires an understanding of the basic processes of communication and the organizational structure that furnishes its environment. These were our goals in Chapter 6. There, we examined the six steps in the communication process and continually stressed the desirability of two-way communication and feedback. Advantages and disadvantages of oral and written communication, as well as the often-overlooked nonverbal medium, were presented.

Next, we looked at the supervisor's role in formal and informal communication networks. We saw that a formal system for transmitting and receiving information up, down, and across is a basic requirement for any organization depending upon human cooperation. Interwoven with the formal structure, however, is an ever-changing and complicated network of informal communication channels that cannot be ignored.

In Chapter 7, we have tried to further illustrate the complexities of person-to-person communication and the various obstacles to understanding.

The future will doubtless bring increased recognition of the value of effective communication both to individuals and to organizations. As organizations continue to grow more complex and larger, the need for people with communication skills at all levels of management will also increase. We are now at the point where lip-service to the need for effective communication is no longer adequate. We must begin practicing it. Regardless of our field of specialization, each of us is in the midst of an information and knowledge explosion, and our communication skills must keep pace.

You will undoubtedly, in time, forget many of the details presented in these two chapters. Make it a point, however, to remember this: There is nothing simple about communication; it cannot be taken for granted. There are so many psychological and physical barriers that the normal result of any communication effort is partial misunderstanding.

No one's communication skills will ever be perfect, but they can be improved; indeed, they must be. All of us must begin with an awareness of our own present level of competence as communicators, one which involves a clear and honest self evaluation of current abilities and practices. Armed with this self-awareness, you can then begin striving for continual improvement.

QUESTIONS FOR REVIEW AND DISCUSSION

1. Recall a breakdown in communication that you have observed or have been a part of. What caused the misunderstanding and how could it have been avoided?
2. How do individual differences affect communication?
3. "The concept of *frame of reference* is the key to the entire communication process." Evaluate this statement.
4. "Most communication serves to reinforce one's already-held beliefs and attitudes." Do you agree? Why?
5. a. Why is semantics a problem in communication?
   b. How can semantic barriers to communication be overcome?
6. Why is it important to distinguish between facts and inferences?
7. What communication barriers are likely to exist between a supervisor and an employee that do not usually exist between friends?
8. How important is *trust* in supervisor-employee communication? Explain.
9. a. What is the function of listening in communication?
   b. What supervisory problems may result from failure to listen effectively?
10. Keep a log of the time you spend engaging in each form of verbal communication —reading, writing, speaking, and listening—during an entire typical day. Compare your results with the percentages reported in this chapter. Do your results confirm the importance of listening as a major component of communication?
11. Is there a relationship between listening and upward and downward communication? Explain.
12. Is good listening by supervisors helpful in their efforts to motivate employees? Explain.

13. Name and briefly discuss the ten common bad listening habits presented in this chapter. Can you think of any others that could be added to this list?

14. a. Why do people tend to react emotionally to certain words and not to others?
    b. What are some words that typically make you "see red"?

15. At times, most of us have been unwilling to accept ideas or information communicated to us only to find later that the communication was, in fact, valid. From your own experience, discuss your reasons for rejecting such a communication. As a group, try to determine if your reasons are similar or if each group member has individual reasons for rejecting a communication.

16. What suggestions have been offered for improving one's listening effectiveness? Can you make any suggestions that have not been presented in the chapter?

17. Why is it important for a supervisor to listen "between the lines" or with a "third ear"?

18. At which of the six steps in the communication process discussed in Chapter 6 do you feel that most barriers to effective communication occur? Defend your answer.

19. Both Chapters 6 and 7 have suggested that the communication process is more complex than we usually think. Can you recall personal experiences in which you were conscious of the difficulty in communicating? In what ways were these situations different from those that did not seem difficult?

20. What benefits could be derived in an organization in which all relevant communication is passed to the right people?

REFERENCES

1. Davis, Keith, *Human Relations at Work,* 4th ed. New York: McGraw-Hill Book Company, 1972, pp. 417–18.

2. O'Hayre, John, *Gobbledygook Has Gotta Go.* Washington, D.C.: U. S. Government Printing Office, 1966, pp. 17–18.

3. Stieglitz, Harold, "Barriers to Communication," *Management Record,* Jan. 1958, pp. 2–3.

4. Kirkpatrick, Donald L., *No-Nonsense Communication.* Elm Grove, Wisc.: K&M Publishers, 1978, p. 22.

5. Diller, N. Richard, "Improving Communications On the Job," *Manage,* August 1966, p. 53.

6. O'Hayre, *op. cit.,* p. 27.

7. *Ibid.,* pp. 25–26.

8. The framework of this presentation is taken from: Ralph G. Nichols, "Listening Is Good Business," *Management of Personnel Quarterly,* Winter 1962, pp. 2–10.

9. *Ibid,* p. 6.

10. *Ibid.*

11. Sigband, Norman B., "Listen to What You Can't Hear," *Nation's Business,* June 1969, pp. 70–72.

Suggested Additional Readings

Driver, Russel W., "Issues in Upward Communication," *Supervisory Management*, Feb. 1980, pp. 11-13.

——, "Opening the Channels of Upward Communication," *Supervisory Management*, March 1980, pp. 24-29.

Gelfund, Louis I., "Communicate Through Your Supervisors," *Harvard Business Review*, Nov.–Dec. 1970, pp. 101-104.

Gemmill, Gary, "Managing Upward Communication," *Personnel Journal*, Feb. 1970, pp. 107-10.

Hall, Edward and Mildred, "The Sounds of Silence," *Playboy*, June 1971, pp.138ff.

Haynes, Marion E., "Becoming an Effective Listener," *Supervisory Management*, August 1979, pp. 21-28.

Horovitz, Bruce, "Why Not Say What You Mean?" *Industry Week*, Dec. 10, 1979, pp. 61-62.

Kikoski, John F., "Communication: Understanding It, Improving It," *Personnel Journal*, Feb. 1980, pp. 126-131.

McCaskey, Michael B., "The Hidden Messages Managers Send," *Harvard Business Review*, Nov.–Dec. 1979, pp. 135-148.

Rogers, Carl R., and F. J. Roethlisberger, "Barriers and Gateways to Communication," *Harvard Business Review*, July–August 1952, pp. 46-52.

Siegel, Alan, "Fighting Business Gobbledygook: How to Say It in Plain English," *Management Review*, Nov. 1979, pp. 15-19.

Thompson, Donald B., "The Ultimate 'Word': The Grapevine," *Industry Week*, May 10, 1976, pp. 29-35.

Weiss, W. H., "Breaking the Fear Barrier," *Nation's Business*, July 1971, pp. 64-65.

Zeyher, Lewis R., "Improving Your Three-Dimensional Communications," *Personnel Journal*, May 1970, pp. 414-418.

CASES AND ROLE-PLAYING EXERCISES

INTRODUCTION TO
THE STUDY OF CASES

The cases in this section of the book place you in a simulated position of a decision maker handling practical supervisory problems. What is a case? A *case* is a description of people and events in a realistic situation that represents a problem to be analyzed and a decision to be made. Although the names of people and organizations have been disguised, the cases in this book are based on problems and events that have actually taken place.

The case method of learning forces you, not the instructor, to do in-depth analysis of a particular situation. The major responsibility for analysis rests on you; learning is promoted by your search for solutions to problems. Thus, the case method *requires full learner participation;* its effectiveness is entirely dependent upon each group member's willingness to become *involved.*

This approach is based on the principle that learning that draws upon the learner's personal initiative and involvement produces more lasting and effective results than learning that is acquired simply through passive absorption of knowledge. In other words, learning is enhanced if the learner takes an *active* part in the process.

The instructor's role in case analysis is keeping the group aware of its responsibilities, posing questions, suggesting additional lines of exploration, and summarizing progress. The instructor's role is *not* to spoon-feed the group, supply it with pat answers, or impose his or her opinions upon the participants.

EMPHASIS ON
DECISION MAKING

One of the prime objectives of the case method is to sharpen your decision-making skills. This objective is of no small consequence because decision making is one of the most important functions of any supervisor.

In pursuit of this objective, all cases in this book are descriptions of situations calling for a *decision on future action,* along with an appraisal of past action. It is not enough to criticize what has transpired in the case; instead, you must decide *in detail* what should be done to improve the current situation in the case.

Each case calls for a careful review of the situation in terms of defining and analyzing the problem, weighing alternative courses of action, and offering a feasible solution. The stress is on logical analysis, developing a framework for decision making, and the necessity of thinking through problems in a straight-line manner.

SUGGESTED APPROACH TO SOLVING CASE PROBLEMS

There is no one best way to study and prepare a case problem, nor is there necessarily a standard outline or form in which to present a case analysis. But here are a few suggestions that should prove helpful, whether you are preparing a written or oral analysis.

First, *read* the case thoroughly and carefully—usually several times and as far as possible in advance of when you plan to do a *serious* analysis. Think about the situation and try to involve yourself in it. Then put the case aside for a while and let it "incubate." Allow the facts to simmer in your mind and let your subconscious work them over. Then *reread* the case. You'll likely find that your second impressions are somewhat different from your first.

Throughout the process of analyzing the case, ask yourself questions. Questions for consideration might be: "Why are the people in this situation acting like this?" "Why has the present situation developed?" "What is the basic problem in this situation?" "What caused this conflict?" "What alternative solutions are available to solve this problem?" "What are the chances of success for the various solutions?"

Additionally, you are encouraged not to disagree with *facts,* but to "read between the lines" in a case and question the *opinions* and *judgments* of the people quoted in the case.

To start your thinking and help you to explore as many areas as possible, questions are appended to each case. These questions are by no means meant to limit you. In fact, some of the questions may never even be raised in a discussion of the case.

In keeping with the objective of improved decision-making skills, here is a suggested model for case analysis that has been well tested in actual practice and may be used as a general outline to guide your thinking:

1. **State what appear to be the major issues in the situation.** An *issue* can be defined as "the question to be resolved" or "the decision that must be made." Examples of issues are: "What additional training does Sue need in order to perform up to standard?" "What steps should be taken to insure employee acceptance of the new cash registers?" Or, "How can we help Joe improve the quality of his work?"

2. **Diagnose the problem(s) underlying the major issue.** Decision making is always related to a problem, a difficulty, or a conflict. Whenever things are not going as expected, there is a problem. Decisions bring about an answer to the problem or a resolution of the conflict.

Thus, the first—perhaps the most difficult and often overlooked phase—is a thorough diagnosis of the problem. The question of problem definition is very important; unless the problem is wisely defined, a poor case solution is almost inevitable.

A common error in diagnosing problem situations is confusing *symptoms* with the problem itself. Essentially, your task in problem diagnosis is finding the *root causes* for the current situation in the case. The same symptoms can result from numerous causes. Clearly, if the wrong causes are assumed, your solution will also be ineffective.

In trying to find this root cause (problem), it may be helpful to view the process as a "gap" between *what we would like to happen* (i.e., our ideal state or objective) and *what is happening now in the current situation*. What *obstacles* are standing in the way of reaching the desired objective?

For example, consider a department that is experiencing a high degree of turnover. A superficial diagnosis might indicate the problem to be "low morale." Of course, an even less sophisticated response would be "the problem in this situation is high turnover"! What is *causing* high turnover? What is *causing* low morale? Low morale is not the problem; it is only a *symptom* of the problem. Perhaps the real cause of the situation is lack of proper training. Again, however, would this be the *root cause? Why* is training inadequate?

Hence, we should continue moving from *superficial causes* (symptoms) to *root causes* (problems). A good way of getting beyond symptoms to the problem itself is to keep asking, "Why?" "*Why* does John have a poor attitude?" "*Why* is Larry a lousy communicator?" "*Why* is Mary continually late for work?"

So, in analyzing the problem, the question should *not* be, "What should be done in this situation?" but rather, "*Why* did this situation develop? What *caused* it?" To put it simply, problems are the reasons for your having to resolve the question or make the decision that you have stated in Step 1.

3. **State all alternative courses of action available for resolving the problem.** Decision making necessitates a choice between two or more alternatives. If there is only one solution available, then there is really no decision to be made. In a problem situation, there are always numerous possibilities available from which we must make a selection.

Imagination and originality are needed at this stage. The goal in this step should be *quantity* of alternatives, not particularly *quality* of alternatives. Don't reject an alternative because at first glance it seems improbable or impractical. There may be elements in it that can contribute to the ideal solution. Only by considering all possible alternatives can you be confident you have not overlooked any opportunities to get the results you want.

4. **Select and state the two or three most reasonable alternatives available**. Evaluate briefly the several courses of action stated in Step 3. From them select the two or three most reasonable proposals.

   The first alternative that occurs to you probably represents your usual approach to this type of problem. But remember that the seemingly "one" right or obvious solution is not always the best answer, because the first idea to come to mind is frequently triggered by preconceived notions held before the problem was analyzed.

5. **Analyze and compare the alternatives**. Weigh the *advantages* and *disadvantages* of each alternative. Consider the *probability of success* and the *risk* of complications for each and forecast the consequences. Determine both the *strengths* and *weaknesses* inherent in each course of action. All pertinent data should be assembled and related to these alternatives.

6. **Make your decision and plan for its implementation**. After weighing the pros and cons of each alternative in Step 5, decide which course of action promises to be the most successful. Also consider *how* you would carry out your plan of action, what steps should be taken, and so on; in other words, give thought to the *implementation* aspects of your course of action. Remember, a poorly implemented good decision may be no better than an expertly implemented bad decision. Whenever possible, translate the course of action into a complete statement indicating *who, what, when, where, how,* and *why,* as appropriate.

Notice that each step in the above model for solving case problems builds on the foundation of the previous steps. Success at each step depends on the successful achievement of the preceding step.

COMMON ERRORS
AND FRUSTRATIONS
TO AVOID

Inadequate definition of the problem. By far the most common error made in case analysis (as well as in decision making in general) is attempting to recommend a course of action without first adequately defining or understanding the problem. Whether presented orally or in a written report, a case analysis must begin with a focus on the central issue and problem represented in the case situation.

In a traditional classroom situation, we normally expect the instructor to state the problem. In using cases, on the other hand, the problem is usually buried under a large number of facts and opinions that confuse and complicate the process of problem definition. Realistically, this is as it should be; in the real world of the supervisor, as opposed to a pure classroom environment, problems are seldom easily identifiable.

As stated earlier, unless the problem is adequately diagnosed and defined, there is little chance of proposing a useful solution to the problem.

The search for "correct answers." Most of us are used to receiving set answers to questions and problems raised in a classroom. Yet, in using cases, there are no clear-cut solutions. Thus, this approach to learning often tends to be frustrating at first.

Keep in mind that an objective of case studies is learning through discussion and exploration (and, occasionally, even argument). There is no one "official" or "correct" answer to a case. Rather, there are usually several reasonable alternative solutions—some perhaps better than others. Depending on the problem situation and the individual skills of the problem solver, many approaches or solutions could be successful in a particular situation.

Therefore, it is quite normal for group members not to agree on a single black-and-white solution or not to reach a neat conclusion at the end of a case discussion. Indeed, you can never, even after the most conscientious analysis, *be sure* your solution (or anyone else's) is correct.

Even though this lack of a "correct answer" tends to be frustrating, it is ironic to note that when classroom cases *do* provide answers there are almost always strong objections from participants who claim that the answers given are wrong!

"I need more information." You may often complain that there isn't sufficient information in some of the cases to make a good decision. There is justification for not giving you "all" of the information. As in real life, supervisors seldom have all the information they would like. Time and financial constraints dictate that supervisors often must make decisions with only the information available at the time. The challenge is to find a feasible solution *in spite* of limited information.

Certainly, it will be necessary to project yourself into the case situation and make *assumptions* based on the facts provided. But in all the cases in this volume, sufficient information is provided to allow you to select alternative courses of action and to reasonably predict their chances of success.

Use of generalities. In analyzing cases, *specifics* are necessary, not *generalities*. For example, a suggestion to resolve a particular problem situation by "calling the employee in for counselling" is unsatisfactory and quite naive. *Specifically,* how will you attempt to solve the problem by counseling? What will you do and say?

"If the situation were different. . . . " Considerable time and effort are sometimes exerted by participants contending that "if the situation were different, I'd know what course of action to take." Or, "If the supervisor hadn't already fouled things up so badly, we wouldn't be in this mess." Such reasoning ignores the fact that we cannot change the events in the case that have already happened. Even though analysis or criticsm of past events is necessary in diagnosing the problem, we must in the end address ourselves to the present situation and the decision to be made.

"Narrow vision" analysis. The cases presented in this book are not conveniently categorized into problems of "motivation," "communications," "change," and so on;

they do not merely illustrate the concepts covered in any one chapter. Rather, most of the cases involve application of *several* aspects of supervision and require you to consider all these aspects in your analysis and recommendations. This is by no means unrealistic, in that it corresponds with the whole-problem challenges facing the supervisor in real life. Thus, at times you may wonder why you aren't able to fit a particular case to a certain chapter or why you can't seem to find all the answers to a case in this book. Admittedly, the process can be very frustrating—again, just as real-life supervisory problem solving can be frustrating.

THE VALUE OF
GROUP DISCUSSION

Central to the case method of learning is *group discussion* of the cases. Discussions invite and draw out the experiences of group members so that, in effect, they teach one another.

As a group member, you exchange your opinions, attitudes, and interpretations of the case with others. In so doing, you can see a variety of possible points of view about facts you may have considered to be quite obvious. For example, in discussing a case, you may find that you haven't completely explored the problem. Or, you may discover that the group has been able to identify many more alternative solutions than you could find. During an open discussion, you may also find that your ideas (as well as everyone else's) are influenced by individual attitudes and values that are not completely free of bias or prejudice; other group members may challenge these attitudes and values, causing you either to defend or modify your ideas.

By allowing free expression, the discussion exposes everyone in the group to new ideas, new information, and various ways of looking at and solving supervisory problems. It can also help each individual gain insight into his or her personal thought patterns and ways of perceiving the world. Acquiring such self-awareness is one of the keys to becoming a better supervisor and increasing one's capacity to deal effectively with people.

As an additional benefit, skills developed during group discussions are easily transferrable to the job during staff meetings, committee work, and other group problem-solving situations.

GUIDELINES FOR
ROLE PLAYING

As you analyze the cases that follow this, notice that many of them ask you to *role-play* the situation. To role-play a situation means to simulate the situation through acting the roles of the people involved—attempting to show their attitudes and reactions to the events of the case. Unlike the possible connotations of the term, role playing is a serious activity with worthwhile objectives. It is particularly useful when it evolves as a natural extension of case discussion and analysis. In trying to portray the people involved in a problem situation or in a proposed decision, participants are forced to use empathy, broaden their perspective powers, improve their communication skills, and sharpen their analytical abilities.

Role playing can be quite helpful in evaluating alternative solutions to a case. In simulating the implementation of a proposed decision, the participants assume the positions of the people involved in the decision. For instance, if the alternative were to "have a talk with Jim to determine why he has been late to work for the past two weeks," the participants would enact the discussion proposed by the decision. It's sometimes easy to say, "I would do 'such and such,'" and quite a different matter actually to carry out that decision. Through role playing, you have an opportunity to see how others interpret and respond to the decision, to see "loopholes" in your strategy, and to understand how your communication efforts are received.

Reversing the roles (taking the position of the other person) helps one to understand the feelings and attitudes of another, thus building ability to empathize and to see how the situation looks from another's viewpoint.

Role playing can also assist in developing ability to find the problems causing an undesirable situation. By acting out the background information presented in the case and putting yourself in the situations that have evolved, you may be able to understand why the people have reacted as they have, to recognize how you might have felt if you were in their situation, and to recognize the factors that influence actions and opinions.

This understanding should make it easier to see beyond the symptoms of the problem. Through analysis of the case information and then putting yourself into the circumstances of the situation, you may be able to spot the root causes of the problem.

In order to role-play a situation intelligently, participants must be adequately prepared. Preferably, most of the case analysis procedure outlined above should precede role-playing activity. That is, the case should have been read several times, the situation analyzed, and alternative courses of action formulated. Therefore, participants will already have a good idea of the attitudes displayed, the actions of the people involved, and the influences that have brought about the situation. Certainly you will be limited in your ability in "being" another person; however, repeated role playing can help to develop your ability to empathize.

Group members other than those actually taking part in the role-play should watch for important happenings. These observers should keep several questions in mind: "What attitudes are being expressed?" "Do my perceptions of the people and events match those being portrayed?" "What was said that resulted in agreement—or conflict?" "What stimulated emotional responses in the participants?" These observations should be valuable in discussing the role-playing activity and making a final decision on problem diagnosis or implementation of alternatives.

Usually, two or three groups will role-play a situation. Almost always someone feels that he or she has an approach to the problem that will result in a better resolution of the question. Observing and analyzing the different approaches develops better understanding of the feasibility of various alternatives.

Role playing increases the opportunity for learning through involvement in a realistic situation. Through enacting a situation, lasting and effective learning can take place. In addition to the experience of analyzing the case and the individual's involvement in case discussion, role playing allows the participant to feel that he or she is actually a part of a situation while attempting to implement a decision.

WHERE TO NOW?

General Hospital is a 400-bed hospital located in a major western city. Established shortly after the end of World War II, the facility has grown and expanded with the area it serves, as have the four other major hospitals in the city. General is a nonprofit organization, governed by a Board of Trustees.

Chief administrator of the hospital, Thomas M. Bryant, joined the hospital's accounting department in 1965, a young man just out of college. After being with the hospital for three years, he left to work toward his master's degree in hospital administration. He returned to General upon completion of his degree, and in 1974 became the hospital's chief financial officer. Upon the retirement of the hospital's administrator in 1978, Mr. Bryant was promoted to his current position. Most of the department heads in the hospital are technically trained personnel with little formal management training. Many are, in fact, "working" department heads. The hospital is highly regarded in the community and boasts fairly up-to-date equipment.

Mr. Bryant sat behind his desk one afternoon, pondering several things that had occurred during the past two weeks.

First, it had been the personnel manager, Elvis Spencer: "Tom, something just has to 'give.' The turnover in the hospital has gone sky high. As nearly as I can tell, we had about a 75 per cent rate during the past year; and it's getting hard to find people. I can't figure what's causing it—our salaries are just as good as other hospitals. Oh, and something else; I've heard that some union organizers are in town looking at the hospitals here. So, that's another worry."

"Elvis," Mr. Bryant replied, "Do you know in what areas the turnover is occurring? How serious is this union business?"

Thinking a moment before saying anything, the personnel manager answered, "Well, the turnover is fairly widespread; but it seems particularly high in nursing, housekeeping, and dietary. 'Course we always figure it's going to be high in the lower-level jobs. But I've done some quick figuring on what this is costing. It looks like every new person we hire is running several hundred dollars—on an average—and probably several thousand or so for a new Registered Nurse. The union? I'll just have to wait and try to find out more about that."

Bryant then asked, "Are you sure about those costs? If your thinking is anywhere near right, that means several hundred thousand dollars a year!—and that doesn't show up directly on a balance sheet. But is sure does *indirectly,* and things are tight enough without that. Seems like our patient care would have to be affected too."

"Tom, I know it sounds high; but I think I'm right. American Hospital Association figures indicate that my guesses may even be conservative on hiring costs. I'll do some more checking on that and the union and get back to you later."

Two days later Mr. Bryant brought up the subject at the monthly department head meeting. "Elvis has done some work on turnover rates, and he tells me it's pretty high. We've got to get to the bottom of this because it's really costing money."

Jim Rich, Housekeeping Department head, immediately answered. "Sure, it's high. And it's going to be high in my department. But it doesn't cost much to replace those people. What burns me up is absenteeism—and having to stay right with them to make sure they're doing their jobs. Now *that* really costs money and time."

Mrs. Bennett, Nursing Director, spoke up next. "My department does the best it can. But it's just a fact of life that a nurse can get a job just about anywhere she wants to, so we just live with it."

Mrs. White, head of the Lab, spoke next. "Well, what really gets me is the way everybody just waits for me to tell them what to do. They're supposed to know how to do their jobs. But if I'm not right there to tell them what needs to be done, or what they're supposed to start next, they just wait for me. Now, can you beat that? Why, I would never do that. I always figured that it was my job to stay busy, but that's not the way it is now with these people."

Glenn Jones, Radiology Department head, bitterly added, "It's all these different people we have now. That's the whole trouble. Used to be that people wanted a job—I sure did. But nobody has a good attitude, except for those who've been around a long time. And you just let me tell one of these kids that he'd better straighten out—and watch out—they'd just as soon walk out as not. I do my job too; we have definite rules about working in my department. And I see that they're enforced. So you can't blame me."

After the department-head meeting, Bryant visited most of the departments and talked informally with some employees and the department heads. Most of the department heads seemed quite capable in the technical aspects of their jobs, and Bryant couldn't quite put his finger on the real problem. Were the managers, including himself, *really managing?* Or were they just taking each day at a time, and reacting to the demands of the moment?

Later, as he sat behind his desk, he reflected on the statements made by the department heads and the personnel manager. He wondered silently, "Why are people leaving? Why do people wait to be told what to do? Why are people absent? What about this attitude of 'just let them leave'? Is it really necessary for lower-level jobs to be high turnover areas?"

Definitely, some problems needed to be solved. The whole picture had to look better. How to accomplish these feats was now the question. Where to now?

GUIDES FOR ANALYSIS

1. Are high turnover, excessive absenteeism, and "don't care" attitudes problems or *symptoms* of problems?
2. Is an attitude of problem solving present in the hospital?
3. What managerial skills seem to be present here? What skills are lacking?
4. What effects might the attitudes of the department heads toward their employees have on productivity, turnover, absenteeism, and so on?

5. Is there any evidence that skill in dealing with people exists among the managerial personnel?
6. Recommend a course of action to Mr. Bryant?

TRY IT: SEE HOW YOU LIKE IT!

David Cisco supervises the first-shift maintenance crew at a large manufacturing plant. The company is in a city that has recently undertaken a campaign to encourage major employers to hire the hard-core unemployed. About 50 people from the ghetto area have joined the company.

One of these new employees has come into Cisco's department. He is Roy Grant, a black man with a wife and four children; according to his personnel forms, this is his first regular work in several years. Until now, he's had odd repair jobs here and there, but nothing with any promise of permanence. His wife, however, has worked steadily.

David talked with Grant before he was hired and felt confident that he had the skills needed to work in his department. He seemed anxious and uneasy, but Cisco figured that was only to be expected under the circumstances. Beneath Grant's nervousness, Cisco could detect a strong desire to make good.

Because the crew is fairly large, Cisco handles most of the scheduling and paper work and lets his assistant, George Klenk, work directly with the employees. Klenk didn't seem too keen on the idea of the company bringing in a group of hard-core unemployed, and few of the workers showed much enthusiasm either. Cisco explained the project to Klenk ahead of time, stressing that it would be up to everyone—himself, Klenk, and the whole crew—to make a success of it. This is a program that top management has undertaken voluntarily, and it'll be watched closely. Cisco didn't stress the fact that normal hiring standards would not apply to the project, but it was common knowledge anyway. It was fairly obvious that Klenk wasn't enthusiastic about the idea, but David hoped that he would come to accept Grant as just another worker.

After Grant came to the department, Cisco introduced him to Klenk and recommended that he be put on carpentry jobs, as Grant had said those were what he did best. From time to time after that, Cisco asked Klenk how he was coming along, and Klenk said, a bit grudgingly, that Grant seemed to be okay.

It's now three weeks since Grant started working, and Cisco was thinking a little while ago how satisfied he felt at the way his hiring Grant seemed to be working out. As if that were a bad omen, Klenk burst into the office just then, obviously steaming over something.

"This stuff about hiring the hard-core might sound great to people who don't have to work with them," he exploded, "but I just want to know if I have to take whatever they hand out!"

"Now, hold on, George. Just what are you talking about?"

"That new guy, Grant. He's been real touchy all week, and this morning when I corrected him for something, he blew up. If I have to use kid gloves on him, I don't want him! This is a shop, not a nursery!"

"Did you correct him any differently from the way you correct the others?"

"Heck, no! I just made a routine check of the work he was doing and pointed out something he'd overlooked. It was no big thing, but he blew his stack. Look, I treat him the same as anyone else. Maybe I didn't think so much of the idea of bringing all these inexperienced people in, but that's beside the point now. I've got one of them, and I don't want problems with him any more than from the others."

"Okay, George. Why don't you cool down and ask Grant to come by here so I can talk with him."

A few minutes later, Grant was in Cisco's office. He looked apprehensive yet defiant. Cisco motioned for him to sit down, and began by asking how he liked his work so far. Still cautious, Grant said he liked it just fine.

"Klenk says you're doing a good job," Cisco added. "But I understand you and he have had a few words. Is something or somebody giving you a hard time?"

Grant hesitated, then said, "Not so much in the open. But I know how they feel about me being here. For a while I thought things were working out real fine. Then, last Friday, I went to my locker after coffee break to put my Thermos away and I heard two or three guys on the other side of the partition. They were talking about the hiring program, bringing in people like me. One guy said his nephew tried to get a job here and was turned down, that they told him nothing was open. He said he guessed you have to be black or a dumb dropout to get work these days. Somebody else said we were nothing but lazy bums, why didn't we go back where we came from and let people have the jobs who deserved them.

"Well," Grant continued, getting more heated, "I'm not as dumb as they think! I was working the best I could before now—a job here, a job there, whatever I could get. And my wife was working steady all the time. How do you think that feels—my wife keeping a job and I couldn't? I know they don't want me here, and I know they're watching me every minute, looking for mistakes to show up to get me tossed out. I've been thinking about it all week, and when Klenk said something about the job I was doing, I thought he was in on it, too, and I blew up. This is the first real job I've ever had, and I'm not letting anybody take it away from me!"

"I think you're overreacting to this," Cisco said. "After all, it is Klenk's job to check the work and if something isn't right to point it out."

"I know that," said Grant, "but it was the way he did it. He seemed glad he found an oversight. Another thing, how come he calls everyone else by name—but always calls me 'boy'?"

It's obvious by now that the tension has reached an explosive point as far as Grant is concerned. David didn't doubt for a minute what Grant says he overheard; he knew the other workers well enough to know that many of them would feel just that way about it.

Cisco wondered what he should do now. Grant promises to be a good worker; but with this atmosphere, it's likely that a fight will break out which could lead to Grant's discharge. That is, unless Cisco can think of a solution.

1. Why do the other workers react to Grant as they do?
2. Can Cisco change the attitudes of the crew by talking with them?
3. Is Grant overreacting to the situation? How would you feel if you were in his place?
4. Recommend a course of action to Cisco.

ONE ROTTEN APPLE

"The trouble is they're just kids," thought Bill Massingale, the second-shift foreman, as he headed toward the shouting and laughter coming from the Section 20 electrical cable test area. "And it's that wise guy Harvey Harrington who's taking them down the path."

The sounds grew louder as Massingale hurried up the aisle toward the test pens. Just as he rounded the corner of the safety fence, Randy Deckert and Diane Hanley, the two youngest employees on the shift, came whizzing past, one pushing the other in a dump cart. Heading toward the wall, the cart and its occupant sped right past the foreman, missing him by inches.

Massingale released his breath slowly; a bit closer and he would have had a broken leg. "Deckert, Hanley," he said with as much control in his voice as he could muster. "Put that cart back and get to work. You're wasting time and you could have hurt someone pretty badly with that thing. Who put you up to this foolishness?"

Massingale didn't need to ask that question; he could hear the sound of barely muffled laughter as he slowly turned to look down the aisle of the test area.

There at the end he could see Harvey Harrington busily sweeping up cable scrap. He knew, although he couldn't prove it, that Harrington had started the horseplay.

That was the real problem. These were good workers, but Harrington just seemed to be turning them bad—fast.

The whole crew had been warned before about their fooling around, but Massingale didn't want to fire all of them, nor could he without causing a lot of headaches. Good workers were scarce. Nevertheless, he had to do something before Harrington, who seemed to be their natural leader, completely corrupted the rest of them. But what?

Then he had an idea. Give him some responsibility. It might just work.

The next night he called Harrington aside. "I'm going to make a deal with you," Massingale began. "Even though I know you've been at the root of all the goofing off around here lately, I'm—"

"That's not true, and you can't prove it," Harrington interrupted as he played with his cigarette lighter.

"Never mind that," replied Massingale, trying to keep his cool. "Let's just say from now on bygones are bygones. Anyway, I think you have leadership potential, and that's why I'm appointing you temporary shift leader for this crew."

"You're kidding," Harrington said, smiling incredulously.

"No, I'm dead serious. But I warn you, Harvey, I don't want any more horseplay.

You'll be responsible for the performance of the crew. I won't accept any alibis. What do you say?"

"Suits me." Harrington thought for a moment. "But wait a minute." Harrington rubbed his fingers and thumb together and looked at his foreman inquisitively. "There's a little extra bread, isn't there?"

"A fifty-cents-an-hour increase," said Massingale a little abruptly.

"Well, that sure ain't much, but I'll take anything I can get. When do I start?"

"As of right now the crew's your responsibility," said the foreman and turned on his heel and walked away.

For the next several nights Department 20 functioned like a carefully run machine, the crew buckling down to the job of packing and moving the drums of cable. Bill Massingale began to think his gamble was paying off.

But one evening, about a week after he had appointed Harrington shift leader, the foreman suddenly became aware that the test area was too quiet.

"Matter of fact, I haven't heard a sound from that crew for the past three hours," he muttered to himself.

Sure enough, there was no one in sight as he surveyed the row after row of unwrapped drums. A forklift stood in the center of the aisle, its motor turned off.

At that moment he caught a glimpse of cigarette smoke curling up from behind a large cable drum in test pen nine. Massingale walked quietly over to the pen, squeezed between two cable drums, and peered along the gap between the row and the wall.

There, protected from prying eyes, sat Harvey Harrington and the rest of the crew deeply absorbed in a poker game.

Massingale stood looking at them for a moment, unnoticed until Harrington happened to glance up. Not taking his eyes off the foreman, he slowly laid down his cigarette and began casually to shuffle the deck of cards. The rest of the crew followed his gaze, but then looked down at the floor guiltily.

GUIDES FOR ANALYSIS

1. Was Massingale's idea of giving Harvey responsibility a good idea?
2. Did Harvey and the crew know what his new responsbilities were?
3. What do you think of Massingale's "let's make a deal" approach?
4. Is there any hope left for Harrington?
5. If you were Massingale, what action would you take?

THE SUBSTITUTE SUPPLY CLERK

It was one of those days in the supply department at the Crescent Chemical Company. Everyone in the plant and office seemed to have requisitions that should have been filled the day before. The four order clerks were busily trying to fill the requisitions that kept coming in one on top of the other.

Supervisor Jackie French appreciated the way her people were working, but she realized that some more help would make it easier on them. Her eyes caught young Lynda Donnell, who checked invoices and supplies as they came from the vendors. That Monday, Lynda had her usual work load and was working at her normal pace while the other people were really pushing it.

Noticing that the supply clerks were falling further behind, French went over to Lynda and said: "Lynda, I need you to give the supply clerks a hand. Go over there, and Jim will show you what you have to do." Half to herself French mumbled as she started to turn away, "Why does everybody have to have everything today?"

"I have some more of my own work to finish," Lynda said.

"I said I needed you over there now," French retorted, rather frustrated at Lynda's stubbornness. "We've got to keep this place running and that work has to be done immediately."

"But what about these supplies I have to check in?"

"Just leave them there. Anyone can handle that job. You can do it later when you get a chance. Filling these requisitions is more important," French almost yelled at her.

Lynda somewhat reluctantly walked over to Jim Atkins, the supply clerk. "What do you want me to do?" she asked sullenly.

Jim quickly pulled out a bunch of requisitions and showed Lynda how to fill them in. Lynda worked the rest of the day without saying another word—not to French, not to any of the other employees. Even at lunch time, she ate by herself in the company cafeteria. And at the end of the day, she walked out of the office without her usual cheery "Good night." Everyone was so busy they hardly noticed.

The next day Lynda was back checking incoming supplies and invoices. The department was back to normal, but Lynda's mood hadn't changed. She grumped only the most perfunctory greeting to her co-workers and didn't even nod in French's direction. She was usually very accurate, but this day Jim found three miscounts when she was filling requisitions.

As the week went on, everyone in the department knew that something was bugging Lynda. Wednesday, Jackie French stopped Lynda. "Lynda, you're way behind. Just look at this mess around here." Lynda just shrugged her shoulders and walked off. French was really puzzled. What could be causing this, she wondered. Something was surely wrong, because Lynda wasn't her usual self. Lynda had been a friendly, outgoing person, and always seemed to pride herself on doing a good job. All this week, supplies and invoices were stacked around her. She'd done only about half her work, and you couldn't get a decent word out of her. One of her co-workers was convinced that Lynda was having a hard time at home. Another felt that she must be having trouble in the night-school classes she was attending. But no one was sure.

On Friday, Lynda went to the Office Manager, Pete Mason, and asked to be reassigned to another job, preferably as a supply clerk.

"I thought you were happy with the work you were doing, Lynda. We've been very proud of the job you've been doing, and we really don't need another permanent supply clerk, either. What made you decide to ask for a change?"

1. What was Lynda's attitude toward her job before becoming a substitute supply clerk?
2. What was Lynda's attitude toward her job after serving as a supply clerk?
3. What possible reasons could exist to make her attitude change?
4. Did Jackie French contribute to the change? Did she do anything to hurt Lynda's morale?
5. Recommend a course of action to Pete Mason.
6. Be prepared to role-play Lynda's and Mason's following conversation.

BRIGHT YOUNG MAN GOES "PFFFT"

Betty Lawson had been very glad—and felt very lucky—to welcome young Jerry Robinson to her division. Betty, accounting division manager for Stephens', a local chain of department stores in a large southwestern city, had long needed another ambitious young employee in her division.

Robinson, a 22-year-old veteran, had just completed two years of college. Recently married, he had decided that his new responsibilities required him to work full time and continue his education at night. An accounting major with some part-time work experience, Robinson represented "a real find," Lawson thought.

Lawson introduced Robinson to Jim Positan, head of the section to which Robinson had been assigned. "Jim, here's that young man we've been looking for. After you work with him a while, I know he's going to take a real load off your shoulders. By the way, take care of him, will you? His sister is my friend Joan, the buyer for the women's department in the downtown store."

Positan was glad to have some help, but Joan Robinson's brother! He knew that Betty Lawson and Joan Robinson had worked together for about five years and had become close friends. "Well, guess I have to tread lightly with this one," thought Positan.

A couple of months later, Jim Positan was ready to agree with Betty Lawson's introductory remarks. Jerry had proven himself to be a hard-working, ambitious young man. Seemingly anxious to learn, he sometimes stayed after hours studying procedures in the department.

Lawson, during the early months of Robinson's employment, had left Jerry and Jim pretty much alone. About six months after Jerry came to work, though, Lawson kept noticing Jerry "coming and going" a great deal. It seemed like every time she looked up, Jerry was walking down the hall, out the door, going somewhere. Betty decided to ask Jim about it.

The next week, though, because of a store-wide clearance sale, everything in the division was rather chaotic. She was so busy, she just forgot to speak to Positan about Jerry.

155

Immediately after that, Lawson went to the downtown store for a company management meeting and ran into Joan Robinson.

"Say, Betty, how's my little brother doing? Some kid, huh? He's a smart one—always making the dean's list at school, right in the middle of the student government at college."

Betty felt almost trapped; she hadn't talked to Positan so she hadn't been able to check on Jerry—and all that running around—"You're right, Joan, with all that 'smart' he really ought to go places."

"Well," replied Joan, "I really hated to see him have to quit going to school full time, but after he got married he just couldn't keep up all his activities and make a living, too."

Betty returned to the store and immediately contacted Jim Positan. "Jim, how's Jerry doing? I've been meaning to talk with you about him, but you know how it gets around here."

Remembering Betty's friendship with Joan Robinson, Jim decided that he should be a little tactful. "Jerry's ability is tops, he catches on fast, and his first few months he really jumped into it. Lately, though, I don't know. Maybe he's just settling down into a routine or something, but a lot of his 'fire' seems to be fading."

"Exactly what have you had him doing?" interrupted Lawson.

"Mainly," responded Positan, "he works on the accounts receivable, but he actually does several clerical jobs that I've assigned him. Sometimes lately, he gets a little behind with some of his work."

"Did he have any trouble learning the new assignments?"

"Well, no, not really; he seems to be a little careless about some of it now, though. I didn't want to say anything, but I had to talk to him about a few mistakes he made—nothing serious, understand."

"Jim, why don't you send Jerry down here and let me talk to him. Maybe he'll open up and talk. I'll tell him I saw Joan downtown. That might make him feel a little easier."

"Great," replied Jim, "I don't know what to do with him. I'll go back and send him down." Positan was glad to let Lawson talk to him—after all, she was his friend, maybe she could straighten him out.

Within five minutes, Jerry strolled through Lawson's door. "Well, Betty, I hear you reported to Joan," he began.

Lawson, rather surprised at that as a beginning, replied slowly, "Yeah, I ran into her at a meeting downtown. She seems to be pretty proud of you. Well, tell me, Jerry, how are you doing here with us?"

"Oh, I don't know. It seems easy enough, not really hard at all. That Positan, though—just make one little mistake and you hear about it. But I guess he told you about that."

"Actually, Jerry, Jim told me a few months ago that you were getting right after it. Did something happen?"

"He thought I was doing okay?" questioned Jerry. "I never heard a 'peep' out of him; he just sorta threw some work at me and didn't say a thing till I messed up a few times. Considering all the help he gave me, I thought I did pretty well."

Lawson thought she might ease away from an obviously touchy situation, "How about the work—what you're doing—do you like it and the department?"

"Oh, sure, it's okay, I guess. Nothing exciting especially. I wouldn't mind getting a promotion though, something a little more challenging. And the extra money would help. I'd really like to move up before long. With Joan doing so good with the company and everything. . . . " he trailed off.

"Okay, Jerry, I'll talk with Positan. Maybe we can figure out something. We'll get back together."

After Jerry left the office, Betty decided that she and Positan would have another talk tomorrow. After all, Jerry did have the ability. Maybe together they could figure out what was going wrong.

GUIDES FOR ANALYSIS

1. What do you think Jerry Robinson wants from his job?
2. What could Jim Positan have done to keep Jerry from "losing fire"?
3. Has Betty Lawson played a role in forming Jerry's attitude?
4. Recommend a course of action that might resolve the situation.

WHAT, ME WORRY?*

When he arrived home Friday evening, Max Gerson immediately took a tranquilizer tablet. It was an hour later before he was relaxed enough to tell his wife of the latest incident involving Terry Mellon, the young new supervisor of the Information Services and Data Processing Unit.

Gerson is now Director of Administration after 23 years with Amercade Products. Starting as a production stockroom clerk right out of high school, he performed all tasks given him with efficiency and filled a dozen or so positions over the years. Gerson had known and worked for just about every type of supervisor: dictators, egomaniacs, perfectionists, slackers, politicians and softies—the good guys and the bad—and he had learned a little from all.

Above all, Max Gerson had learned that you eventually get to the top by hard work; that even a college diploma (which he earned after seven years of night school) couldn't guarantee success. Hard work also meant playing ball with the Boss—no matter what!

Gerson felt that he had fewer personnel problems than most managers, but Mellon was something else again. . . .

*Reprinted with permission from the August, 1971, issue of *Training in Business and Industry* ©MCMLXXI Gellert Publishing Corp., and the author, Robert D. Joyce.

As his wife, Edith, listened attentively, Max recalled the six weeks since Mellon was hired.

"He certainly made a good impression during the employment interview. He was neatly dressed, aggressive but not overbearing, and relaxed as if he already had the job. He obviously knew his business, too—a B.S. and an M.S. in Information Theory, plus solid progressive positions in two prior companies. I felt he would be an outstanding choice as our Supervisor of Information Services although he had no prior supervisory experience.

"About two weeks after he was hired he began to wear sport shirts and came to work several times in sandals with no socks. Then there was the beard! We had a long talk at that point about the interests of the company, his role as a supervisor, and his personal rights. He kept the beard, but I got him to wear socks.

"Later, when Mellon became involved in a complex simulation project, he started working all hours of the night and came in at one or two o'clock the next afternoon. He also had some of his people doing the same thing and there were times when their work area was practically deserted. I was about to read the riot act to him when he announced that his group had completed the simulation programming except for documentation! Under Ben Otter, the manager prior to Mellon, the group had fooled with that same problem for months and appeared nowhere near a solution."

"I knew that," Edith responded. "What happend this week?"

"Well," sighed Gerson, "it started on Monday. I was reviewing some classified material with Terry when he went off on a tangent about the foolishness of security. He rambled on about how we keep documents on government projects classified secret—you know, key drawings, specifications, and so forth—only to find the same information later on page 10 of an aviation magazine or a perfect small-scale replica plastic model kit of the thing sold to kids.

"He had a point and I agreed that some of our security practices were poor. I thought the whole matter was over and done with, but Tuesday I heard him joking in the cafeteria about how he had gotten into the facility that morning by quickly flashing a pack of cigarettes to the guard instead of his badge! I told him that he was out of line and that this would have to stop immediately. He apologized but appeared surprised that I didn't see anything funny in the incident."

Gerson continued. "Thursday the whole area was giggling over another Mellon antic. He evidently clipped a picture of that comic-book character Alfred E. Neumann—you know, that "What, Me Worry?" boy with the moronic face—and pasted it over his own picture on his badge. Apparently he wore it that way all day before anyone noticed. I was ready to have it out with him once and for all, but by the time I saw him the picture was gone.

"This morning about 8:15 I received a call from the guard at the main entrance. He said that Mellon didn't have his badge when he arrived and refused to accept a 'temporary.' The guard told him that no one entered that plant without a badge and he had his choice of a temporary badge or going home. Then he said that Mellon turned abruptly and walked off. Terry Mellon never showed up today at all and wasn't home when we called.

"Edith, this guy borders on genius but he's a *kook!* I don't know what to do with him."

"You want my opinion?" asked Edith.

"Yes, I do."

"Fire him! You've got enough other problems. If you continue to be soft, he'll make you the laughing stock of the company."

GUIDES FOR ANALYSIS

1. How would you handle this situation?
2. Could the problem have been prevented? How?
3. Would you answer this differently if:
   a. Mellon were a programmer and not a supervisor? Explain.
   b. Government security were not involved? Explain.
   c. Mellon were not so talented? Explain.
4. What is the attitude of your organization relative to unusual dress or work habits?
5. Can restrictive organizational policies limit individual creativity? Explain.

HORTON'S DEPARTMENT STORE

Horton's, a local full-line department store, is one of a chain of ten stores located mostly in medium-sized cities throughout the Midwest. In the three years that Jim Owens had been the store manager, the store's business had just about doubled, as had the population in the area that the store served. The store had 100 regular employees and usually added another 30 temporary workers for holiday help.

Jim Owens was known among his managerial staff as an efficient person, although he left most of the day-to-day operations to his division managers. He wasn't one to fritter time away on anything that wouldn't contribute to the growth of the business and spent a great deal of effort in doing public-relations work in the community. He served, for instance, as president of the local Kiwanis Club. Although he presented a rather cold image to most of the employees, most of the "old-timers" felt a certain respect for him.

The staff of the store included an accounting department (three employees), three secretaries, a personnel manager, and the two division managers, Charles Stout in hard lines and Judy Laird in soft lines.

Jim periodically reviewed all phases of his operation. Right now, he was looking over a review of the labor turnover figures that the personnel manager, Carolyn Lyons, had given him. Part of the labor picture was fairly stable: Lyons had been with the store for four years, Stout and Laird had been there three years. The accounting department and secretarial pool suffered from a high turnover rate; in fact, there had been 10 different people in the three secretarial positions in three years. Accounting department employees seemed to last about six months.

What really bothered Owens, though, was the turnover in salespeople. To maintain an employment level of 70 regular salespeople, they had hired 165 people during the past year. Part-time employees seemed to last about three months. Of the 30 temporary helpers employed, only five had ever returned for another holiday season.

Extremely disturbed over these high turnover figures, Jim decided to call a meeting of the division managers, department managers, and the entire office staff to see if they could present any ideas for this costly situation. He set the meeting for early the next morning.

Jim greeted the group the next morning and proceeded to lay his cards on the table. He wanted to give them the facts and find out the true story behind the picture. Having presented the labor turnover situation, he continued:

"I just don't understand what's happening and perhaps you can tell me. Our salary scale is 50 cents an hour higher than the other retailers in town, and we've tried to take care of our employees. Last year we set up the new employees' lounge—even put in a television set and vending machines so they could relax on their break—and started the new vacation program after a year's service. So what is it?"

There was silence around the table in Owens' office. Finally, Stout spoke, at first hesitantly.

"Good, hard-working people just don't want to work for what we can pay them," he commented. "Why, I have to keep a constant watch on every one of mine, or they'd just let customers wander off without even trying to sell anything." He seemed to warm to the subject and was about to continue. Therese Rich, Ladies Accessories department manager, interrupted.

"You're right, Charles. Just last week I had to terminate one of my people. When she made her fourth error on the cash register in a week—well, that's just too many. They're so bad they can't even learn a simple thing like ringing up sales!"

Charles Stout broke back in, "Most of them don't care if they do what they're supposed to do or not, and when you try to tell them where they're wrong, they just quit."

Jim Owens, not believing that the employees were all incompetent people, pondered, "Well, what about the suggestion system we started last year? Did we get any ideas from that about what we could do to improve the situation?"

"No, not really," interjected Judy Laird, soft-lines manager. "I heard a lot of them laughing about it, though. I told them they would get a reward for a good suggestion, but very few were submitted."

Carolyn Lyons, personnel manager, had kept quiet. But now she added, "You just don't get good applicants any more. It seems that we used to have about five applications for every job, but not now. And what you can get just want to show up, and that's all! Having to put up with part-timers is a real pain, too. Most of them don't want to work in retailing as a career. They're just here to make some spare money. Just try telling some of them what to do, and they're gone in a flash."

Karen Oxford, one of the secretaries, spoke up. "You all sound alike—and just like her," nodding at Lyons. "She isn't even my boss, but no matter what the secretaries do, it isn't right. She's always telling us that she does something another way."

Lyons, obviously disturbed, jumped up. "Somebody has to tell her how to get things done around here. If it weren't for me, none of them would ever do anything right."

Jim Owens, seeing the heated atmosphere between the two women, decided that he'd better break it up at once. Still, he was concerned; he wasn't sure that he had heard the real story. He interrupted.

"Let's close this meeting now. But I want you to be thinking about the situation; surely there must be some answers to this turnover problem. After all, ours, according to industry figures, is way out of line. I'm going to do some investigating and thinking of my own. Ask one member from each department to come to a meeting at ten in the morning, and I'll see what I can learn from them. You people (indicating the entire group present) come up with some ideas before we meet again next week."

At ten the next morning, the departmental representatives slowly gathered in Mr. Owens' office. There was a steady buzz of wondering what the meeting was all about.

Jim Owens greeted the group cordially, attempting to put them at ease. "I know you are all curious about why you're here. We have a real problem that simply must be solved. I've talked with the managers and asked them for their ideas. Now perhaps you can help too," Glancing around he noticed several wary looks and continued.

"Our labor turnover rate is extremely high; our employees seem to leave just about the time they're broken in. It's bound to be affecting sales and that means it affects you. Can you help me find out why so many people are leaving?"

Blank, hesitant faces stared at each other. They certainly hadn't expected this.

Finally, Harold Samuels from the TV department commented. "Well, we lost one man last week. He was a pretty fair salesman—he'd had some sales training before he came here. But he and Mr. Stout just didn't see eye-to-eye on some things. He just couldn't take any more and quit."

Lee Davis of the men's department looked up. "Mr. Owens—you really want to know why we quit? The money isn't much, but mainly, oh, I don't know, just the way some people act around here. . . . " he trailed off.

Suddenly, Marty Simmons of the girls' department blurted: "It's the managers!" She stopped, as though backing off. Slowly, she began again, "Sometimes they're a little rough on you, you know, jumping on you for little mistakes, giving orders. . . . "

Mr. Owens, feeling uncomfortable, slowly came to his feet.

"I wonder if this attacking of supervisors is really getting us anywhere. We're all in this together and we have our problems. You have a job to do, maybe everything your managers do isn't right; but perhaps if you did what you're supposed to do, they wouldn't jump on you. I'm about to think this meeting was a mistake. Even so, if any one of you have any good, constructive ideas about why people quit, I'd appreciate your coming by and telling me."

Jim Owens dismissed the meeting in a state of confusion. The managers complained that the salespeople wouldn't work; but something was definitely wrong. Just what did these employees mean about the managers? He determined that he would have to get some help in finding out the real problems that existed.

The next day, six salespeople gave notice of quitting. One of the six was Marty Simmons, who had said a few things at the meeting. This time she accepted his invitation to let him know how she felt. She left the following note for Mr. Owens:

> Mr. Owens, you wanted to know why we quit. Since I'm leaving anyway, I guess I can tell you without it hurting anything—it's already ruined anyway. Being dirt under anybody's feet is no fun, being yelled at is embarrassing. Everybody expects you to know how to do everything—automatically! And when you don't—watch out. Probably a lot of others have left for the same reasons.
>
> Marty Simmons

Jim Owens scanned the note and pondered all the things it could mean. Sadly he shook his head and wondered, "What now?"

GUIDES FOR ANALYSIS

1. What attitudes are displayed by the two groups toward each other?
2. Can you draw any conclusions about the seeming lack of a training program?
3. Have the managers, including Owens, contributed to the problem?
4. What appears to be the philosophy of management displayed in the store?
5. Recommend a course of action to Jim Owens.

WHAT DOES IT TAKE?

Grady Hull carefully parked his new Corvette in the company lot and walked across the road. His work clothes were clean, his lunch pail full. In three years, he'd come a long way from the Kentucky hollow he'd lived in until he was twenty-four.

The stainless-steel mill here in northern Indiana was the greatest thing that had ever happened to Grady. He was making more than twice as much money as he'd ever made, the work was twice as easy, and everyone acknowledged that Grady ran the angle-straightener better than anyone else and put out far more production to boot.

The straightening machine had long been a headache to Claude Miller, supervisor of the processing department. For years he had mentally groaned whenever he saw a large order for angles on his schedule. The machine was old, its adjustments were wrong and there was no tried-and-true way to run it. Yet, angles were a minor part of over-all production—not important enough to justify the purchase of an up-to-date straightening machine, according to the plant manager.

But Claude's headache had eased considerably when Grady Hull arrived. This lean mountaineer knew instinctively, it seemed, exactly how to make that machine behave. The operators on the other two shifts continued to have their difficulties, though, and whenever possible Miller moved them to other machines in the department, giving Grady overtime. Of course, this brought some protests from the other employees—but not as many as if the other operators had been anywhere near as capable as Grady. There was no question, Grady was in a class by himself.

There hadn't been an assistant foreman's job open until recently. And that was when the trouble started. Grady had ambitions. He'd long since made sure Miller knew that he thought he deserved to be made assistant foreman and would like to be considered for it when an opening came. But Claude Miller, however much he respected Grady as a worker, simply didn't feel he was foreman material. If he'd had to put it into words, he'd merely have said, "He isn't the type." Of course, he'd have denied that it had anything to do with Grady's being a "hillbilly," although he would have admitted that the other workers didn't have much use for hillbillies in general or Grady in particular. Not that Grady minded. Loners never do.

So last week Miller had picked Ronnie Ball. Ball was a crane follower. As such, he'd had to keep track of all the orders on the floor, take a finished bundle of steel from a machine, put it where it was supposed to go next, and replace it with whatever other bundle the schedule called for.

But he'd never been a ball of fire. Many's the time both operators and foremen had to go scouting for him when they wanted something moved. Still, he made few mistakes. And he did have a pretty good understanding of what went on in the entire department. Besides, he was captain of the bowling team and had once run a gas station, factors that carried a lot of weight with management.

To Grady, however, Ronnie Ball was just a goof-off—someone who would go far out of his way to avoid a good day's work. In fact, he'd argued with Ronnie over many an unmoved bundle. Ronnie's getting the job came as that much more of a blow.

Last week, when he'd heard the news, he'd told Claude, "I can see that the way you get to be a foreman around here is by goofing off."

Claude gave this little thought until he began noticing Grady's production figures. Formerly, Grady had always turned out at least twice as much as anyone else on the job. But for the past week, his production rate had dropped to what would be normal for the other operators—in other words, not nearly enough. If it kept up, Claude estimated, his schedule would be in serious trouble soon!

Sure, he'd confronted Grady with the figures. "What about this, Grady?" he'd asked. "Haven't you been feeling well or something?"

"Been feeling fine, Claude," Grady had replied. "What makes you think I haven't?"

"Look how you've dropped off."

"I don't know what you mean, Claude, I'm doing just as good as the others, aren't I?"

It was true. Grady was doing as well as the other operators. That was just the trouble.

The supervisor sat down at his desk and tried to figure out what had gone wrong and, more important, what he might do to right it.

Had he, a production-minded supervisor, really considered Grady for the job? Or would he have favored Ronnie no matter what Grady's qualifications? Had he, Claude

Miller, done as much as he might have these last three years to help Grady make himsel more promotable? Ah, no sense crying over spilt milk. But he still had to find some way to get Grady back on the beam again.

GUIDES FOR ANALYSIS

1. From Grady's viewpoint, what should be the basis for promotion?
2. Why did Miller select Ronnie Ball for the job?
3. What did Miller really think of Grady?
4. Does the supervisor have a responsibility for developing his or her employees?
5. If you were Miller, what would you do now?

UP THE LADDER

"Fallon? Good kid, really good kid. I spotted him the first day he started as a genera helper over in Department 20. When I had an opening I asked the foreman to release him for a transfer. Haven't been sorry yet," said Art Eversole, trim and assembly departmen foreman, to Sid Hazleton, the casting department supervisor. "He's smart, you know?" Eversole winked and tapped his head. "And ambitious. Reminds me of myself fiftee years ago."

Hazleton smiled and relit his pipe. "Glad to hear it, Art. I noticed him working th other day, and he looks like he can handle that trim machine."

"He sure can. Took him about a day to reach production on it, and now he's my best employee. I'm telling you, Sid, that kid's on the ball. You know what he buttonhole me for after lunch? He wants to move up to an assembly machine! Really gave me a sale talk. After only three months on the trimmer, he's the fastest one in the department, an now he figures he's ready for the assembler."

"He's hungry," said Hazleton, puffing on his pipe.

"I know it, just like I was when I was his age. His wife's got a baby on the way, an he wants that 60-cents-an-hour increase. Well, he's earned the job. Matthews is transfer ring to nights next week, and Fallon can have his spot." Eversole sat there musing for a moment. "You know, if I just had one or two more kids like him, my department migh start setting some production records around this place."

"Art, you'd better enjoy it while you can. Up-and-comers happen along only onc in a while, and when they do, they don't usually stay in one department too long They're always ready to jump at the next spot up the ladder. And Fallon will do just that He wants to learn, and he needs the money, too."

"Look, with his speed he'll make out on that assembly machine like a bandit," sai Eversole, irritably. "He'll be making more money than most young people around here and he'll want to stay on the assembly machine for at least a couple of years, once he get the hang of it. If I'd had the chance to make that kind of dough when I was starting out you can bet I wouldn't have jumped around so much."

"Yeah, and you probably wouldn't be a foreman right now, either—and hoping to make assistant supervisor in a couple of years," replied Hazleton with a chuckle.

Almost six months went by, and Hazleton began to wonder if he hadn't been wrong. Young Fallon had seemed to settle down to the trim and assembly department for an extended stay. After the first couple of months learning the ins and outs of the assembler, he had, according to Eversole's glowing accounts, increased his productivity until he was number two operator in output. From what Hazleton could observe, Fallon appeared to be a team player in trim and assembly, getting along well with the other workers and his boss and enjoying his work. But then a few weeks later Hazleton found Fallon waiting for him near his office on his return from lunch. "Do something for you, Eddie?" "Hope so, Mr. Hazleton. Hear you got a slot open on one of your casting machines, and I'd like to try out for it."

"Yes, I do, Eddie," said Hazleton, stuffing his pipe into his shirt pocket, "but I thought you were doing real well on that assembler."

"I am. I'm making the highest rates in the department now," he said proudly. "But now I think I'm ready for a casting machine, and I'd sure like to get a crack at that 30 cents more an hour."

"It's okay by me, Eddie, but you better let me talk to your foreman first about a transfer. He'll probably be a little unhappy to see you go." Hazleton realized what an understatement that was when he went into Eversole's office a few minutes later and saw an angry man hunched over his desk.

"You already know what I came over here for, don't you, Art?"

" 'Course I do. The kid was over in your department, wasn't he? What else was he there for except to ask for that casting-machine job?"

"Well, I said I'd try to get him the transfer," said Hazleton, a little warily.

"You did, huh? Listen, friend, I can't spare him. He's the best operator I got, and he stays in this department. Now, if you don't mind leaving, I got some work to finish."

GUIDES FOR ANALYSIS

1. Why does Eversole want Fallon to remain in his department?
2. Does Fallon's achievement record say anything about his goals?
3. Eversole has gladly encouraged Fallon's progress within his department; does he have a responsibility to let him go on up in the company?
4. What would you do if you were Sid Hazleton? Remember, Eversole spent months training Fallon to be a productive member of his department.

ASSEMBLY TWO

Ellen Hagen is the supervisor of the assembly department of a medium-sized electronics company, Space-Age Industries. The company has been a fast mover in a rapidly growing industry. Until four months ago, all of the assembly work was done in a single department with about 55 employees. Then Space-Age developed a new product, something really different in the industry, that required a new assembly department.

To keep a balance of experienced employees in both departments, Hagen transferred 15 of her veteran, though average-producing, employees to the new department. All of them seemed happy to make the change—in fact, several others wanted to change, too. New employees were hired for both departments, 15 new employees for each.

The production standard for the old department—now called Assembly One—is 100 units an hour. The employees receive a 1 per cent hourly bonus for each unit they produce over this standard. Each employee in Assembly Two must perform two additional operations, and the work is slightly more complex. Methods engineering therefore set their production standard at 80 units with the same incentive bonus.

Hagen and Doug Turner, a member of the Training Department, trained the 30 new employees. Turner spent ten days in the new department, while Ellen divided her time between the new employees in Assembly One and helping to train in Assembly Two. Both were really amazed at the progress in Assembly Two. Training time to reach standard in Assembly One had usually run about five days, but Hagen had expected Assembly Two to take a month to reach that, since they had to do not only more operations but more complex ones, too. Assembly Two employees really caught on to their jobs.

Within 10 days they were producing up to standard; at the end of the first month, they were averaging 100 units per hour for a 20 per cent bonus.

It looked like everything was rolling along smoothly. Until yesterday. That was when Hagen heard the "buzz group" in Assembly One. As they returned from their afternoon break, Ellen heard Jill Hawthorne, one of the veteran assemblers, talking to Tom Crawford, one of the new employees in Assembly One.

"I average 110 units for a 10 per cent bonus, and that's just about right for Assembly One, as we are now called. But you know, Tom, those people in Assembly Two get a 20 per cent bonus for less work," complained Jill.

"That doesn't seem fair for them to turn out less and get paid more," agreed Tom. Some of the other workers chimed in their general agreement, too.

Ellen started to talk with them, to try to understand what was going on. But the telephone distracted her.

Ellen knew she should have been prepared. The next day, Jill, Tom, and five others stopped her on her way through the department. Jill led the discussion and repeated just about what Ellen heard the day before. Jill continued, however, "We think the standard rate for us ought to be reduced to 80 units or their standard in Assembly Two raised to 100. It's not right for us to get less for more work."

Not really knowing how to answer the argument (and realizing that the other employees really had made standard quickly), Ellen promised, "I'll check with Methods Engineering to make sure that they couldn't have made a mistake in setting the standards." The employees weren't too happy with that, but it seemed to pacify them.

Well, Ellen wondered, what else? Oh, yeah, those rumblings in the nonincentive workers—mainly in Quality Control. They aren't on incentive because their work requires analysis and problem solving, elements that can't be timed. Most of them were at the top of their salary range. Even though they earned more than the employees in Assembly Two, they felt the difference was too little.

Ellen returned to her office and called Larry Schmidt in Methods Engineering.

"Larry, recheck your standards for my new Assembly Two, will you? Those workers hit the standard mighty fast, and I'm about to have all kinds of trouble with my people in Assembly One."

Larry countered, "I have the figures here, Ellen. Those standards are correct. I was especially careful with that. In terms of the additional operations and their complexity, those workers in Two have a lot more to do than those in One. There must be something wrong in One, but it isn't the standards. They're right for both sections."

Hagen spent the next hours mentally reviewing Assembly One. She couldn't think of anything wrong there—till this gripe came up, anyway. There wasn't anything there to keep them from making just as much bonus as those in Assembly Two; the work is easy, there's nothing to delay them, she concluded.

Well, thought Ellen, there has to be an answer. She had to find it. She'd told Jill and Tom that she'd talk with them tomorrow. Maybe by then something would show up —or even they might give her some clues.

GUIDES FOR ANALYSIS

1. Why might employees have asked to change to the new department?
2. What factors may encourage higher production in Assembly Two?
3. Recommend a course of action for Ellen Hagen.
4. Be prepared to role-play Hagen's meeting with Jill and Tom the following day.

SIMMONS SIMULATOR CORPORATION

The Simmons Simulator Corporation was founded in 1942 by Lionel Simmons, an aeronautical engineer, to provide simulator panels for training naval pilots. Since its inception as a single-product war baby, Simmons has grown into a multimillion-dollar company with sales and rentals on more than 17 basic simulation systems. These systems range from small, relatively inexpensive devices used for testing depth perception and reflexes, to elaborate systems used in the aircraft, missile, and space industries. The large systems typically are rented at fees of more than several thousand dollars a month.

The Simmons company sought not only to build high-quality equipment but also to assure its productive use by developing an outstanding service organization. As the company expanded into more and larger systems, Simmons saw even greater importance in guaranteeing major customers immediate service and maintenance. Building a team of service people with an intimate knowledge of Simmons' equipment has proven to be a costly but invaluable step in the company's continuing growth and profit. Several of Simmons' customers have commented that, while other companies offered comparable equipment at lower cost, they have stuck with Simmons because of assurance of quick and competent maintenance.

To assure this service, Simmons has developed a highly trained, well-paid group of 60 to 70 "Service Engineers" who operate out of 16 district offices. As the major customers are closely clustered around ten of these offices, Simmons normally is able to put a Service Engineer in a customer's facility in less than two hours after notice of difficulty. Given the extremely complicated nature of the system, however, it may take as many as six hours to diagnose and remove the cause of a system's failure. Although such a situation is unusual, when it does occur, typically it is in a large, rented system. Thus, every hour spent on diagnosis is costing the company dollars of lost profit and, typically, is delaying important tasks in the customer's facility.

In an effort to increase the speed and accuracy of diagnostic work by the Service Engineers, George Nichols, director of service engineering, has worked with a large computer company on a "diagnostic assistance" program.

The reason for, and mechanics of, this program are given in the following memorandum from Nichols to the ten district managers reporting to him:

> To: District SE Managers
> From: G. W. Nichols
> Subject: Diagnostic Assistance Program
>
> As a result of the increasing difficulty in the maintenance and repair of our large rental systems, we have virtually completed plans for the installation of a diagnostic assistance program. Please arrange your schedules to make it possible for you to be in Houston on October 20 in my office for a two-day briefing. More detailed plans will be forwarded to you prior to the 20th, but it may be helpful to give you an overview of the program as it is now envisioned.
>
> With the introduction of the Series G simulator last year, our records indicate a 15 per cent increase in the average time required to isolate causes of systems failure. Moreover, with the Series F-A2 simulator now being used in the Neptune project in three locations, we have been experiencing increased problems in locating the causes of systems failure. Fortunately, with both systems, we have had a very low failure rate, but we cannot expect to hold our market without improving the speed and accuracy of diagnostic work. As you know, Sim-Test has been our strongest competitor in both of these markets and is bragging about its "larger and better-trained" field staff.
>
> I recognize the pressures our Service Engineers are under and do not want to appear critical of their work on these series. Rather, the diagnostic assistance program is designed to make their job a little easier. We have virtually completed a program for our home office computer which will allow for extremely rapid and accurate diagnostic assistance. We plan to connect your offices directly to the computer on January 1 of next year for data-processing purposes and will use the same input-output devices to handle diagnostic problems.
>
> In a nutshell, the system will allow your field people, when they encounter a system

failure which is not readily diagnosable, to call your office and provide symptom data which you will send through to the control computer in Houston. Based on tests of this system in several computer companies who use it to repair their own equipment, you should get a request for additional data or a diagnostic estimate within 15 seconds after sending in coded symptoms.

There are many bugs in the system that we will have to work out, and I will look forward to getting the benefit of your ideas on October 20.

One final point: until we have completed our review of the project, I would prefer that you do not discuss it with your people. After the recent incident in San Diego, we do not wish further trouble due to misunderstanding.

The San Diego incident referred to by Mr. Nichols caused quite a stir in the company. Although hourly workers in Simmons' plants are unionized, the Service Engineers are not. Three months ago, 9 of the 16 service engineers working in the San Diego branch office requested the right to hold a representation election to determine whether the Service Engineers wished to join an international electronics workers' union. The company's director of labor relations, Alex Michak, advised them of their rights, and after several days' discussions the matter was dropped by the engineers. Michak reported that it really had stemmed from a "misunderstanding about company policy on tuition refunds for technical courses." Michak explained:

> Tom Snow, who has been with the company for 17 years, is one of the top Service Engineers in the San Diego branch. For more than six months he has been trying to get permission to take a new course in electronics under the company's tuition-refund program. His district manager, Bart Dunn, had sat on the request because he didn't want Tom tied up in a course when he might be needed for emergency overtime because of problems with the FA-2 simulators. Besides, Bart told me that the only reason Tom wanted to take the course was so that he could qualify to be put on the new Series G simulator. Bart told me that he didn't really need Tom for Series G work since he had two new men who had just joined the company and who had the academic background to specialize on Series G maintenance.

When Snow learned that Dunn had not acted on his request, he and several others of the older Service Engineers in the district became quite upset about the way they "got pushed around" and sought the union election. Snow said:

> I've been with this company a long time, and I like the work because it's always a real challenge. You really have to know the equipment inside out to maintain and repair it. If something goes wrong, it's a real test to see whether you can figure it out and fix it. We know that the faster we do our work, the more our customers like us and the more revenue for our company. But for most of us the real challenge is knowing we figured it out. Well, by now I know the Series FA-2 simulator inside out and, while there's an occasional tough one to fix on the Neptune project, I can handle that equipment blindfolded. The challenge has gone, and I want to go over to the new Series G stuff and see whether I can handle it.

George Nichols calmed Snow and the others down by assuring them that there was no company policy against high-senority employees taking courses under the tuition-refund program. He pointed out, however, that the company found it much harder to shift people like Snow to the new systems because they were so good in their present specialties. "Besides," he pointed out, "the pay's the same regardless of what system they work on."

Tom Snow is presently enrolled in the technical course, which meets after working hours, and two other senior Service Engineers in San Diego have applied for the same course next term.

Nichols was quite relieved when things settled down because, as he put it, "Experienced people like Snow are scarce as hen's teeth. Sometimes they act more like prima-donnas than service people, but right now they're in the driver's seat."

GUIDES FOR ANALYSIS

1. To what extent will the new program conflict with the needs of the service engineers?
2. Discuss the possible informal group reaction of the service engineers to the "diagnostic assistance program."
3. How would you recommend that the new program be explained to the service engineers?
4. If you were asked to advise G. W. Nichols, what basic problems do you foresee in the implementation of the new program? Give your recommendations on how these problems should be avoided or resolved.

THE GREAT TICKET TRAGEDY

As usual, the regular Thursday afternoon meeting of the division and department managers of the Westgate branch of Mason's department stores was in progress. Clyde Lowery, from the downtown accounting department, was presenting some new procedures that would be implemented in three weeks.

Sarah Marvin, manager of the furniture department, impatiently drummed her fingers on the table as Lowery discussed the changes. Sarah, who had been "mentally griping," suddenly tuned in on what Lowery was saying:

> ". . . in addition to these new steps to get sales reports to you, your salespeople will begin making the tickets on sales items which are delivered from the warehouse differently. As you know, the warehouse has often charged your departments the regular rather than the sale price on delivery merchandise. To make sure that all the inventory and change records are kept straight, have your salespeople include the regular price, the sales price, and the difference on the tickets."

Sarah, greatly concerned since a large part of her furniture sales were warehouse items, interrupted.

"What? My people will have to do all that? Isn't the merchandise number and sales price enough? Can't you keep the warehouse straight on the other stuff? We shouldn't have to do all those calculations."

Lowery, slightly startled by the outburst, replied, "Yes, we could and do try to supply the warehouse with price information. This way, though, we can be sure that every charge against your department is correct. Now, some sales information and price changes are overlooked."

Sarah, still not satisfied, slumped back and muttered, "Looks like that's that. Just something else for us to do that they can't handle."

Rhonda Blake, store manager, continued the meeting amidst the stony stares of Sarah Marvin and the somewhat less than enthusiastic expressions of the Home Improvement manager, Joe Mattern, and the Major Appliance manager, Jeff Stubblefield. These three departments sold mostly warehouse items.

At the conclusion of the meeting, Sarah Marvin left hastily, thinking to herself, "Well, Lowery said to tell the salespeople now about the tickets. You bet I will. They won't like it, but it's just like always. Those guys figure they can change things around, make us do more work, and be real bigshots."

Mattern and Stubblefield likewise went to their departments to explain the new procedures. Both, however, before talking with their salespeople did some thinking. They recognized that Lowery had been right—there were mixups and this would probably help the problem. Not that they were overly enthusiastic about it; surely it meant some extra work. Both decided that the advantages were worth the trouble. After explaining the procedures, the employees in their departments generally accepted the idea.

When Sarah got to her department, though, it was a different story. Striding briskly into the department, she called loudly to the two salespeople present: "Nancy, Doug, come over here."

Reacting to Sarah's apparent upset mood, Doug inquired, "What's up, Sarah?"

Sarcastically, Sarah replied, "We just had our meeting; and Lowery, the chief accountant, just put the monkey on our backs. Starting in three weeks, you're going to have to make out the tickets for the warehouse differently. From then on, you have to put the regular price, the sales price, and the difference on the tickets. Just because the warehouse can't keep their prices straight, we have to figure all that. I don't see what they're up to—probably trying to see if we're pushing sale merchandise or something. Who knows what!"

Nancy ventured, "Just like those guys—think we don't have enough to do. If they did their jobs they wouldn't have to spend so much time checking on us."

"I don't like it any better than you do," replied Sarah, "but I just work here too...."

The grumbling continued later in the day when Sarah relayed the message to the other employees in the department. For the next few days, the new ticket procedure was the main topic of discussion in the department.

Three weeks passed, and almost everyone had just about forgotten about the situation. Sarah received notice that the new procedures were to go into effect. "Okay, gang, this is it," she told them that morning. "You remember the new warehouse tickets—start that mess today. Don't gripe to me. I can't help it."

Doug, Nancy, and the other employees shrugged their shoulders and walked off.

Two weeks passed. Whenever Sarah happened to write up a ticket, she grudgingly but silently followed the new procedure. She didn't mention it to the others.

Thursday afternoon came and the managers meeting convened. Rhonda Blake distributed the various reports to the managers, including the warehouse distribution sheet. Attached to Sarah's was a stack of tickets.

"What's all this on here?" questioned Marvin, pointing to the tickets.

"Well," replied Blake, "rather than give you an incorrect accounting of your warehouse sales costs, they sent copies of the tickets back."

" 'Incorrect' . . . 'costs' . . . what are you talking about?" sputtered Sarah.

"They weren't sure what may have been sale merchandise, because of all your department's tickets only yours have all the calculations on them. All the others are figured like regular price."

"What? That makes my profit ratio look bad! I told those people to figure the tickets the new way," retorted Marvin.

"Maybe they didn't get the message, Sarah," replied Blake. "If you want a complete accurate picture, you'll have to figure out the best way to get the information."

Sarah was stunned. She wondered, "Those dummies—why did they mess up all these tickets?"

Meeting over, Sarah left determined to give her people "a piece of her mind." "Make me look bad, will they?" she thought.

Bitter over the embarassment she had faced at the meeting, the extra work she faced, and her employees' failure to follow instructions, she rushed toward her department.

GUIDES FOR ANALYSIS

1. Why do you suppose the employees in Sarah's department failed to make out the tickets properly?
2. Did Sarah in any way contribute to the situation?
3. Did the attitudes of the other department managers toward the change influence the way they presented the new procedure to their employees?
4. Stop Sarah before she gets to her department. Recommend a course of action for her to follow.
5. Be prepared to role-play Sarah's meeting with her employees,
   a. without having heard your recommendations.
   b. with your recommendations.

THE GUILTY PARTY

"Five hundred and fifty today, Dad. How many did your people push out?" The speaker was Len Bagley, the young assistant foreman—one of two in the fractional motor department.

"Enough," Dan Ross replied without looking at Bagley. He was the other assistant foreman in the department. "And don't call me 'Dad,'" he added.

"Why not?" asked Bagley, grinning. "After all, you're plenty old enough to be my father—not that I need another father!"

"Don't think for a minute I'd want a wise-guy like you for a—oh, forget it."

"What's the matter, Dan?" asked Bagley, walking with the older man. "You don't look like you feel well."

"I'm just a little tired, that's all," said Ross.

"Could be the competition is getting to you, Dad," Bagley's voice returned to its former mocking tone.

"Listen," muttered Dan Ross in a savage undertone. "I don't know where you get this idea you and I are competing, but my advice is to cut it. My people put out a decent day's work, and that's all a decent foreman can expect of 'em—and Phil Blocker is pretty decent. Now, if you want to stay on your people's tails all the time just so you can make a hero out of yourself, that's your business. I'm not built that way."

"Okay, okay—don't get yourself shook," said Bagley. "Tell me one thing, though. If Phil is so damned decent, how come he set it up like this in the first place?"

"What are you talking about?"

"You know what I'm talking about. He didn't have to split the line up into two parts, right down the middle, so that we'd have almost the same equipment and manpower to work with."

"The way he's got it set up is his business," said Ross. "He's the foremen, isn't he? Besides, common sense would tell you that two of us splitting it down the middle is the only fair way."

"You think there's always going to be two of us? We're the only department that has this set-up. When Phil moves up to assistant super, there's gonna be one foreman—the guy that's got the best record. *Me.*"

"Baloney. Phil doesn't think like that. He's always told me that how you get along with your people is just as important as production."

"You just go on thinking that," said Bagley, taking off his shoes. "But some time, get Phil to show you the chart he keeps on both of us."

"I got other things to do besides stick my nose in where it doesn't belong," muttered Ross, uncomfortably.

Three days later, Len Bagley was in Phil Blocker's office. "Look, Phil, if anyone else besides Pete Case has spotted this I'd have never come to you. But you know what a bigmouth Pete is, and I thought you'd better hear it from me before he blabbed it all over the place."

"You're sure there couldn't be any mistake about this?" asked Blocker.

"I just wish there was, Phil. I saw Dan transferring those cases from the reject bin back to the on-line rack for two days running. Hell, you can probably spot him yourself if you keep an eye out after shift goes off tonight."

"I guess that's what I'll have to do," said Blocker, thoughtfully. "Dan's been with me for over fifteen years."

"I know how it must be Phil," said Bagley. "But I think he's been doing it because he's worried about keeping up with my unit production. This way, he wouldn't have that rework time on his record. I thought there was something funny about the way he was turning out way more than he used to."

"You're the last guy I thought would ever pull a stunt like this, Dan," said Blocker the next day.

"So am I," muttered Ross, his misery plainly showing on his face. "I don't suppose it would do any good to say it'll never happen again?"

"Maybe, if just you and me knew about it; but it's already gone all over the plant. I wouldn't be surprised if the Old Man has gotten wind of it."

Dan Ross sighed. "I guess I'm just out of luck. I should never have let that Bagley kid get to me with his talk of who was going to make foreman around here."

"What did he say?"

"Something about how you set it up so that whoever got the most stuff out the door would make foreman."

"Well, I did have something like that in mind," Blocker replied after some hesitation.

"I wish you'd told me about it, Phil. Then I might not have had to play catch-up all of a sudden."

Ross looked directly at Blocker. "Okay, I'm guilty," he said. "What happens next?"

GUIDES FOR ANALYSIS

1. Is high production over a short time indicative of good leadership?
2. Would you blame yourself in any way for the situation if you were Phil Blocker? If so, how would that affect the way you handled it?
3. What does happen next? What would be your course of action if you were Phil Blocker?
4. Be prepared to role-play the ensuing converstion at the end of the case when Dan Ross says, "What happens next?"

THE PRIMA DONNA

It was just a month ago that Bill Jordan, head of Research and Development for Quality Chemicals, had given Paula Elkins the good news that she was to become the supervisor of Quality Control the next week.

"Paula, you've only been with the company five months," Bill had told her, "but we feel that with the unusual flair you've shown for engineering you shouldn't have any trouble with the department. That's a pretty sharp group over there."

Paula and Bill reported to Quality Control the next Monday. After Bill introduced Paula as the new supervisor, Paula went into her new office. She felt that she really had a lot to learn; the former supervisor was already gone, but Paula reasoned that surely she'd be able to find out how the department really worked if she studied the records.

The employees in the department hadn't exactly welcomed her as she would have liked. She hadn't gotten to know them personally. Right now it seemed more important that she learn the operation of the department; she could get to the "personal bit" later. Anyway, the employees seemed to accept the fact that she was the new supervisor.

The past month had gone pretty well. Paula reflected as she sat in the office that she really would have to consider herself off to a good start, and she couldn't see any real problems ahead. She felt pretty secure in the job; studying the records and procedures had really helped. Then, too, Bill had been right about the crew—they were a pretty good bunch who seemed to be able to carry the ball without too much from her. Even though she had stayed in her office most of the time since she'd been there, she had a pretty good feel for their capabilities from the test reports.

Suddenly, the phone rang. It was Bill Jordan.

"The testing section will be running a special series on load capabilities starting Monday," Bill told her. "They need someone from your group to help keep an eye on it. It'll be a temporary assignment, probably no more than two or three weeks. But they need someone with a lot on the ball. I hate to say it, but what we need is the best you've got."

Paula hesitated a moment. "Then I guess that would be Gene Hock. I hate to lose him right now, but he seems to do a good job and be on the ball."

"Good, that's whom I had in mind, too. It's a pretty important series, and they need someone who can think," replied Jordan. "Have him report to Testing on Monday."

Paula hung up the phone, glanced at the clock and noted that it was late—right at quitting time in fact. Well, she'd better go to see Hock. Here it was Friday—that wasn't much warning.

"Hi, Gene," Paula said as she approached Hock's station. "Got a moment?" Hock put down the part he was inspecting and said cautiously: "Sure, what is it?"

Paula began, "Jordan just called me. They need someone in Testing starting Monday. They're going to be doing some special series for about three weeks. They need someone from our department, so I told them I'd send you. Bill said they'd give you all the details when you report first thing Monday."

Gene turned slowly and began, "Just some more bother, huh? You told them you'd send me?"

Slightly puzzled by Gene's seeming reluctance, Paula replied, "Yeah, just go over there Monday like I said."

Hock stared, glared actually, then very loudly said, "Why pick on me to go over there? Aren't I doing okay here?"

Paula started, really startled at the reaction, "Of course, you're doing okay here, but they needed. . . . "

Gene interrupted, "I probably know more about this job than you ever will. But as soon as somebody says they need an extra body, who gets sent? Hock! Yeah, I know, as far as you're concerned, I'm dispensable. All you need is your little stack of reports. We just do the work."

By now there was quite an attentive audience. The other inspectors had stopped their work to listen.

Paula, struck silent by the outburst, thought, "He looks like he's got a lot more to say; what brought this on? I'd better do something fast!"

GUIDES FOR ANALYSIS

1. What does Gene Hock feel that Paula Elkins is saying to him?
2. Why has Hock misinterpreted Elkins' feelings about him?
3. What can Elkins do now to straighten out the situation?
4. Be prepared to role-play the rest of the conversation between Hock and Elkins.

SOUTHWESTERN FABRICATORS

Southwestern Fabricators, a division of a large national concern, employed about 200 people—most of them skilled workers. The nonunion company had a history of fairly good employee relations. In fact, Bob Portwood, production supervisor, was proud of his company's low turnover. Of course, the company paid good wages and had a good fringe-benefit package for all employees.

However, Bob was slightly puzzled right now. Last week, production in the machine shop had been very erratic—up one day, down the next—and there just wasn't any logical explanation for it. This week, it was even worse. Something was going on, he knew, because at least three times during the week he'd noticed clusters of his people engaged in rather heated discussions. He hadn't been able to learn what they were talking about because the groups always broke up whenever he appeared. Once he had inquired if they needed him to work out something, but they had just sort of mumbled and gone back to work.

Portwood did notice that most of these groups had one thing in common, however, and that was Larry Walker, a veteran lathe operator. Walker had always been a satisfactory performer, above average in many respects, but whenever there was a controversy in the department, it was a good bet that he'd be involved in some way. Walker had been with the company for about ten years and seemed to know everyone who worked there. Many of the younger workers in the department seemed to look up to him and regarded him as "someone in the know."

On Friday, Portwood once more encountered a group of workers. This time, though, he heard a little of what was being said before they rapidly broke up; they were talking about a layoff! Portwood decided to take Walker aside and try to get to the bottom of these meetings and the "layoff talk."

"Larry," he asked, "what do you know about this talk about a layoff?"

Walker looked at him for a moment and then smiled. "Finally going to give us the news, eh? Well, I just know what I hear—a layoff's in the works and it could hit any time. Now's the time, huh?"

"Wait a minute. I didn't say there was going to be a layoff!"

"They already laid off five people in the other shop. I heard about that last week," countered Walker.

Portwood bristled. "Well, you're wrong this time. Dead wrong." He wanted to add that he thought Walker was at the bottom of the talk but thought better of it and didn't.

"No layoff?" Walker asked in mock amazement. "Come on, Bob, you can level with me. I've been around here long enough to know a layoff's coming when I see it. All you've got to do is look around you—there're signs all over the place. It's as plain as the nose on your face."

Portwood knew that Walker was probably referring to two ominously empty work stations from which machines had been removed a couple of weeks ago. "If it's those machines we took out that're bothering you, why didn't you people ask me about them before you went off halfcocked and jumped to crazy conclusions? That equipment was so outmoded it was pathetic—you know that—so we got rid of it."

"Well, the last time you took out some machines was right before that layoff," interrupted Walker.

"But we've got some replacements ordered, and they should be here in a few weeks. As for those people in the other department, they were trainees who just didn't have it."

"No kidding?" Walker asked, still not convinced that he wasn't right about the impending layoff. "Well, if that's the case, I guess the workers in the other shop were wrong. I heard that everybody would be cutting back just like they did. Maybe nothing's behind all this we've been hearing. Just been worrying for nothing." And with that he went back to work.

Portwood wasn't sure that he'd been able to convince Walker, however. After all, the department had been hit by a layoff a few months before, and it always took a while for confidence to rebuild after something like that. At any rate, he'd made up his mind that he'd have to keep an eye on the situation.

His nagging suspicion that there might be problems was confirmed in less time than he imagined possible. Tuesday morning, Sherry Cook, a young worker who'd been stationed near Walker, handed in her notice.

"I thought you liked it here," Portwood told her. "Is something wrong?"

"Sure I like it here," Cook answered. "The work's great. But I've only been here a few months, and when the layoff hits I'll be one of the first to go. The other three who started when I did feel the same way. I might stick it out and take my chances; but I've got a family to think about, too. So I lined up this job over at. . . ."

"Layoff!" Portwood blurted. "What layoff? There's not going to be any layoffs around here."

"But, I've been hearing about it for weeks," Cook told him. "What with those workers in the other shop going and taking the machines out. . . . "

"Well, you can forget about what you've heard," Portwood said heatedly. "Look, have you actually agreed to take this other job? Because if you haven't, I want you to sit tight. And as far as that layoff goes, you can take it from me that there isn't going to be one."

"Well, I don't know," responded Cook. "I would rather stay here. I'll think about it for a couple of days. I don't know about the others, though. Larry Walker told us about the layoff, and he seems to know what's going on around here."

Until Cook tried to hand in her notice, Walker's storytelling had always struck Portwood as being harmless—the sort of thing that goes on in every shop. But now he could see that it was affecting morale and that something would have to be done before it got any further out of hand.

Now, to find Walker and talk to him!

GUIDES FOR ANALYSIS

1. What position does Larry Walker hold in the work group?
2. How has Bob Portwood created this situation? Or has he?
3. What was the worker's source of information?
4. What has management communicated to the employees?
5. Advise Bob Portwood on the course of action that he should follow.
6. Be prepared to role-play the coming confrontation between Portwood and Walker.

SO, DO ME SOMETHING

Jack Orman, the sub-assembly foreman, read the petition on his desk for the third time in the half hour since he'd received it. He'd been a foreman now for six years, and this was the first written protest he'd ever received from his crew.

The petition was from the workers on the "E" line—one of the five five-worker groups that did the sub-assembly wiring on the vending machines that the company made.

It read: "We, the undersigned, do not want to work with Louis Walsher any longer. He has been a disrupting influence ever since he was hired and assigned to break in with us a year ago. Furthermore, although he has learned the work, he deliberately works slower than the rest of his fellow employees and impedes their progress, thus preventing them from making their full rates on the pool. We, the undersigned, have tried every way we know how to get this fellow employee to cooperate, but he just does not want to do so. Therefore, either we would like to have him replaced with someone who can get along with other human beings or we want to be transferred to another department."

"This is pretty bitter stuff," said Jack Orman to Al Lauder, the lead assembler of the "E" group and one of the signers of the petition. "And it's also a hot potato that you've dropped in my lap. You know as well as I do how closely the Big Boss has been working with the state handicapped-workers program. That's how come Lou is working here in the first place. And it's supposed to be a compliment to you guys that you'd be understanding enough to take in a guy like Lou. Don't think the front office hasn't been keeping an eye on how he's getting along—him and all the other handicapped we've hired."

"That's the reason we all signed this thing, Jack," said Lauder. "It isn't as if only one or two of us feel this way—we all do. And don't think we don't feel lousy about the way it's turning out. The thing of it is, it's not the fact that he's in a wheelchair that's causing the trouble—it's the guy's personality. He is just no damned good. He's a trouble-maker. He can do the work all right, but all he's interested in is lousing the rest of us up. Hell, we've even told him to get lost somewhere, but he just sticks around and gets in our way. Believe me, we've tried everything we can think of."

"Have you invited him in on all the different things you do?" asked the foreman. "Maybe you've been making him out to be a cripple, and he doesn't like it."

"Come on, Jack—you know better than that. We wouldn't do that to anyone. He won't play cards with us, he won't stop for a beer, he won't do anything. We've tried to get him to go bowling with us, but he just makes one of those sarcastic remarks of his—something about bowling being for creeps like us—and he won't eat lunch with us—just goes off and listens to that transistor radio of his. We've given it a good try, but it just hasn't worked."

"There must be something we can try that'll make this thing work out." The speaker was Kay Drucker, the personnel director. She, Orman, and Walt Frost, the superintendent of Orman's department were sitting in Drucker's office. "I don't mind saying that this isn't going to look good for anyone if we have to get rid of Walsher or transfer the rest of the crew."

"I don't care so much about looking good, Kay," said Jack Orman. "I just don't want to lose my best group of assemblers."

"You may," said Frost, "unless you can get them in line. The way I understand it, there's a lot at stake in this handicapped program. There are some mighty good customers of ours in back of it."

The personnel director nodded. "That's about the way I see it, too. We've got to make more of an effort than we have so far."

"You'll get it when I'm good and ready!" Lou Walsher's voice came loud and clear and irritably from the section in which he and the rest of the group were working.

"Damn it, I just have to tighten this one flange up," said one of the other assemblers. "You can spare that wrench for two seconds."

"The hell I can!"

Jack Orman walked up to the work area where the argument was taking place. His intention was to have a heart to heart talk with Lou Walsher. "Why can't you let him use that, Lou?"

"Because he's got one of his own that he lent to someone, that's why. Now he's just gonna have to wait till I get through. I got my own work to do."

"But you're all supposed to be working together as a team," said the foreman.

"So go ahead and do me something," said Lou Walsher, sitting in his wheelchair.

GUIDES FOR ANALYSIS

1. Why may Walsher have declined to take part in the group's activities?
2. Should a group be prepared by management for the addition of a "different" worker such as a handicapped person?

3. Is Lou Walsher's attitude understandable?
4. Is the group's attitude understandable?
5. What would you do now if you were in Jack Orman's shoes? You're not permitted to replace Walsher. On the other hand, if you don't do something about his attitude toward the rest of the crew you stand to lose them all.
6. Be prepared to role-play the confrontation between Walsher and Orman at the end of the case when Walsher says, "So go ahead and do me something."

THE FRIENDLY SUPERVISOR HEARS NO EVIL

While driving to work, Bill Dossey, day-shift supervisor in Maintenance, remembered that this morning he had an appointment with Dave Snell, one of his arc welders. Dossey recalled that Snell, who had been with the company about five years, had asked at least a half-dozen times for "conferences" with him. They usually ended up with Snell asking about some trivial matter, like the time he took 20 minutes to ask for a new pair of safety gloves. "Well, I guess I'll have to go through with it and see what he has to complain about," Dossey thought to himself.

He prided himself on being friendly and putting his people at ease when they wanted to talk to him, even though most of them didn't seem to have any really important problems to discuss. In fact, half the time most of them just wanted to talk about their families or fishing or something like that. He knew them pretty well and always made it a point to go to their informal department gatherings.

Later that morning, Snell walked into Dossey's office. "Sit down, Dave," Dossey said. "Say, did you watch that movie on television last night?" the supervisor asked. "I don't remember when I've laughed so much."

"No, boss, I didn't. What I came in here to talk with you about is. . . ." Snell began.

"The trouble with old movies is that they remind you of how quickly time flies. We were all 15 years younger when it first came out," Dossey said, leaning back in his chair. "What I wouldn't do to be 15 years younger. Know what I mean?" Dossey asked, chuckling to himself.

"Sure thing," Snell answered. "Mr. Dossey, for the past couple of weeks my wife hasn't. . . ."

"Say, how is Marilyn?" Dossey interrupted. "I haven't seen her since our Christmas party. We really had a good one—we'd better all be getting together again soon."

"Well, Marilyn's what I wanted to talk with you about." Snell said quickly. "You see, for the past couple of weeks she hasn't felt well, and Monday I finally talked her into seeing a doctor."

"Nothing serious, I hope," Dossey responded, leaning forward on his desk.

"No, it's not serious, but the doctor suggested that she take it easy for a few weeks and. . . ."

"Oh, glad to hear it. You just never know these days. Seems like so many terrible things happening around you all the time. Give her a good rest and it'll be okay though, huh? That's good news."

Just then his telephone rang. "Dossey speaking," the supervisor said. "Oh yes, Mr. McDonald. . . .Sure I can come up right away. . . .No, I'm not busy. One of my employees is in here, but it's not that important. I'll be right up."

"Uh, Mr. Dossey, what I wanted to ask you was. . . ."

"Save it for later, Dave. When the boss calls, I've got to move."

"But Mr. Dossey, I've got to. . . ." Snell almost pleaded.

"Come in and see me anytime, like tomorrow afternoon. We'll get to it then," Dossey said, slightly irritated, as he got up from his desk and started toward the door.

Heading for Bob McDonald's office, Dossey wondered what Snell had wanted. All he had done was give him a rundown on his wife's health; probably wanted to complain about the doctor bills.

That afternoon, Dossey received a second call from his boss. "Bill," McDonald said, "if there's no one in your office right now, I'd like you to come up here."

When Dossey walked into his office, McDonald got right to the point. "Listen, Bill, one of your employees was just in here to see me, and he was pretty upset."

"I don't know what or who you're talking about," Dossey began, obviously puzzled.

"I'm talking about Dave Snell," McDonald said.

"Snell! I saw him this morning. He told me something about his wife being ill, but that the doctor had said it wasn't serious. I gather that all she needs is a few weeks of rest. That's all he had to say. Oh, yeah—he wanted to complain about the doctor bills or something, but I needed to come up here."

"Well," McDonald said, rather irritated, "I don't know exactly what happened in your meeting, but Snell feels that he received short shrift. The whole point of his wanting the appointment was to ask for permission to take time off to drive his wife to her sister's house. He thought she could take care of her. He wasn't looking for sympathy or to give you doctor's reports. He was making a perfectly reasonable request, which you evidently turned down."

"But he never asked for time off; so I didn't turn him down. I would have let him off for something like that. Why didn't he get to the point?" Dossey asked, his face flushed from the dressing down.

"Well," McDonald continued, "I told him I would talk to you about the situation, so we'd better figure some way to straighten this out and see that it doesn't happen again."

GUIDES FOR ANALYSIS

1. Why did Dave feel that he had been treated "poorly"?
2. What did Bill communicate to Dave? How?
3. Why did Bill feel that his employees "usually didn't have any important things to discuss"?

4. What do you recommend that Bob McDonald do to "straighten this out" and "see that it doesn't happen again"?

WHAT AM I DOING HERE?

James Monroe had suddenly begun to ask himself, "What am I doing here?" After his promotion and transfer to the southwest branch of Barrington's, a local department-store chain, James' life had been in a continuous state of turmoil, all seemingly coming to a climax this afternoon. "What have I done to deserve this mess?" he again pondered.

Only nine days ago, he had been quite contented as Housewares Department Manager at Barrington's downtown store. The Christmas season was only a couple of weeks away when the personnel manager, Mr. Sewell, unexpectedly informed him of his promotion to Area Manager at the branch store, making him responsible for a total of 13 departments.

Mr. Sewell mentioned something during their conference about the present Area Manager at the branch store being replaced suddenly because "he just couldn't handle the job." He also commented on the man's "loose operating style" that the company apparently was not pleased with. The personnel manager had continued, "I have full confidence, James, that you're ready for the move and can handle the new situation. There are some good department heads at that store, and I know they'll help you get started in any way they can. It'll take you a little while to get oriented, but that's to be expected. If you hit any snags, let the department heads help you out; they know their operation, so don't hesitate to ask their advice if you need it."

At first, it was too great to believe. At age 28, James had thought it would be at least another year before he could even be considered for promotion; he had had his own department for only slightly over a year.

The first week on the new job had been spent in trying to get a grasp of his new duties and responsibilities as quickly as possible; twelve- to fourteen-hour work days became common for James. He made an effort to meet as many of the personnel in his area as he could and tried to know everyone by name. Contrary to what Mr. Sewell had said, however, the department heads weren't all that cooperative. It almost seemed that they considered him to be in their way.

James was determined to gain control of the situation, however. In an effort to gain the support of everyone in the area and to communicate his methods of operation, James sat down at his typewriter and composed a memo that was distributed to all area department heads and sales personnel. (A copy of this memo is presented in Exhibit 1.)

The memo had been sent out two days ago, and yet everything seemed to be going wrong today. "What is wrong with these people? Surely, they've read the memo by now." thought James.

The day had started out all wrong when James had walked into his office only to find a stack of miscellaneous notes, invoices, and other papers strewn across his desk. It had taken him almost an hour to shovel through them and file them properly.

barrington's

houston, texas

From: J. Monroe   To: Area Staff

Greeting from the new idiot of your areas. Even though I've talked
to most of you already, I'd like to say now pleased I am that I am
now in the new areas. Of course, most of you realize that all of
these areas are "Christmas Areas" and that I am totally unfamiliar
with the merchandise, personnel, stock areas, figures, and even the
department numbers. I urge all of you to help me learn as fast as
my feeble mind will allow me to do. In the same turn, I am a total
new "project" for you, and you do not know my way of managing, methods
of operation, expectations, and goals. Thus, the age-old problem of
mankind--that of co-existance is forced upon us. This means, we must
each try to live with each other, understanding, helping, and most of
all cooperating with each other for the bettermend of the area. (*and our jobs*)

First of all, I feel that I do not have 13 departments (or whatever the
exact total might be) but that I am responsible for an area. I feel
that each of you are qualified for movement into another area (not
technical areas, such as cameras) but from one into another. Even
though, previously, you were a china lady, or silver lady, etc, but
now I expect each of you to remain in your most familiar area, but
remember, you are not tied there. If I should ask you to move areas
to cover a lunch, break, or while stock is being cleared, I do not
want to hear "that's not my area," because it is, as long as I am
responsible for area 4, 14, and 10.

I have also requested that all 5:30 totals be called in by Barbara
White, and then put on my desk. On her day off, she has assigned
that task to someone else.

Any paperwork, (transfers, _and_ new orders coming in) that accompanies
merchandise into my area will be put in the bottom drawer of my file
cabnat, according to the department number. Also, any merchandise
leaving the area, (exxept BITUC) the pink copy will be put into the
file in the top drawer marked "Goods Transferred Out).

When I receive a "Price Revision Notice" I take it from my mailbox
and make a Xerox copy at once. I then put that copy in my file in
the top drawer, marked New Mark Downs, Ups,.....and then put the
original in your mail boxes (on my desk top also)....when you have

Exhibit 1

completed the counts you will go to the New File, remove the copy, and
fill it in according with the figures on the original copy and replace
it to the file marked "Markdowns Completed"....and put the original
in my mail box on the right hand side of the desk.

I have a pet-peave about having things left it on my desk that have
no messages, reasons, or instructions left with them....so please, if
you leave anything on it...please let me know why, or what it is
there for.

When I receive a proof from the ad department, I usually look over it,
then place it in your mail box, and ask if "we're well stocked, or
have enough, etc! If we are in trouble...LET ME KNOW IMMEDIATELY....
so that I mightxxxxxkx take the necessary steps to help us out of it.

On my right hand drawer, I keep a file of Advertising by the month...
it is up to each individual to see that you are aware of what is
"happening" in your individual department...you might get a little
notebook, and write down what ads are running when, so that we can be
on the "lookout" for any trouble that might arise....such as no
merchandiss. These are usually 2 weeks in advance, but occasionaly *(like every 3 days)*
change, so check it periodiocally and we wont slip up. *((and a name)*

If I receive phone calls on the floor, and you cannot find me, ask
them if they can leave a message, or a phone xxxxxx number, so that
I might call back. DO NOT say that you dont know wheere I am and let
it go at that.....that makes you look a little silly, and me a ghost.
THE Take the message and leav it on my desk as soon as you get a free
moment from all your custommers, or if you should xxk spot me coming,
hand it to me personally.

Finally, if I am with another person, Mr. Metcalf, Knapp, another Area
Manager, buyer, and I have a phone call, ask them for a message also,
and give it to me, but do not   , (unless of course it is extremely
urgent) walk up and say that I have a phone call....merely give me a
message on paper, and I shall handle it.

I"m sure that these seem a little harsh as compared to some of your
previous rules and regulations, but I am a very organized persnn (or
try to be ha ha) and get very "uptight" when xxxxxkk anything is "out
of order" or in total confusion.

As far as our stock rooms go, I will be asking each of you for a little
more manual labor this week and next, as you know Gourmet Shop is set
up on Monday, and all of our Christmas Gifts, Candles, Records, Candy
etc. is coming in each day in great quanity, and I'm being xx bombarded
with questions on "where to put it"....I certainly wish I knew....so
please, bear with me.

houston, texas

Again, I"m very pleased with my new areas, and I only hope that we
can accomplish a good x rapport between us....and please, IF ANYONE
HAS ANY QUESTIONS, GRIPES, PROBLEMS, ETC.......TELLXXME....AND IF
I CAN XN ANY WAY HELP YOU I WILL, IF NOT I"LL SXND YOU TO SOMEONE
WHO CAN....BUT DONT WAIT TILL LXST TO TELL ME...THAT WONT SOLVE
ANYTHING......

In case we"re so swamped in the near future, or should I have a
nervous breakdown by then end of December......Merry Christmas.....

J. Monroe

Several of the papers pertained to the Linen Department, so James walked over and asked the manager, Mrs. Craig, if she would please file the paperwork in the appropriate places as he had requested in his memo.

Although James thought he had asked her in a reasonable tone of voice, the woman exploded, "I don't have time to be your file clerk; I've got a department to run."

"I fail to understand your attitude," replied James, nearly in a state of shock. "It was a reasonable request, I believe."

He decided to let the matter drop for now, but knew that some action would have to be taken later.

On top of that, he received a phone call from Mrs. Kravitz, the store manager, asking why James had failed to return her phone message informing him of a management meeting that took place earlier in the morning.

James uttered clumsily that he had not received the message and was quite sorry he had missed the meeting. Just then, he spotted a scrawled note taped to his door reading simply, "Call Kravitz."

As if all this weren't enough, two salespeople in the Lamp Department called in with what was supposedly the "flu." He had asked Mrs. Thompson of the China Department to fill in in the Lamp Department. She whined, "I can't do that Mr. Monroe; I know absolutely nothing about lamps. I'd do more harm than good in that department."

James threw his arms in the air, hung his head and shook it slowly, wondering half aloud, "What is the. . . ." as he heard the incessant ringing of his phone in the background. Stumbling to the office, he snatched the phone and answered with a very gruff "Hello."

"James," came the startled voice from the phone, "this is Mr. Sewell. You sound a little upset. Is something wrong?"

"No, Mr. Sewell, everything's fine—just great, in fact," James replied wearily. "All I have to do now is figure out what I am doing here!"

GUIDES FOR ANALYSIS

1. Has James created any problems for himself? If so, how has he done so?
2. What did James' memo communicate to his employees?
3. Have the employees reacted as you would have predicted?
4. Recommend a course of action to James.

LARKIN'S LAST LAUGH

Annie Larkin was furious. She'd been a lead assembler for almost five years; and now that there was an opening for foreman of her department, they were trying to tell her that she wasn't even going to be considered for the spot. "You say it's tradition!" she said, angrily. "I say it's prejudice! That's right—PREJUDICE! Pure and simple. But go ahead and laugh all you want. We'll see who has the last laugh around here!"

"But I wasn't laughing at you, Annie" said Stan Shutz, her general foreman on the first shift. "All I was saying was. . . ." But she'd decided that she'd heard enough, so she didn't wait to hear Shutz finish. She stormed out of his office, slamming the door behind her.

"Boy!" exclaimed Stan, laughing to himself. "Women!"

Bert Strong, the day foreman that Annie wanted to replace, laughed with him when Shutz told him about the incident. "I've heard some screwy ideas in my time, but I never thought I'd be hearing them come from Annie. I always thought that she was pretty level-headed as a rule."

"Yeah, but they're all alike, basically," said Shutz. "Once they get it into their heads that you're trying to do 'em out of something, they try to get back at you any way they can. I'll bet you dollars to doughnuts that the next guy to hear about this is Al Sloan."

"Think he'll listen to her?" asked Strong.

"Al? Not a chance," answered Shutz. "He didn't get to be top man on this shift because he hasn't got good sense, you know. All Annie's got to do is hit him one time with that screwy idea of hers about being foreman, and he'll throw her right out of the office—politely, of course. Come to think of it, he might even take her lead assembler job away from her. I wouldn't put it past him, you know. He doesn't have time to fool around with crazy ideas like that."

"He'll break her heart if he does," commented Strong. "She waited a long time for that job, and I know it means a lot to her."

"Well, no one asked her to stick her neck out like she's doing," commented Shutz, emphatically. Whew! When I think of what might happen if she ever got that job—I don't even like to think about it.

"I wish you hadn't told her that you're being transferred over to the other plant, Bert. It would've been better for everybody if she'd found out about the opening after we'd already found somebody else to fill it. Of course, who'd ever have thought that she'd think of putting in for it?"

The doors opened and Jake Dobbs, one of the inspectors, walked in. Spotting a chance to get some supporting evidence for his point, Shutz asked him, "How would *you* like it if you had to work under a woman foreman, Jake?"

"Are you kidding me?" asked Dobbs in return. "You'd better be, because it'll be a cold day in hell before you'd catch me working for a woman. My brother did for a while; and from what he told me, I don't want any part of it. Besides, my old lady pushes me around enough at home. I figure good jobs aren't that hard to come by."

Shutz looked at Strong and smiled. "What'd I tell you?" He knew he'd made his point. Annie could try all she wanted to get a foreman's position, but the men would never accept her. And that meant that she'd never get it.

Shutz was right about Annie Larkin. When she left his office she was steaming with rage. She knew that she was the most qualified candidate for the vacancy, and she wasn't going to let them pass over her just because she happened to be a woman—at least, not if she could help it. So, she went straight to Al Sloan to have it out with him. When she finished telling him her story, he told her that he was sorry that she was so upset and that he'd look into the matter as soon as he could.

Later that afternoon, as Annie walked through the shop to the section where the women did the assembly work, she was greeted by some men who'd heard about her run-in with Shutz. "What do you say, boss lady?" called out one, and another brought himself to attention and gave her an exaggerated salute. "All right, all right," said Annie, trying to pass it off with a smile. But by the time she reached her section, she was beginning to wonder whether she hadn't made a mistake by saying anything about that foreman's job in the first place.

Early the next morning, she was called into the office of Sid Trask, the company's personnel man. "I'm only talking to you because Al Sloan has asked me to," he told her. "I don't really have much to add to what you've been told already. You see, we've always had a man in that spot, and I don't think that we're ready to change that policy at the present time. I understand that the boys on the floor have been giving you a rough time since they learned about it."

"That doesn't bother me, Sid," answered Annie.

"Well, I can tell you that it sure bothers me," Trask commented. "My job is rough enough without any new problems popping up, especially problems like this one. As I said, it would take a change in company policy to get you this job, and the policy isn't going to be changed. And if you're thinking about taking it to a higher court—like Mr. Ramsey—I can tell you right now that you'll be wasting your time. I had a hard enough time as it is convincing him that you were qualified to handle the job you've got."

Annie's jaw thrust forward. "Well, I can tell you that I definitely was thinking of going to him about it," she said defiantly. "Especially since all I've been getting so far is the runaround. This company has government contracts that state in black and white that you can't have any discrimination because of race, color, creed, or sex. I've been a lead assembler for five years, and I know that you don't have anyone that's more qualified for the job. And what's more, I think a court of arbitration will agree with me—if it has to go that far!"

"Court of arbitration?" asked Trask, "Where'd you hear about that?"

"In the newspaper, that's where," she answered, as defiant as ever. "There was a case almost exactly like mine out in California last month. Would you like to guess who won?"

"All right, Annie," said Trask, grinning. "Why don't you let me talk to the Old Man about it. I can't promise you that anything will come of it—just don't be too surprised if he blows his top, though."

Two days later, Stan Shutz called Annie into his office. He didn't look very pleased. "I'm not sure what you told Trask or what he told the Old Man," he said grimly, "but you're our new foreman—or perhaps I should say 'forewoman.' God only knows what's going to happen now. We'll probably have half the crew quitting by the end of the week—that or asking for transfers to other departments."

As Annie left the office, Stan wondered what he should do now.